PENTAGON PRESS

COMMITTED TO SERVE THE ARMED FORCES

Insights into Evolution of Contemporary Pakistan

Insights into Evolution of Contemporary Pakistan

Editors

Satish Chandra
Smita Tiwari

INDIAN COUNCIL OF WORLD AFFAIRS

PENTAGON PRESS

Insights into Evolution of Contemporary Pakistan

Editors: Satish Chandra, Smita Tiwari

ISBN 978-81-8274-842-2

First Published in 2015

Published by
PENTAGON PRESS
206, Peacock Lane, Shahpur Jat,
New Delhi-110049
Phones: 011-64706243, 26491568
Telefax: 011-26490600
email: rajan@pentagonpress.in
website: www.pentagonpress.in

Branch
Flat No.213, Athena-2,
Clover Acropolis,
Viman Nagar,
Pune-411014
Email: pentagonpresspune@gmail.com

Printed at Avantika Printers Private Limited.

Contents

Preface

In the backdrop of the momentous May 2013 elections in Pakistan, the Indian Council of World Affairs created a Core Group on Pakistan comprising eminent scholars and former diplomats. The Group decided to steer clear of the bilateral India-Pakistan relationship; instead, it devoted itself to a better understanding of what drives Pakistan. Accordingly, it focused on Pakistan's politico-military dynamics, military build-up, economy, the challenge of ethno nationalism confronting the country and radicalisation within the state and developed articles devoted to each of these issues, which are duly compiled as a book. It is hoped that this offering will further a deeper understanding of Pakistan at a critical juncture in its evolution.

The first article on "Pakistan's Politico-Military Dynamics" is authored by Rana Banerji, IAS (retired) and formerly Special Secretary (R&AW). With his long experience of studying Pakistan, Mr Banerji has meticulously delved into that country's fractious civil military relations through an event based prism. After a brief historical perspective, his focus is quite appropriately on the more recent developments, such as Memogate, dealings with the TTP, the happenings in Baluchistan, Musharraf's trial, etc. He concludes that the jury is still out on whether or not the military and the civilian leadership will be able to work together harmoniously. While Nawaz Sharif, with his popular mandate, has the opportunity to establish civilian supremacy, a strongly entrenched military may not be in the mood to let go.

The next article entitled "Pakistan's Military Build Up", has been developed by Shalini Chawla, who has been a Senior Fellow at the Centre for Air Power Studies since 2006, and who not only specialises on Pakistan, but also has published work to her credit on the military in Pakistan. The article painstakingly details the extent to which Pakistan's arms acquisitions, both conventional and nuclear, have been facilitated by foreign assistance. In the process, it underlines that this exercise has primarily been driven by the military, which has projected a threat perception from India as a means to justify its massive quest for high tech weaponry and unsustainably high levels of defence spending. While Pakistan's arms imports have been diversely sourced, the major weapon suppliers to Pakistan have been China and the USA. The former is, however, by far the largest supplier and has also been the main supplier of knowhow, materials and equipment enabling the nuclearisation of Pakistan. The article also addresses in some depth the details and logic of Pakistan's nuclear doctrine and its India centric nature.

The third article entitled "Pakistan's Economy: An Unviable State" is by Sushant Sareen, Consultant, Pakistan Project at the Institute of Defence Studies and Analysis and Senior Fellow, Vivekananda International Foundation. Sareen is one of India's leading Pakistan experts and has an academic background in economics. The article presents an in depth and graphic account of economic developments in Pakistan. The picture presented by him is inevitably gloomy as Pakistan, under PPP rule, experienced average GDP growth of 2.5 per cent, fiscal deficits of over six per cent and double digit inflation. Pakistan's economic crisis is nothing new and the country, over the last two decades, has been lurching from crisis to crisis. Historically, its economy has prospered only when there have been large infusions of assistance. This is so because the economy is largely consumption driven and until and unless the structural problems of the economy in the form of the savings-investment deficit, the expenditure-revenue deficit and the import-export deficit are tackled, it will continue to be troubled. The situation is further complicated by the crippled energy sector and the issues of terrorism, sectarian strife, etc., which are an impediment to foreign investment. Since Nawaz Sharif, contrary to popular expectation, has done little to address these basic issues, an upturn of the economy is not on the cards. His success in getting about $10 billion in foreign assistance is nothing more than a band aid and its impact will only be to temporarily tide over the current crisis.

The fourth article entitled "Identity Conflict in Pakistan: The Challenge of Ethno-Nationalism(s)" is by Savita Pande, who is a Professor in the prestigious Jawaharlal Nehru University's School of International Studies and heads its Centre for South Asian Studies. She is a specialist on Pakistan and has written and spoken extensively on it. The article dwells upon the very serious challenges posed to Pakistan by the forces of ethno nationalism. In so doing, it underlines the irony of the fact that Pakistan, which came into existence on the basis of identity, notably Muslim nationalism, is "still struggling to find its identity." Thereafter, it assiduously details the strength of various ethno nationalisms, which have assailed Pakistan since its inception, most importantly those of the Bengalis, Sindhis, Pushtuns, Baloch and Seraiki. Pakistan's denial of these movements and its endeavour to sweep ethnic differences under the blanket of a single religious identity can only be at the peril of its unity.

The final article entitled "Radicalisation in Pakistan" is by Alok Bansal, a retired naval officer with 26 years of commissioned service, whose prime area of interest has been South Asia with a special focus on Pakistan. He has been with the Institute of Defence Studies and Analysis as Member (Navy) and is currently the Executive Director of the National Maritime Foundation. The article posits that radicalism constitutes "an extreme world view, backed by aggression, force and possibly violence, which also encompasses complete rejection of alternate view points and has extremely low tolerance for ambiguity." In the context of Pakistan, terms like fundamentalism and extremism are substitutable with radicalism of which Talibanisation is a major manifestation. The article rejects the view that radicalism in Pakistan had its origins in General Zia ul Haq's policies and makes a persuasive case that it started right since the country's inception and traces its evolution till the present day. It suggests that radicalism is not only accentuating the sectarian divide and aggravating the persecution of minorities, but also challenging the writ of the state and its institutions. It concludes that there is a distinct possibility of the withering of the Pakistani state and consequential internecine warfare and large scale bloodshed.

Satish Chandra

Contributors

Rana Banerji is former IAS and was Special Secretary in Cabinet Secretariat. He has dealt with security and intelligence, with focused expertise on South Asia. Mr Banerji headed a Task Force on Intelligence Reforms at the Institute for Defence Studies & Analyses (IDSA). He has also worked as Visiting Professor, Pakistan Studies Programme at the Academy of International Studies, Jamia Millia Islamia University, Delhi. Mr Banerji has attended several Track II dialogues &international conferences on Indo-Pak Military to Military Experts' CBMs, Trans National Crimes, Money Laundering & Terrorism, Indo-Pak-Afghan Policy dialogue, and on 'The Terrorist Threat from ISIS: Strategic Issues & Growing challenges' at the East Asia Summit in Singapore.

Dr Shalini Chawla is a Senior Fellow and Project Director *Pakistan and Afghanistan: Present and Future* at the Centre for Air Power Studies (CAPS), New Delhi. She was a research scholar at IDSA, 1999-2002. She worked as a free lance defence analyst from 2003-2005 in Colombo, Sri Lanka. She is also the Project Director for an ICSSR Project - *Afghanistan: The US withdrawal and Beyond.* She is a member of the *Core Group on Pakistan* facilitated by Indian Council of World Affairs. She is a member of *Policy Group on Afghanistan* by Friedrich-Ebert-Stiftung (FES). She has authored three books titled - *Pakistan's Military and Its Strategy* (2009), *Nuclear Pakistan* (2012) and ed. *India's Sentinel: Select Writings of Air Commodore Jasjit Singh* (2014).

Sushant Sareen has been a close observer of the political situation in South Asia, specialising on Pakistan. He was the Executive Editor, Public Opinion Trends. He has also been Associate Editor, southasianmedia.net, a South Asian news portal being run by the South Asian Free Media Association (SAFMA). He is currently a Consultant with the Pakistan Project of Institute for Defence Studies and Analyses (IDSA). He is also Senior Fellow, Vivekananda International Foundation.

He is the author of the book: "The Jihad Factory - Pakistan's Islamic Revolution in the Making". He has contributed papers on the situation in Pakistan, India-Pakistan peace process etc. for many reputed journals and Indian news papers. He has also delivered lectures and talks at many premier institutions.

Professor Savita Pande is presently working in the Centre for South Asian Studies, School of International Studies, Jawaharlal Nehru University, (JNU), New Delhi, India. Her area of expertise is Pakistan's Domestic and Foreign Policy, Regional Security in South Asia and Indian Foreign Policy. She joined as Associate Professor, South Asian Studies, in the year 2000 and was promoted as Professor in 2008. Prior to coming to JNU, Professor Pande was at the Institute for Defence Studies and Analyses since 1993 where she worked in different capacities reaching to Research Fellow. In 2012, Prof Pande was Visiting Professor, India Chair, at Tara Shivchenko National University, Kieve, Ukraine. She has written extensively, contributing to various Books and Journals, which include her books, *Regional and Ethnic Minorities in Pakistan*, *Pakistan's Nuclear Policy*, etc. She has also done research projects for University Grants Commission and Indian Council for Social Science Research. Prof Pande has also traveled extensively in and outside the country

Alok Bansal is Director India Foundation, New Delhi and the Executive Director of South Asian Institute for Strategic Affairs (SAISA). He is also the Professor of Strategy and International Relations at New Delhi Institute of Management (NDIM) and facilitator of India Policy Group (IPG) on Afghanistan for Track II Dialogues by Friedrich Ebert Stiftung. He has been a Visiting Professor at the Pakistan Studies Programme of Maulana Mohammed Ali Jauhar Academy of International Studies at

Jamia Millia Islamia. He has been the Executive Director of the National Maritime Foundation (NMF) and has worked with the Institute for Defence Studies and Analyses (IDSA), and Centre for Land Warfare Studies (CLAWS). He has authored a book titled *Balochistan in Turmoil: Pakistan at Cross Roads* in 2009 and has co-edited three books titled *South Asian security: 21st century discourses, Pakistan Occupied Kashmir: The Untold Story* and *Sri Lanka: Search for Peace.*

1

Pakistan's Politico-Military Dynamics

Rana Banerji

The May 11, 2013 elections to the National and Provincial Assemblies marked a significant political watershed in Pakistan[1], representing the first ever smooth transition to a newly elected civilian government without military intervention. There was a 'normal' transition to a new civilian government after completion of a full term by a previous civilian government, itself elected democratically in 2008.

The election results were a boost for conservative forces in Pakistan. Right of Centre political parties did well, especially in Punjab and Khyber Pakhtunkhwa (KP). The Pakistan Muslim League (Nawaz-PML-N) got a total of 129 seats out of 272, with 118 from Punjab alone. Imran Khan's Tehrik-e-Insaaf (TeI) won 17 seats out of 35 from KP, cobbling together a coalition government there. Parties like the Awami National Party (ANP), People's Party of Pakistan (PPP) and Muttahida/Mohajir Quami Movement (MQM-Altaf), which could be deemed either centrist or moderate/'secular' were not allowed to canvass freely due to threats from the Taliban and suffered reverses, except perhaps in Sindh.

In another sense, the results accentuated ethnic regionalisation of mainstream political parties, diminishing their spread to provinces of their traditional strength. The PML (N) hardly has a presence in provinces other than Punjab. The PPP has been confined to Sindh, 29 out of its 31 seats coming from there.

Why No Democracy – The Historical Context

However, viewed in historical context, it can be argued that though there has been much active politicking in Pakistan, democracy has failed to strike roots in the country.[2]

One explanation commonly given by historians is the early demise of Mohd. Ali Jinnah, whom many scholars considered representative of a modern, secular and liberal tradition. Absence of a charismatic politician contributed to insecurity and led to the nation building process being overtaken by Islamic and authoritarian trends.

The elites, who played the most active part in creating Pakistan, migrated from Muslim minority areas in undivided India, but had no indigenous roots there (Mohajirs). They were reluctant to initiate a democratic process in which they could lose out their control over the levers of power. Deliberations in the Constituent Assembly were influenced by the fear that if Pakistan went in for unadulterated democracy straightaway, in sheer numerical terms, Muslims from East Bengal would have dominated any elected legislature.

It seemed almost as if legislators, who sat in the Constituent Assembly, were bereft of any sense of democracy or any ideal form of government they should work for. The only commonly shared notion of nationhood was Islam. Though political leaders of the day were often forced to fall back on the slogan of Islam to bring order out of chaos, the central dilemma of Muslim Leaguers was that they did not want to go much further or interpret any particular variant of Islam as officially sanctioned. The religious parties seemed better qualified to do that but none could agree on what type of Islamic State or Islamic constitution Pakistan deserved.[3]

The most well organised institutions in the newly created country were the Army and the civil bureaucracy. Both soon grew impatient of the perpetual bickering of politicians in the Constituent Assembly and convinced themselves that they alone were best suited to take Pakistan forward in terms of its economic and strategic goals. The pattern of civil-military bureaucratic capitalism, which unfolded in Pakistan during the early years of the Ayub Khan dictatorship, saw the emergence and consolidation of many political groups and economic classes, which quickly made their peace with authoritarian political dispensations.

Though Bhutto's 'roti, kapda aur makaan' slogan in 1967 initiated a new political party and started a somewhat different trend, feudals of south Punjab and Sindh survived the PPP's land reform measures and the civil bureaucracy carried its way back into Bhutto's favour. The Military too had to be used to curb rebellion in Baluchistan. The Zia-ul-Haq take-over in 1977 crystallised the hegemony of the civil-military bureaucracy. They were the main beneficiaries of the regime, along with the urban and rural middle classes as their political and administrative roles extended into the economic domain.[4]

The role of the military changed gradually – earlier, it was playing more of an administrative role but now, progressively, it became more visible in the economic sector. Many lucrative positions in the private sector were made available to retired military personnel, as 'Mil bus' (Military Business) spread roots. The tradition of concessional land allotments to military personnel in prime urban as well as rural areas was formalised during this period.[5]

This fusion of economic and political power did not have much to do with democratic politics. It was more a manipulation of political actors, processes and results by 'agencies'. While the middle classes got gradually economically empowered, military governments, which were non-elected, un-democratic and authoritarian were preferred. Civil-military relations in Pakistan alternated between direct and sometimes brutal domination by the military and reluctant power-sharing agreements with civilian governments.[6] Political parties, not in power, kept running to the Military with tales of 'bad governance' and pleas to take over. Members of civil society seemed eager to be co-opted to serve in successive Military governments. This Pakistan could best be described as a 'praetorian democracy'.[7]

Repeated Civil-Military Strife

The civil-military relations in Pakistan have remained fraught with tensions, first on account of the Army's disdain of bickering politicians, as they delayed

Constitution making and later on account of ineptitude in governance, perceived double standards and pursuit of pelf during brief interregnums when civilians came to power. The latter have sought to incrementally seek political space, but the powerful military establishment was not prepared to forego its role in formulating and controlling vital areas of security and foreign policy. Conflict occurred frequently on issues of governance, especially on matters pertaining to the control of the State's security apparatus and secret agencies. Approaches differed widely on how to tackle questions of alienation and quests for autonomy, as in Baluchistan.

The interregnum of 1988-99 saw four elections being held within a short period. Not all of them were entirely 'free and fair'. The Inter-Services Intelligence (ISI) of the Pakistan military helped create an alliance of political parties (Islami Jamhoori Ittehad-IJI) to oppose Benazir Bhutto's PPP. Benazir had to accept a retired General, Sahibzada Yaqub Khan as Foreign Minister. She brought in a retired General, Shamshur Rehman Kallue as the Director General, Inter-Services Intelligence. This was not liked by the then Army Chief, Gen. Aslam Beg. Kallue was soon ousted and replaced by Asad Durrani. The PPP's relationship with the Muhajir Quami Movement (MQM) was destabilised. A 'Combined Opposition' was goaded to accuse the first PPP government of corruption, particularly Benazir's husband, Asif Zardari, who earned the notorious 'Mr Ten Percent' sobriquet. President Ghulam Ishaq Khan, a quintessential representative of the old civilian bureaucracy, which had colluded with the Military, promptly used Art 58(2) of the Constitution, introduced under the 8th Amendment of 1985 by Zia-ul-Haq, to dismiss the PPP government. Nawaz Sharif came to power in the 1990 elections.

During Sharif's first premiership, from November, 1990 to July 1993, Gen Asif Nawaz was the Army Chief. Several issues of discord came up. Asif Nawaz had to sometimes cater to unwarranted recommendations on postings, promotions of senior officers. Apprised about rumours circulating that the Ittefaq Group was distributing BMW cars as 'Abba ji's (Nawaz Sharif's father, Mian Mohd. Sharif) gifts' to cultivate gullible Generals, the Army Chief confronted Nawaz, who did not deny the allegation, rather he offered the keys of a new BMW to Asif Nawaz, urging him not to keep driving his old Toyota Corona as it was not` befitting' for the Chief! Asif Nawaz politely returned the keys and walked away.[8]

Quoted in a vernacular publication, '*Ghaddar Kaun*', Nawaz Sharif described Asif Nawaz as 'a headstrong individual, who did not give him due regard as PM'. The PM and the Army Chief were not on the same page over handling of the situation in Sindh and the splintering, infighting between Mohajir Quami movement factions (Altaf vs Haqiqi). Nawaz brought in his father's Tablighi acolyte, Lt Gen Javed Nasir as the new DG, ISI without consulting Asif Nawaz.

When the latter died suddenly after a heart attack in January, '93, there were allegations of arsenic poisoning. Begum Asif Nawaz received anonymous letters from waiters at Nawaz Sharif's Raiwind house claiming use of special 'poisoned' cloth to polish plates on which the Chief was served refreshments. Though Asif Nawaz's body was exhumed and an inquiry was held by US forensic experts, these allegations could not be substantiated.

Both President and PM have to go

When Gen Abdul Waheed Kakar was appointed the next Army Chief, Nawaz Sharif did not agree with President Ghulam Ishaq Khan's choice. Relations between the two soured further, leading to Nawaz's dismissal in April'93 with the President using his powers under Art 58(2) (b) of the Constitution. Nawaz challenged this in Court and Supreme Court Chief Justice, Nasim Hassan Shah deemed the dismissal illegal. Later, the Army Chief, Gen Kakar had to mediate, leading to a situation where both Ghulam Ishaq Khan and Nawaz Sharif were made to resign and Pakistan went into fresh elections, which brought Benazir Bhutto back in for her second tenure as PM.

In the 1997 National Assembly elections, Nawaz Sharif's PML (N) received a massive mandate – 45.9 per cent votes and 155/207 seats, with PPP getting only 18 seats. This brought to fore Nawaz's authoritarian streak – he introduced the 13th Amendment, doing away with the President's powers to dismiss the PM and dissolve Assemblies.

A new chapter of confrontation was opened up with the Supreme Court Chief Justice, Sajjad Ali Shah, whose court was stormed by PML (N) supporters. The Army Chief, Gen Karamat refrained from responding to Justice Shah's call for assistance from the Army.

More differences surfaced. Lt. Gen Khwaja Ziauddin Butt was brought in as the new DG, ISI, once again without approval of the Army Chief. In a speech at the Naval Staff College, Lahore in October,'98, Karamat criticised profligacy of certain grandiose civilian government schemes and demanded setting up of a National Security Council. This incensed Nawaz Sharif and he called in the Chief to remonstrate. Karamat quit as Chief without taking this issue back to his Corps Commanders [This dismissal was quite out of character with the generally accepted behavior of the Army. In later analyses, a view was espoused by retired Army Generals that if Karamat wanted, his senior officers would have stood by him in another pre-emptive coup].[9]

Musharraf was appointed the new COAS over the heads of two seniors – Chief of General Staff, Ali Kuli Khan Khattak and Lt Gen Khalid Nawaz Malik, ostensibly because he was a Mohajir. Nawaz was advised by his close confidants that Musharraf would not be too dominating, as he was a Mohajir and Nawaz could reach over his head to appeal to Punjabi Other Ranks and officers.

Kargil – To What Extent was Nawaz Sharif on Board?

Though Musharraf claims Nawaz Sharif was taken on board and kept informed of the Kargil incursion, before Indian Prime Minister Vajpayee's Lahore bus yatra (February '99), the operation remained a closely guarded secret. In later Pakistani post-mortems, it was seen as the handiwork of 'the Gang of Four' – a coterie of Generals close to Musharraf, which included Maj Gen Javed Hassan, GoC of the Force Command, Northern Areas; CGS Lt Gen Mohd Aziz and X Corps Commander, Lt Gen Mehmood Ahmed. Even the DGMO, Lt Gen Tauqir Zia was the 'odd man out' and the DG, ISI Ziauddin admitted sensing something grave was brewing much later.[10]

Distrust increased between the civilian executive and the military leadership, to the spectacular extent of the DG, MI bugging the ISI chief and the latter returning the compliment. In September '99 matters came to head as Musharraf sacked XII Corps Commander, Lt Gen Tariq Pervaiz, a close relative of Raja Nadir Pervaiz, Communications Minister in the Nawaz Sharif Cabinet and a 1965 war hero, on charges of leaking minutes of Corps Commanders' meetings to the political executive. Nawaz sent brother Shahbaz as emissary to the United States to focus on apprehensions of a coup attempt, urging US mediation. A last minute attempt was made to appease Musharraf by appointing him conterminously to the vacant four star slot of Chairman, Joint Chiefs of Staff Committee.

The Kargil Review Committee (KRC) commented on the decision to undertake the military operation. They found that it could not have been made without close consultation with the Pakistani political leadership at the highest level, though it acknowledged there was no clear evidence on the basis of which to assess the nature and extent of Nawaz Sharif's involvement in the adventure. The balance of probability suggested that he was fully in the picture. Those, who knew Nawaz Sharif personally, believed that he had a limited attention span and was impatient with detail. Accordingly, it was reasonable to assume that Nawaz Sharif was at least aware of the broad thrust of the Kargil plan when he so warmly welcomed the Indian Prime Minister in Lahore.[11]

Musharraf's First Coup

After the 12th October, 1999 coup, Nawaz Sharif was taken prisoner, hauled in chains on a seven hour flight from Islamabad, via Multan to Karachi and back, before being lodged in solitary confinement, first in Adiala and later in Attock jail. Saudi intervention and a commitment not to return to politics for 21 years led to exile in Jeddah. Subsequent mediation by a Pakistani arms dealer, Brig (retd) Niaz, enabled Nawaz to move to his London home.[12] His political banishment was reduced to 10 years and he was able to return to Pakistan after 8 years – taking advantage of the burgeoning civil society/lawyers' agitation on the Judges restoration issue, which saw the ground under President Musharraf's feet disintegrate quickly.

Charter of Democracy

In May, 2006, while Benazir Bhutto and Nawaz Sharif were both in political exile in London, they concluded the Charter of Democracy, pledging to work for the establishment of genuine democracy in Pakistan and promising not to destabilise each other.

Signs of Shift in Civil Society Ambience

The 2008 National Assembly elections saw mandates sufficiently large, though short of absolute majority for the two major, mass-based parties in the country – the Asif Zardari led PPP and PML (N) of Nawaz Sharif. Though the coalition government formed between them broke down soon over differences on the modalities of restoration of the superior Judiciary, the government of the day survived. During this period, despite widespread public perceptions of mal-governance or involvement in corruption, politicians stopped running to the Army with complaints urging them to intervene or seeking to oust the party in power. Nevertheless, the Army continued to call the shots, especially on vital security policy issues, such as India, Afghanistan, nuclear policy and relations with the United States.

Judiciary-Army Tensions

When Supreme Court Chief Justice, Iftikhar Chaudhry was ill-treated by Musharraf, there was unexpected turmoil in civil society. As this imbroglio broke into the open, it created widespread consternation and disgruntlement among the emergent middle classes. These sentiments found expression in the lawyers' agitation for re-instatement of the Chief Justice and other senior Judges after the November 03, 2007 proclamation of a 'conditional emergency' by Musharraf.

At this time, another controversy surfaced about whether Musharraf could continue in uniform while holding on to both posts – President as well as Army Chief. Demands grew that he should relinquish his uniform to preserve the sanctity of constitutional provisions. Faced with a brewing confrontation with the judiciary, Musharraf tried to defuse the issue by handing over the military baton to his selected nominee, Lt. Gen Ashfaq Pervez Kayani, then DG, ISI.

The successful restoration of the Chief Justice and other Judges, in March 2009 was a landmark in Pakistani politics, with the judiciary giving up its age-old 'doctrine of necessity'. This doctrine had been used to validate a succession of military takeovers on grounds of public interest. Every time there was a martial law takeover, the military's actions were indemnified by the Judges and validated under Art 270 AA of the Constitution; but the Nov 03, 2007 emergency proclamation was not. Though Chief Justice

Dogar's order validated Musharraf's proclamation of conditional emergency from Nov 03 – Dec 15, 2007 in February, 2008, this was struck down by the Supreme Court in August, 2009.[13]

The Eighteenth Amendment to the Constitution, passed by the National Assembly in April 2010, saw this emergency validation clause (Art. 270 AA) being repudiated entirely.

NRO and Judicial Over-reach

The controversial National Reconciliation Ordnance (NRO), issued by General Musharraf in October 2007 granting amnesty to politicians, political workers and bureaucrats accused of corruption, embezzlement, money laundering, murder, and terrorism between 1 January 1986, and 12 October 1999, was also struck down by the Supreme Court in 2009.

The PPP leadership faced a hostile and intrusive judiciary seeking closer scrutiny of executive actions. A sitting Prime Minister was hauled over the coals for contempt of court, for not writing a letter to the Swiss authorities over cases of corruption pending against President Zardari, despite the Constitution granting immunity to a serving President under Art 248.

Though Justice Chaudhry 'legitimised judicial activism', his frequent use of 'suo moto jurisdiction' 'declined into institutional trespass', the 'acme being the firing of a sitting Prime Minister' for contempt and almost 'forcing his successor to commit hara-kiri in the same manner'. This was 'populist justice', which vulgarised it while 'settling scores despite knowing that the opposite of justice is not injustice, but revenge'.[14]

The SC under CJ Chaudhry took undue interest in government policies regarding postings and transfers of civil servants, professional consultants and experts. Indeed, it went so far as to order that the government appoint a committee of neutral and credible persons to scrutinise and appoint the right man for the right job. This step stemmed perhaps from the need to stop cronyism and corruption, but it curtailed the executive's right to take decisions in the light of its own political requirements.[15]

Limitations of Judicial Activism

Despite a generally well respected activism, question marks remained over the Iftikhar Chaudhry Court's attitude towards cases touching on Islamic radicalism. All courts were reluctant to readily accept prosecutors' presentations at the charging stage against persons arrested as suspected terrorists unless cast iron evidence was forthcoming. The Prosecuting Judge trying the Salman Taseer murder case sought security cover and eventually had to seek exile in Saudi Arabia even as rose petals were bestowed by lawyers on his assassin, Mumtaz Qadri. In many such cases of preventive arrests, the civilian police and even military establishment were put on the defensive and could not get convictions. Also, though the Court took on the civil-military establishment in the 'disappearance cases', this remained a populist measure designed to appease agitating families, whereas no serious punitive actions were taken against uniformed personnel, especially of the Army and para-military forces. Though Gen (retd) Aslam Beg and former DG ISI, Asad Durrani were made to appear in Court in the Asghar Khan case alleging misuse of secret service funds to create the Islami Jamhoori Ittehad (IJI) in 1988-89, no punitive action was specified in logical culmination against them. The Army remained a sacred cow before this new found judicial activism.

With the appointment of Justice Tassaduq Hussain Jilani as the next Chief Justice of Pakistan, there is now an expectation in political circles that 'the era of undue intervention in civil-military affairs and political arena may come to an end', as Justice Jilani may 'prefer judicial vigilance over judicial populism'.[16]

Justice Jilani's term would last till early July, 2014 with the baton passing thereafter, in orderly successions, to Justice Nasir ul Mulk and Justice Mian Saqib Nasir. It is believed that judicial activism may not die down immediately though the tumult of the 2007-2012 years may not be repeated.

'Memogate'

The hiatus between the civilian executive and the military was brought into sharp focus in the 'Memogate affair'. Zardari's appointee as Pakistan's Ambassador to USA, Hussain Haqqani had to be peremptorily sacked as the Army leadership took umbrage over his alleged involvement in drafting a secret memorandum seeking assistance from US authorities to remain in power and requesting the military leadership in Pakistan to refrain from ousting the civilian government through a military coup. In return, the civilian regime is reported to have assured to follow policies desired by the US, inter alia promising to acquiesce in intrusive inspection over Pakistan's nuclear assets and ending safe havens to terrorists being used as 'non State actors' on the Afghan-Pak and Indo-Pak borders.

The controversy saw the old streak of politicians complaining to more powerful tiers of the Establishment re-surface. Opposition leader Nawaz Sharif filed a petition in the Supreme Court demanding an inquiry. The Supreme Court lost no time in opening up a broader inquiry into the origins, credibility and purpose of the memo. The DG, ISI Lt Gen Ahmed Shuja Pasha rushed to London, ostensibly only on the authorisation of the Army Chief without seeking permission from the civilian executive, where he held secret parleys with Mansoor Ijaz, a businessman of Pakistani origin in USA with whom Haqqani allegedly colluded while drafting the memorandum.

The Army Chief and DG, ISI filed an affidavit before the Supreme Court through the Defence Secretary, without approval of either the Defence Minister or PM. Yousuf Raza Gilani dismissed Defence Secretary, Lt Gen Naeem Khalid Lodhi and brought in a senior civilian bureaucrat, Cabinet Secretary Ms Nargis Sethi to hold dual charge of Defence. The Prime Minister lamented in a forceful speech in the National Assembly that no organ of State could claim to be "a State within the State", asserting that "decision making is done only by Parliament" and "all institutions of the county remain answerable" to it.

A somewhat bitter after-taste of this fracas was reflected in the tenor of self-congratulatory speeches of newly elected legislators after the May '13 elections, which focused on the need to limit the role of the hitherto 'all-powerful' civil-military bureaucracy (pejoratively referred in common vernacular political parlance as 'Aamriat').

Kayani takes notice

The senior Army leadership may have been forced to take cognizance of this sentiment of civil society. This became evident also in some recent speeches of the Army leadership just before the 2013 elections. Speaking to a group of officers at GHQ on Nov 05, 2012, Kayani acknowledged 'mistakes made in the past'. Emphasising that 'armed forces draw their strength from the bedrock of public support', Kayani cautioned against 'any effort to wittingly or unwittingly draw a wedge between the people and the Armed Forces of Pakistan', which would tantamount to 'undermining the national interest'. In what could be seen as a reaction to increasing recent judicial activism, directed also against past actions by the Army, Kayani mentioned in another speech, "While individual mistakes might have been made by all of us in the Country, these should be best left to the due process of law. As we all are striving for the rule of law, the fundamental principle; that no one is guilty until proven, should not be forgotten. Let us not pre-judge anyone, be it a civilian or a military person and extend it, unnecessarily, to undermine respective institutions.'[17]

Army Still the Best Bet?

Just before the May 2013 elections, reports appeared in Pakistani media on views expressed by Kayani at a closed door lunch with selected senior journalists and Editors, sometimes in the end of February or in early March, 2013, Kayani is reported to have opined in favour of free and fair elections. He denied that the Army had anything to do with propping up of either Tahirul Qadri (cleric now resident in Canada) or Imran Khan. He said that the Bangladesh model of Caretaker government had failed and did not have applicability in Pakistan, but he indicated that the Army would intervene in difficult internal situations like in FATA & Baluchistan only if asked to by the civilian political leadership.

Kayani also clarified that the Army was not in cahoots with, but supported talks with the Tehrik e Taliban Pakistan (TTP). However, these would have to be within the ambit of the Constitution. Issues that could be discussed included laying down of arms and a ceasefire. Civilians would be in the driving seat, but no agreement could be concluded with civilians without the military being on board.[18]

Ominously enough, while talking to these media editors, Kayani gave a long list of civilian failures, which read almost like a charge sheet against politicians. He clearly did not want to share the blame for civilian mismanagement. He lamented why civilians in Pakistan still remain much too scared of the ISI and why they do not use or depend more on civilian agencies like the Intelligence Bureau (IB). He opined that the Election

Commission (EC) was still quite weak and recalled the irony of having to identify himself as the Army Chief in his audience with the CEC, 'who was too old'![19]

Media and political analysts present at this meeting felt that Kayani was deliberately creating doubts about the capacity of civilian politicians and in a larger sense, the very efficacy of democracy as a system. It seemed as if he was not really in the mood to let the Army continue taking a back seat or create adequate space for the democratic process to settle in. The impression conveyed was that only Army Generals have the sagacity and vision to lead the country. What Kayani perhaps left implicit or unsaid in this interaction was that may be, at a later date, military rule could again become more acceptable.[20]

Abbottabad Enquiry Report

After the US raid killing Osama bin Laden, the Abbottabad Commission of Enquiry report handed a surprisingly scathing indictment concluding that Pakistan's Military and political leaders 'collectively displayed a degree of incompetence and irresponsibility, which was truly breathtaking'. This was described as the country's 'worst failure since 1971'. There was 'extensive complacency, inefficiency and negligence' not only of local civil administrative, police or military officials, 'but comprehensive and sustained failure of intelligence and security agencies' in not being able to detect OBL's presence.

Unerringly flagging the historical course of civil-military relations in the country as a contributory factor, the report blamed the 'military's exercise of authority in policy and administration, for which it neither had constitutional or legal authority, nor necessary expertise and competence'. It held it "unnecessary to specifically name them (those responsible) because it is obvious who they are" adding that "it may be politically unrealistic to suggest punishments for them (!)". It suggested 'grave complicity at an undetermined level' for this 'collective failure of the military, political and civil administration'.[21]

Among recommendations for the future, the Commission cautioned against a revival of the Army's Green Book ideology of too pervasive a role and suggested instead, 'honest, competent and consultative' leadership to democratically enunciate 'a national security policy, establish a National Security Council and bring in comprehensive intelligence and police reforms'. It also advocated 'dismantling of terrorist infrastructure', which has had such deleterious 'blow back effects' on the security establishment in recent years.

Though speculation in Pakistan media suggests this was a deliberate leak of one version of the report authored by ex-diplomat, Ashraf Jehangir Qazi, while the final version was apparently written out by the retired General, Nadeem Ahmed,[22] these recommendations about overhauling the legislative framework within which the security agencies operate, establishing accountability and shifting control of defence policy to civilian authorities seemed to strike at the core of Pakistan's security establishment. Controversy about who authored the report notwithstanding, it can hardly be seen to have been a whitewash; rather it definitely provided a long-overdue jolt to the system. The army, naturally, was not amused.

In this backdrop, the new civilian political executive under PM Nawaz Sharif is once again faced with the question whether it would like to traverse down the hazardous path of trying to bridle the Military and how soon or how effectively it would be able to do so. A number of problem areas can be identified where this politico-military dynamics can play out with unpredictable consequences: (i) how to deal with the Taliban – in Pakistan and Afghanistan; (ii) Military's role in governance and (iii) handling of complex, chronic problems like burgeoning sectarian strife, and the simmering insurgency in Baluchistan.

Dealing with the Tehrik e Taliban (TTP)

One of the foremost issues where differences of approach have been evident is on how to deal with the threat of Islamic terrorism.

In the past, the Army in Pakistan used the 'Islamic crutch' for symbolism – touting mottos of 'iman' (belief), taqwa (fear of Allah, righteousness of conduct), and 'jihad-fi-sabilillah' (fight in the cause of Allah) to justify repeated unconstitutional abrogation of the democratic process. It often turned a 'blind eye', not only because it was using Islamic parties to justify its domestic political repression, but also because it was using some of these groups as 'non-State actors' to sponsor low grade 'proxy' trans-border insurgency movements in Afghanistan, Indian Punjab and Kashmir. The situation changed after 9/11, when under US pressure, terrorist outfits operating across the Afghan-Pakistan border became targets, albeit selectively.

The Army's initial attempt to tackle the Tehrik e Taliban (TTP) militants in the Federally Administered Tribal Areas (FATA) through use of force had mixed results. After suffering initial reverses in 2003-2004, morale dipped to an all-time low. Even as Islamic militants continued to attack security convoys with impunity, desertions or tame surrenders of ill equipped policemen or FC personnel continued. Several 'peace accords' with the militants were concluded – Shakai (April '04), Sararogha (Feb '05), North Waziristan (Sept '06) and Swat (May '08) – but these proved short-lived.

Pashtun Army officers at senior management levels began to question the wisdom of lukewarm battle tactics in counter insurgency operations in FATA and Swat. Some Brigadiers and Major Generals asked for a re-examination of outdated doctrinal inhibitions and advocated a more wholehearted, classical military response, with strength in numbers. It was decided to deploy larger formations hitherto reserved for facing the Indian threat from the Eastern border to FATA. The Army geared up its counter-terrorism (COIN) capabilities in FATA and KP by bringing in sizable forces from its Eastern sector, to undertake 'clear, hold and build' operations.

The Frontier Corps, with Pashtun officers and ranks was given more teeth. In Waziristan, tribal rivalries between Mehsuds and Wazirs were played up, serving or retired Inter-Services Intelligence (ISI) intermediaries were deployed to work out local peace pacts, not all of which sustained over time.

However, the situation changed in 2009-2010, when the TTP started targeting the Military and Police establishments in Rawalpindi and Lahore. A mosque within Army Headquarters in Rawalpindi frequented by senior Army officers, Police Training schools in Lahore, buses carrying Special Services Group (SSG) personnel outside its headquarters in Cherat and civilian employees from Kahuta being carted through a crowded street of Rawalpindi were attacked by Islamic radicals.

The tribal militias were well armed and they retreated to the hills or across the border into Afghanistan every time they were confronted by a major operation of infantry forces in superior numbers, living to fight another day. If uneasy peace prevailed in Waziristan, trouble erupted in Bajaur, Mohmand or Orakzai. Swat was cleared through precision operations and an overwhelming force presence but Maulana Fazlullah escaped to Kunar, in Afghanistan. He continued launching attacks against security forces from there.

In a daring jailbreak at Bannu (April,2012), TTP militants released a large number of militants including Adnan Rashid, former air force employee accused of plotting the abortive assassination attempt against former President Musharraf in 2003. In July, 2013 in another daring jailbreak at Dera Ismail Khan, TTP claimed to have released over 230 prisoners. Though warned by intelligence agencies, police deployed at the jail failed to react. There were reports of reluctance even among army personnel asked to join in hot pursuit operations after the incident.

Since 2001, the Army has suffered 12,829 casualties in the war against terror, including 3097 killed – with an unusually high ratio of officers – one for every 16 soldiers killed – since it began fighting the Taliban. Total Army officers killed were estimated at 194.

These 'ghosts now haunt the top military leadership in Pakistan'.[23] On the one hand, the senior Army leadership has remained conscious of the need to maintain the Army's image as 'defender of Islam'. On the other, it has had to address morale issues and takes firm enough action to hit back when directly confronted in ground combat. This dichotomy continues to plague the Pakistani security forces. The Army leadership has to continually look over its shoulder to take cognizance of the sentiment of a majority of Pak Army personnel – officers as well as other ranks (ORs) not sympathizing with the war on terror.

After the May, 2013 elections, the new civilian politicians, who came to power appeared keen to pursue peace talks with the TTP. The PML (N) was perceived to be soft on Punjabi sectarian radical groups like the Lashkar e Jhangvi (LeJ) and other Punjabi Taliban, who were found to have links with the TTP and helped them to attack the Army and police in the past.

While Nawaz Sharif was not initially very specific about how he would deal with the Taliban, Imran Khan talked of extending an olive branch to the militants. During the election campaign, he was persistently critical of

US drone attacks in FATA. To gain populist mileage, he led a 'peace procession' up to Dera Ismail Khan, before being stopped by the Army from venturing further into FATA on grounds of security. Both Nawaz and Imran explored the option of roping in the Jamiat (JuI) Maulanas, Fazlur Rehman and Samiul Haq, as well as the Jamaat e Islami (JeI) leadership (Munawwar Hussain) for mediatory sallies to the TTP. A lot of confusion in approach seemed visible.

The proposal to hold an All Party meeting (APC) on July 12, 2013 did not fructify as Imran Khan proceeded to UK for medical treatment for his spine injuries, which was apparently pre-scheduled. He was demanding a separate briefing for himself by the Army Chief before attending any such APC. While the generals kept urging the civilians to "take ownership" of the war, neither Imran Khan nor Zardari seemed particularly interested in bailing out the Nawaz government when it comes to speaking with one voice on terrorism, just as Nawaz Sharif did not hold out a helping hand to Zardari when he was in the hot seat. They were apparently bent on paying back in the same coin.[24]

An APC was finally held on September 09, 2013. This time, Nawaz Sharif and Gen Kayani briefed Imran Khan separately just before the APC meeting. The APC resolution resolved to initiate an inclusive dialogue with all stakeholders to bring peace to the region. It also opposed drone attacks by USA and urged the government to take up the matter in the United Nations. The Nawaz government and the Army agreed to resort to political dialogue with the TTP. Gen Kayani was quoted to say, 'The Army will follow whatever decision is taken by the government'. Imran claimed that he persuaded Kayani to gradually thin out Army presence from FATA.[25] The TTP too welcomed this announcement though later, some factions introduced conditions, not accepting a unilateral ceasefire with renouncing of weapons and demanding a stoppage of drone attacks by America.

While political commentators in Pakistan initially commended this approach to 'talk to reconcilable militants', appreciating this 'rare civil-military partnership' to deal with the problem, others criticised the rather vague commitment to deal with hard line militants. They wondered whether this 'Munich/Chamberlain style appeasement' will lead to a different solution this time.[26]

The killing of 17 Div GOC, Maj Gen Sanaullah Khan Niazi in an

IED explosion on September 11, was claimed promptly by the Swat branch of the TTP. It again raised questions about the durability of the peace process. Army Chief Kayani warned sternly that though the Army wanted to give peace a chance, its rectitude should not be interpreted as a sign of weakness or incapacity to respond. The Army reacted strongly also against the Jamaat e Islami's depiction of only the terrorist as 'martyr' and not the Army soldier. This also caused revulsion among common people, akin to the anti-Taliban sentiment, which surfaced after flogging of women in Swat became public in 2009.

The killings of top TTP leaders, Waliur Rehman and Hakimullah Mehsudin drone attacks in North Waziristan were a big setback for the TTP and effectively put paid to the peace talks, at least in the short-term. A hardliner like Maulana Fazlullah was appointed the successor to Hakimullah Mehsud despite not being a Mehsud and not having a base in Waziristan. The new TTP leadership has been increasingly faction-driven in subsequent months. Not only were the Mehsuds of Waziristan not reconciled to the imposition of a leader from outside in Mullah Fazlullah, rival leaders emerged from the Hakimullah and Waliur Rehman factions and their supporters clashed several times. The Nawaz government also faced difficulty in enunciating its new security policy and in deciding how to co-ordinate decision making – whether through the Defence Committee of Cabinet (DCC) or by reviving the National Security Council (NSC), as has been an old demand of the Army.

On October 25, 2013, a Pakistan Protection Ordinance, 2013 was promulgated, listing special offences, which could be deemed crimes against the State and arming police with special powers to apprehend those suspected of waging war against the security of the State. The Opposition parties in the Senate have been reluctant to give a green signal to these draconian powers.

The newly set up National Counter Terrorism Authority (NACTA) drafted an Internal Security policy document. There has been talk of setting up a 'Task Force' to deal with the problem of terrorism, in all its facets and the need to focus on capacity building in the police, improvement in intelligence co-ordination, morale, provision of better equipment and training. There is mention of the need to introduce the narrative of peace and de-radicalisation as well as steps to re-integrate reformed terrorists into the mainstream.

A decision was announced to set up a new Counter Terrorism force comprising crack commando officers from the Army on deputation. Also, there is a near revolt in the Punjab Police, with officers up to the rank of Deputy Superintendent of Police agitating and lamenting neglect and erosion of its powers in the name of empowering a new anti-terror outfit. Some analysts described this attempt as 'a quick-fix formula'.[27]

After closed door deliberations between the new civilian leadership and the Army, it has apparently been decided to follow the Indian model of referring these crucial matters to the Cabinet Committee on Security (CCS), where all three Service Chiefs and the Chairman, Joint Chiefs of Staff Committee would be present, but the civilians would be in a numerical majority. The first meeting of this Committee was held after Kayani's retirement, with new Army Chief, Gen Raheel Sharif in attendance.

While these steps may be well intended and reflect, perhaps, a seriousness of intent to deal with this grave threat, it remains to be seen how effective it will prove in implementation.

Seasoned academics, who have long studied civil military relations in Pakistan, claim that the country's counter-terrorism policy must observe certain essential principles. First, violence and terrorism must not be tolerated. Second, the primacy of the State must be asserted over all organisations, groups and individual within its territory. Third, the Military must assert its control over the tribal areas. The confusion over whether the current impasse there is 'a problem of capacity' or 'a matter of policy', with militants being given 'space to survive' must end. Fourth, dialogue with TTP must be within the Constitution and fifth, as Pakistan faces different types of terrorism – religious, ethnic, sectarian and nationalist – different strategies would be needed to deal with them.[28]

Visiting the Corps Headquarters Peshawar on December 21, in his first policy statement on the all-important issue of the war on terror, Gen Raheel Sharif declared that the "military will not tolerate terror attacks and effective response will be given to the terrorists".[29] Subsequently, the Army has hit back at TTP in FATA through aerial bombardment and local ground actions.

On Jan 28, 2014, Gen Raheel Sharif, COAS met the PM. Nawaz Sharif addressed the National Assembly on Jan 29, 2014 in what was widely expected to declare finally the government's resolve to deal with the terrorists firmly, but it ended re-iterating that one more attempt would be made to resume talks with the Taliban. A four-member Committee of Interlocutors was named on behalf of the Government, this time including individuals with some experience and understanding of dealing with the problem – namely veteran journalists, Irfan Siddiqui and Rahimullah Yusuf Zai, Capt. (retd) Aamir, formerly with ISI and Rustam Shah Mohmand, a retired civil servant and former Ambassador of Pakistan to Afghanistan, some of whom were known to oppose the military option.

The TTP Shoora named its own representatives to the talks, resuscitating Maulana Samiul Haq and Jamaat e Islami's KP cleric, Prof. Ibrahim, but after a stuttering start, the talks stalled over unreasonable demands relating to prisoner release, leaving areas of 'no go' territory free for the Taliban in FATA and imposition of Shariah, on none of which the Army leadership was prepared to yield ground. Since then, the Army persuaded Capt Aamir to withdraw from the government's interlocutor team.

It seemed for a while that the PML (N) was covering its flanks before finally plumping for an eventual military option.[30] The PM's reluctance stemmed possibly from a fear of TTP backlash against military reprisals focused exclusively in Punjab. Since then, factional differences within the TTP have been exploited by intelligence agencies and the Army has hit back through aerial bombardment and limited ground offensives to re-establish their writ in parts of North and South Waziristan. Presently, though Interior Minister, Chaudhry Nisar Ali has still not jettisoned the talks' process formally, the new Army leadership appears to have convinced PM Nawaz Sharif about the need for eventual firm though limited military action to contain the TTP. Doubts remain about the results, which may or may not ensue from this fresh attempt of talks.

The strategy that finally emerges will also have to factor in the evolving situation in Afghanistan as US/ISAF troop withdrawals continue in 2013-14. Both the Pakistan Army and TTP seem on board to continue providing safe havens to the Afghan Taliban during this period. However, agreement on the mechanics of peace-making and talks on power sharing with the

Afghan Taliban have proved elusive. Though the American withdrawal will remove a major grievance of the Taliban that the Pakistan Army is no longer acting as a tool of foreign interests, radicals holed up in North Waziristan, the suicide bombers, the support network throughout the country will feel a surge of confidence resulting from the US withdrawal. If there is a perception that negotiations achieve a pro-Pakistani power sharing dispensation, the atmosphere may improve, but the underlying problem will not disappear. A change of government in Kabul may not solve Pakistan's Taliban problem. New equations may evolve between Afghan Taliban sharing power there and the TTP inside Pakistan.[31]

Potential for Civil-Military Conflict in Baluchistan

The Pakistani military establishment has always ruthlessly suppressed Baluch nationalism in Baluchistan, while the civilian governments of the day have helplessly looked on.

Immediately following partition, Mir Ahmed Yar Khan, the Khan of Kalat claimed independence and refused to join Pakistan. Jinnah did not accept this. After many attempts to negotiate a diplomatic solution, the Pakistan Army marched into Kalat on 1 April 1948 and forced Mir Ahmed Yar Khan to agree to accession. His younger brother, Prince Abdul Karim took to arms and fled to the mountains across the border in Afghanistan with 700 men. After a few months of guerilla warfare, Prince Karim was persuaded to return and agreed to lay down arms. The government broke the amnesty, captured and imprisoned Karim and his men on their return to Kalat.

The second outbreak of violence occurred in response to the 1955 "One Unit" plan. The Baluch saw this as an affront to the little remaining power they enjoyed at the provincial level and revolted. Prince Karim, who had recently been released from jail, formed the People's Party and brought local people together to demonstrate against the changes. In reaction to this threat, on 6 October 1958, the Pakistan Army once again marched into Kalat and arrested him. The Pakistan Army again put down the insurrection with force.

Nauroz Khan, Sardar of the Zehri tribe led a guerrilla war in response to the actions of the Army. This time, however, in contrast to the events of

1948-1950, the insurgents enjoyed wider support from the population. The insurgency simmered on for over a year, with no clear victor emerging. Both sides agreed to discuss a ceasefire in the spring of 1960. Nauroz Khan and his band agreed to lay down their weapons in exchange for amnesty. Again the government reneged, arrested and hanged Nauroz Khan along with his son and five other commanders for treason. The Pakistan Army began to increase its cantonments in the province. Sher Mohammad Marri led the next phase of the insurgency, raising a guerrilla army of Marri, Mengal, and Bugti tribals, who controlled 45,000 square miles of land in their respective tribal areas. They attacked weak points along the Pakistan Army's lines of communication, typically avoiding large scale engagements. The Army responded with heavy handed tactics against the guerrillas, when they could find them. They attacked their families, communities, and property when they could not.

In 1969, General Yahya Khan rescinded the "One Unit" policy. As a result, the fighting died down. Sher Mohammad agreed to a ceasefire in 1970 and the status of a "Province" was given to Baluchistan. Provincial elections were held.

The bloodiest uprising in Baluchistan occurred from 1973 until 1978. The impetus was provided by Prime Minister Bhutto's decision to dissolve the National Awami Party (NAP) government after they won the 1972 elections in Baluchistan, on charges of alleged collusion with the Soviet Union, publicising the capture of weapons and ammunition from the residence of an Iraqi military attaché in Islamabad as evidence. Bhutto brought in Nawab Akbar Bugti as the Governor of the province, in an effort to drive a wedge between the Bugti tribes and the numerically more populous Marris and Mengals. These actions infuriated the Baluch people and insulted their sense of personal and tribal honour. The Sardar of the Marri tribe, Khair Baksh Marri, organised Baluch resistance under the banner of the Baluch People's Liberation Front (BPLF). By 1974, the insurgents had control over most of the ground lines of communication entering the province from the east, including the railway, which connected Baluchistan with the Punjab.

Approximately 80,000 troops from the Pakistan Army were deployed in Baluchistan during this counter insurgency operation. Elite commando units of the Special Services Group (SSG) were used, experiencing their first combat. Again, the Army used heavy handed tactics to find and destroy the insurgents. In the summer of 1974, Iran provided Pakistan with thirty AH-1 Huey Cobra attack helicopters along with other military hardware. The Pakistan Army used these gunships effectively to strafe even civilian inhabited areas. A decisive battle was fought in Marri territory on the plains of Chamalang in the northeast of the province. Baluch Marri tribal families, along with males of non-fighting age, had moved to the plains to graze their livestock in the spring of 1974, congruent with their traditional migratory pattern. The Pakistan Army harassed these families in order to coax the fighters down from the hills to engage them in a conventional battle. The ploy worked. On 3 September 1974, the Pakistan military attacked. Ground forces were supported by strafing with Mirage jets and the Cobra gunships. The Baluch fought valiantly, but were forced to retreat to the mountains when they ran out of ammunition. The exact figures of casualties in this battle are conflicting, but conservative accounts assess 3,300 Army casualties and 5,300 Baluch fighters. The insurgency suffered a major setback.

In July, 1977 General Zia ul-Haq ousted Bhutto through a military coup. In 1978, Zia released 6,000 Baluch prisoners and offered amnesty for guerrilla fighters, who were willing to give up arms. Tensions declined as a result. Lt. Gen Rahimuddin Khan (later X Corps Commander in Rawalpindi and whose daughter was married to Zia's son) was made the Governor of the province, marginalising Akbar Bugti. He tried to channelise some foreign development aid into programmes for education, village electrification and women incentives' schemes in the province. The Pakistan Petroleum Company started exploration for gas in the Sui gas fields. Gwadar was notified as a separate district and integrated into the province. While political unrest in the province continued, the armed insurrection and guerrilla actions against the Pakistan security forces abated, but the underlying causes of the Baluch separatist movement were not addressed.

'A' and 'B' Areas – Police versus Levies

Traditionally, Baluchistan was governed by the British under a three-tier security arrangement. Baluchistan Levies, a paramilitary force comprising mostly local tribes, recruited with the help of tribal Sardars were given responsibility of law and order in rural areas, which were categorised as

'B-Areas' (comprising 95 per cent of area of province) while urban parts of the province, (main cities), dubbed 'A Areas' (comprising only five per cent of the area), were placed under the Police. The Levies were initially quite successful in bringing in a concept of community policing in the province. They were considered more reliable, efficient and cheap in setting up and were given rudimentary arms and equipment. They used camels and horses for policing. Some critics contended that they were being misused by the Sardars to perpetrate their own vested interests.

During Musharraf's administration, in 2003, the Provincial Government was pressurised to disband the Levies. Police jurisdiction was extended to the entire province. From 2007 to 2009, the entire province experienced Police rule. The strength of the police force doubled and expenditure increased manifold, yet statistics of serious crimes jumped upwards. This move was opposed by all political parties in the province and was challenged in the Baluchistan High Court. Its order in 2010 restoring the system of Levies was welcomed widely.[32]

In 2001, Musharraf announced plans to locate three new cantonments in Baluchistan, at Sui, Kohlu and Gwadar. More than 500 Chinese engineers and workers came in for the development of Gwadar port. This created considerable resentment among Baluch populace, enhancing fears that the familiar pattern of forcible acquisition of prime agricultural lands, displacement of locals by outsiders, mostly Punjabis and Pashtuns, as had occurred during the construction of the high value Gwadar port and Mekran coastal highway, would be repeated. On May 03, 2004 three Chinese engineers were killed in a rocket attack claimed by a Baluch insurgent group.

In recent times, the main counter insurgency role has devolved on the Frontier Corps (FC), which has deployed 33,600 troops in the province. These include a Special Operations Group. Though formally under the Chief Minister of Baluchistan and accountable to the Federal Interior Ministry, in practice, the DG, FC takes orders from the GOC XII Corps, Baluchistan. Its senior command is invariably filled by officers seconded from the Army, for deputation periods ranging from two to three years. Lower rank and file may be locally recruited, but seldom gets promoted to command positions.

Traditionally, very few Baluch joined the Army, both at the officer level or as Other Ranks. Partly, reasons for this have been historical as the British recruited mostly from the 'martial' races in Potohar (central/ northern Punjab-Chakwal, Jhelum, Campbellpur) and later, Pashtuns from NWFP. The Baluch regiment of the Army retained a heavy Punjabi bias in its senior officer echelons – Gen Kayani is from the Baluch Infantry arm. Several other senior Baluch Regt officers have held important posts, but these officers have not been known to share any empathy for the Baluch.

Since the mid 1990s, efforts have been made to broaden the recruitment base by relaxing educational and physical qualifying benchmarks for Sindhis and Baluch. It was hoped that the representation of Baluch would go up from almost nil to four per cent by 2001. By 2005, though, and under special recruitment drives launched during Gen Kayani's tenure as COAS, more officer recruits from Baluchistan (not necessarily all ethnic Baluch) have been enlisted, to somehow reflect the population distribution of the country – wherein Baluch are shown having reached five per cent in Army recruitment as well. Recent media reports indicate more progress in this direction.[33] Nine thousand Baluch youth were reportedly inducted for training in 2010, relaxing standards of chest width, height and education. Also 2000 Baluch were inducted in the Chamalang Levies. This effort has not yet contributed to lessen Baluch alienation against Punjabi domination in the Army.

On January 2, 2005 Dr. Shazia Khalid, a Medical Officer posted in the Pakistan Petroleum complex hospital at Sui was raped at night, allegedly by one Captain Hammad, a Pakistan Army officer deployed with the Defence Security Guards. Further investigations were hushed up and President Musharraf denied that any Army officer was involved. Though Dr. Shazia was a non-Baluch, the Baluch tribal sense of honour was hurt. They viewed it as one more instance of high-handedness by a Punjabi dominated Army.

Pendency and inadequate payment of Sui gas royalty claims by the Federal government was another issue aggravating Bugti tribesman. They started attacking Sui gas installations and other military installations in the area with rockets and mortars. Between 7th and 15th January, 2005 more than 450 rockets were fired. Responding in typically high-handed manner, the Frontier Corps (FC) moved in additional forces and arrested

80 suspects. The residential campus of Baluch leader, Sardar Akbar Bugti was also fired upon by the FC personnel.

The clashes continued sporadically during the year despite efforts to negotiate a ceasefire with the dissenting tribesmen. On Dec 13, rockets were fired on the Quetta garrison. Though no casualties were reported, the Baluchistan Liberation Army (BLA) claimed to be behind the firing. Shortly thereafter, Musharraf came to Kohlu to address a rally. While he was speaking at the Frontier Corps camp at Maiwand, near Kohlu, again rocket firing was reported in the vicinity. The next day, a helicopter carrying the Director General, Frontier Corps, Baluchistan Maj Gen Shujaat Zamir Dar and his Deputy, Brig Salim Nawaz was fired upon and hit, causing injuries to both. This incensed Musharraf to publicly claim that Baluch Sardars would be 'wiped out' and 'not know what hit them' when the Army retaliated.

In the crackdown, which followed, more than 50 Baluch rebel fighters were killed and 150 injured, including civilians. In mid-March 2006, Akbar Bugti along with his tribesmen moved into the Kohlu hills. On March 26, Musharraf further provoked the Bugtis by organising a resettlement of rival sub-tribes in Dera Bugti district – the Kalpars, Masouris and Rahejas – with whom the Bugtis had been engaged in decades of family strife.

On August 26, 2006, Bugti was killed in what was initially claimed to be an air to surface missile attack by an Army/FC helicopter, while he was hiding in a cave in the hills bordering Kohlu/Dera Bugti districts.

Essentially, Musharraf followed a three-pronged policy, which has been traditionally employed by the Pakistani military establishment to keep Baluch aspirations in check. While keeping the door open for dialogue with political parties, who confined their activities to overt political dissent without indulging in acts of violence, a no-holds-barred military campaign was carried out against Baluch youth – projecting such elements as terrorists. The establishment's response against Baluch nationalists was kept separate from the flank of dealing with Al Qaeda and Taliban of the Quetta Shoora, active along the Afghan-Pak border, who were given safe havens in mosques located on the outskirts of Quetta (Pashtunabad).

After the Bugti murder, the pattern of Baluch resistance has changed. Earlier, it depended more on 'nationalist Sardars' – the Marris, Mengals or even Bugti. The Sardars kept their medieval privileges over their own people intact, inuring them from the modernising influences of 'State generated' development. Since then, there has been a splintering of nationalists. Several factions of Baluch insurgents have sprouted – the Baluch Liberation Army (BLA), led by Hyairbair Marri (currently in exile, in UK), the Baluchistan Republican Army (BRA) of Brahmadagh Bugti (also in exile, possibly in Switzerland) and the Baluchistan Liberation Front (BLF), led by former Baluchistan National Movement student leader turned militant, Dr Allah Nazar. The latter was arrested by the intelligence agencies on March 25, 2005 and remained under detention for over a year. He re-surfaced on August 12, 2006, but was jailed again in Quetta for several months. After his release on bail, he went into hiding. He claimed that he had been tortured in the prison cells and he pledged, going underground thereafter, to 'purge Baluchistan of the Punjabi Army'.

There has been a spate of killings of Punjabi settlers in the province (at least 1200) in last three years, many of whom were working as teachers, doctors, middle-level bureaucrats and professionals. An exodus of over 20,000 settlers, mostly from Punjab, was reported by the Human Rights Commission of Pakistan (HRCP) in 2011. The Military Establishment accused nationalists of killing moderate elements settled in the province. Well known poet, Habib Jalib Baluch was shot by unknown gunmen on June 15, 2010 for which a hitherto unknown group calling itself 'Baluch Mussallah Difai Tanzeem' claimed responsibility. Another moderate thinker, Maula Baksh Dasti was killed a month later, on July 11, 2010. Nationalists deny these allegations and blame intelligence agencies for sending out specially designated 'vigilante squads' to eliminate voices of sanity.

Use of Sectarian Card

Extremist Islamic sectarian outfits like the Lashkar e Jhangvi (LeJ) joined the fray, sending out 'killer squads' targeting Quetta's hapless Hazaras as well as other Shias living in the provinces or travelling for religious purposes to Iran.

Judiciary-Military conflict over Disappearance Cases

Preventive arrests of dissenters by police and intelligence agencies have been common in Baluchistan. According to a recent Asia Society report, authorities in Pakistan have found it difficult to convict suspected terrorists and criminals for want of proper criminal investigation and lack of evidence for charge sheeting of cases.[34] This has indirectly contributed to the phenomenon of 'disappearances'. When families of dissenters raised a hue and cry, either before a sympathetic and receptive media or sought legal remedy in courts, often such quests ended in tragedy with the dead body of missing persons being dumped on the road-side in mysterious circumstances. The Baluch Diaspora abroad and intellectuals have described these as 'kill and dump operations'.[35]

Recently, in new found judicial activism, which may force the FC and Military Intelligence/ISI to behave in a more circumspect manner in the future, Chief Justice Iftikhar Chaudhry held several suo moto hearings in these 'disappearance cases', castigating the nonchalance of both civilian and military intelligence agencies in the investigation and follow up of these cases. The Director General, Frontier Corps, Maj Gen Obaidullah Khan Khattak was asked to appear in Court personally and he was notionally censored. The civil administration and the then Chief Minister of Baluchistan, Aslam Raisani were also criticised for dereliction of responsibility.

The Army has been quick to deny any culpability on death squads, covert or overt military operations or missing persons in their custody. In October 2012, the Inter Services Public Relations (ISPR) issued a press release reiterating the Army's full support for the political process in Baluchistan, as long as this remained within the Constitution of Pakistan.

The fractious vote in the 2008 Provincial Assembly elections saw a government coming to power, with 51 out of 65 MPAs becoming Ministers. While all of them partook of State funds and developmental largesse, there was no impact in addressing larger issues. The 7th National Finance Commission (NFC) Award increased the share of federal revenues for the State from five to nine per cent. The Aghaz-e-Huqooq package and the Eighteenth Constitutional Amendment also announced important steps. However, these political initiatives received two types of responses: outright rejection or skepticism about effectiveness of implementation and have so far remained mostly on paper.[36]

Meanwhile, insurgency continued to simmer. Cadres of different rebel groups numbering about 5,000-7,000 remain in the hills. They are ill-equipped in terms of sophisticated or modern arms held and may also be facing shortage of funds. Baluchistan, thus, represents the 'cumulative consequence of deliberate and exploitative neglect, stupid self-governance, and the arrogant and ignorant use of force, under civilian and military rule, for six decades.'[37]

Returning from three years' self-imposed exile abroad, Baluch leader Akhtar Mengal deposed before the Supreme Court in Islamabad on the situation in Baluchistan (October, 2012). He demanded (i) an end to all overt and covert military operations against the Baluch; (ii) production of all missing persons; (iii) disbanding of all proxy death squads by the ISI and MI; (iv) free political play by all Baluch nationalist parties without interference by ISI and MI; (v) bringing to book all those responsible for killings and disappearances; and (vi) rehabilitation of thousands of Baluch displaced by the conflict.[38]

The May, 2013 elections in Baluchistan again resulted in a fractured mandate in the province. The PML (N) was able to form a government, in alliance with the PkMAP, National Party (NP) of Hasil Bizenjo and Independents. Non-religious Pakhtun parties like the Paktunkhwa Milli Awami Party (PkMAP) of Mehmood Khan Achakzai did better than the Jamiat e Ulema (JuI-Fazlur Rehman) and JuI (Nazariyati). Choosing a leader proved difficult due to competing claims of Sardars – Sanaullah Zehri and Jangez Marri, but finally, a 'non-Sardar' politician from the National Party, Dr. Abdul Malik Baluch was appointed the CM.

The Baluchistan Nationalist Party (BNP) of Akhtar Mengal participated in the polls in the face of threats from more militant nationalists, but could win only two seats at the provincial level. Mengal met Nawaz Sharif on July 11, 2013 to discuss some of these issues, but no details emerged of the road ahead.

After the 2013 elections, a complete overhaul of the police security structure in the province has been ordered. This is easier said than done. There is talk of restoring a single chain of command under civilian authority, but it is not clear whether the Frontier Corps will take kindly to severance of its umbilical cord from the Army. Though the new CM has recently called for an All Party dialogue to deal with the Baluch problem and has said that the onus for further response now rests with the insurgents, there is no guarantee that violent actions by both sides would be stopped.

So far, there have been no clear indicators how the military or the nationalists would behave in the changed political ambience after the elections. There were reports of insurgents attacking Army or FC personnel deployed for relief, rehabilitation work during the recent earthquake in Awaran.

There is no confirmed evidence yet that the Army has stopped being in denial about the extent and depth of Baluch alienation. In this complex backdrop, the Nawaz Sharif government has to find a way to accommodate demands for greater autonomy for the Baluch, while balancing against the Army's reservations about not exceeding constitutional limits. Differences, if any, between the new Army leadership and Nawaz Sharif on how he tackles this issue may well test out, in a broader context, how civil military equations evolve in the country as a whole.

Spreading Sectarian Strife

Pakistan continues to be plagued by endemic sectarian strife. Fanatical groups like the Sipah e Sahaba, now re-named Ahle Sunnatwal Jamaat (ASWJ) and Lashkar e Jhangvi (LeJ) continue perpetrating horrific pogroms of Hazaras in Quetta and Shias, elsewhere in Pakistan. Their leaders – Malik Ishaq and Maulana Ahmed Ludhianvi enjoy considerable latitude from law enforcing authorities despite involvement in criminal actions. There are reports of enhanced support for such organisations within the security forces. This prevents unbiased and objective remedial action by the State to convey a sense of fair play to minority groups in civil society. Observance of Muharram in Rawalpindi this year saw large scale arson and sectarian clashes all over the country. Reprisal killings of Shia and Sunni clerics continue unabated. This violence has cast its shadow on Karachi as well.

Tackling the law and order situation in Karachi has always had the potential of creating civil-military discord. Chronic ethnic and sectarian violence has plagued the greater Karachi urban agglomeration in the last few years, causing economic and industrial downturn in the erstwhile prosperous business hub and main port of Pakistan. During the last six months alone, 1726 persons were killed, compared to 1205 for the same period last year.[39] There are exclusive 'no go areas' in Mohajir resident localities where Pathans cannot go. New settlement of Pashtuns has taken place in outlying suburbs where land mafias operate. Islamic radicals of Pashtun ethnicity have entered newer settlements and set up mosques, which adhere to more violent theological doctrines and preaching.

The Mohajir Quami Movement (MQM) grew phenomenally as an urban political force after the frequent Mohajir-Pathan riots between1978-1984. Earlier, Mohajirs had come out as a united political force agitating against preferential educational reservation policies favouring Sindhis announced during Mumtaz Bhutto's Chief Minister-Ship of Sindh in 1977. Despite factional schisms engineered by the ISI in the mid-1990s, which saw violence erupt between factions led by Altaf Hussain and the Haqiqi group led by Afaq and Badr, the MQM could oust the Jamaat e Islami as a political force from Karachi. Subsequently, its leadership grew increasingly powerful and Altaf Hussain started exercising near fascist control over his satraps despite remaining in exile, in UK.

Despite a fractious past, which saw killing of an Army Major in a Mohajir ghetto of the city, the MQM (A) developed fairly comfortable rapport with the Army leadership during the last decade, both under Musharraf and Kayani. The current DG, ISI Lt. Gen Zahirul Islam was previously Corps Commander in Karachi. Lately however, there have been indications of a cooling off of relations with the Army, for reasons which are not quite evident so far.

The MQM (A) dominated elections in Karachi's 20 constituencies in the last few elections. In 2008, it won 17 NA seats. The May, 2013 elections have seen some changes. Though it went one better in terms of seats held, winning 18 NA seats with 71.56 per cent of the total votes cast, it lost ground to Pashtun backed PTI candidates in some constituencies. The election process was vitiated by reports of violence and several complaints of intimidation, fraud and ballot rigging. In the Sindh Provincial Assembly, it won 37 seats.

The MQM (A) allied with the PPP government at the Centre and in the Province after the 2008 elections. The relationship frayed later, especially over the implementation of the Local Bodies ordinance. This time, it is not currently in alliance with the PPP led Provincial government in Sindh.

MQM (A) leader, Altaf Hussain is in a difficult position following investigations by the British Police in the Imran Farooq murder, search of his house in London and discovery of huge caches of unaccounted foreign currency.

Karachi – Ethnic Cauldron

The Karachi Police has not been able to effectively control the deteriorating law and order situation. Postings to Police stations and other key supervisory jobs in the Police became highly politicised and motivated by monetary considerations designed to preserve various vested interests of crime and drug syndicates. Though there are 106 Police Stations and four DIG Zones in Karachi, the police are hopelessly outnumbered. The Police-people ratio is skewed adversely at 186 policemen per one lakh population, which is below the standard average of 222 for South Asia. It has archaic equipment and its policing records, including vital updates of illegal arms holdings, bad characters' lists, etc. have fallen hopelessly behind the pace of burgeoning settlements.

Federal governments have usually taken the soft option of calling in Pakistan Rangers for more effective policing or curbing of frequent spurts of violence. 12,500 of the total force of 25,000 Sindh Rangers are deployed in Karachi. The Rangers are usually headed by Army Officers on deputation. In the recent past, senior Major Generals have been entrusted the difficult Karachi assignment, often taking over on promotion as three star Lieutenant Generals as GOC of V Corps, Karachi. Demarcation of policing responsibilities between the Rangers and the Police has not always been clearly defined. Special operations of search and seizure do take place sporadically, to cleanse the city of hardened criminals but the effectiveness of these operations wears off in time.

In early September, 2013 the deteriorating Karachi law and order situation forced the Prime Minister and Interior Minister to rush down to Karachi and hold all party parleys before announcing a special de-criminalizing drive, to rein in violent cadres of different political and ethnic forces. Though there was talk, briefly of calling in the Army, which the MQM (A) supported, consensus prevailed ultimately to let the Rangers execute this drive under notional supervision of the Sindh Chief Minister.

Rangers have been tasked to pick up violent offenders afresh, cutting across party lines and ostensibly, without political interference this time.

The Police top officials have been shuffled and new officers brought in. Initial arrests in this new drive have brought forth usual squealing and complaints of partisan action from affected parties.

Though the current Governor of Sindh, MQM (A)'s Ishratul Abad has not been changed so far, relations between the PML (N) and MQM (A) have not been very comfortable, with an undercurrent of persisting ethnic discord and suspicion (Mohajir versus Punjabi) dampening development of close political bonhomie. In the past, the Army could take advantage of discord between the Benazir Bhutto's PPP government at the Centre and the MQM in Karachi. The Nawaz Sharif government will have to keep this in mind while crafting its overall approach to deal with the law and order situation in Karachi.

PPP in Bad Shape

The 2013 elections have left the PPP badly battered and bruised. It was hardly allowed to canvass due to threats from the Taliban. Results showed it had been reduced to mere regional presence with 33 seats from its rural Sindhi bastion. In 1997, it also lost badly to Nawaz Sharif's PML (N) but received 23 per cent of the vote. This time, it has fallen to as low a figure as 15 per cent. It was routed in Punjab, even from urban pockets of strength. Not only did it not execute programmes relating to bread and butter issues dear to the common man and the urban lower middle classes, its leaders remained scandal ridden and hungry for power and pelf.

The lack of any charismatic leader at the helm was badly felt. In the absence of Benazir and with her children still remote from the party, the elder scion, Bilawal was rumoured to have differences with father, Asif Zardari. The latter's 'darbari' culture kept loyal party 'jiyalas' at bay.

Though it may be too early to conclude that this result demonstrates the limitations of dynastic politics in South Asia, the PPP seems denuded from 'a victim narrative', having served a full five-year term. More disconcertingly, a third political force has emerged in the shape of the Pakistan Tehrik e Insaaf of Imran Khan, competing perhaps for the same political space, though right of centre in its orientation. It could even be said that PPP as a political force thrived in opposition under martial law, not in democratic circumstances.[40]

To rise from the ashes, the PPP government in Sindh will have to meet better yardsticks of governance. This may depend on several factors, especially on whether it can forge a new partnership with MQM(A) and also on the evolution of some new leaders from within. Lately, Asif Zardari seems to have decided to project his son, Bilawal as a politically charismatic, 'risen again' Bhutto, who has encouragingly enough, spoken about the need to confront Islamic radicalism in Pakistan frontally.

New Army Chief Selected

In a major decision, PM Nawaz Sharif finally selected Lt Gen Raheel Sharif as the new Army Chief on November 28, 2013, one day before Kayani's retirement. This was a surprise choice as Raheel was third in the seniority pecking order, below Haroon Aslam and Rashad Mehmood. The latter's earlier posting as Chief of General Staff had marked him out as Kayani's favourite. While Haroon was overlooked, Rashad Mehmood has been accommodated in the other, largely ceremonial four stars slot of Chairman, Joint Chiefs of Staff Committee (CJCSC). Raheel Sharif hails from Gujrat, in Punjab. His father was a junior commissioned officer, who was given honorary rank of Major after retirement. His brother, Major Shabbir Sharif was a martyr in the 1971 war with India. Raheel Sharif belongs to the same 'Kashmiri' biradari (sub-caste) as Nawaz Sharif, but is not a relative. He worked under Lt Gen (retd) Abdul Qadir Baluch, a member of the Nawaz Cabinet, who recommended him, ostensibly because he was known to keep a low profile and did not display political ambition.

The Musharraf Treason Trial

When former Army Chief, Gen (retd) Pervez Musharraf returned to Pakistan before the May 2013 elections, there was speculation about how vindictively he could be treated if Nawaz Sharif came to power once again. Apart from possible Saudi pressure restraining such a reaction, Nawaz was conscious that the Army would not take kindly to berating or humiliating a former Army Chief beyond a point. His main problem on this front came from the former Chief Justice, Iftikhar Mohd Chaudhry, who appeared hell-bent to try Musharraf for all his past misdemeanours. The registration of murder cases against Musharraf in the Bugti killing and the Lal Masjid operation strengthened this perception. There seemed to be a vested interest to selectively punish one person alone, who had rendered the judges impotent in the recent past. A recent lower court order however, allowed Musharraf bail in the Bugti case.

The Nawaz government took up treason proceedings against Musharraf under Art 6 of the Constitution for his imposition of a special emergency on November, 03, 2007, dismissing the Judges bench under Iftikhar Chaudhry, despite growing disquiet among retired and serving military personnel. After Kayani's retirement, Musharraf claimed that he had the backing of the Army and was surprised why Kayani did not take a stand against what seemed a clear case of vendetta by one or two persons.[41]

Though the Senate had earlier passed a resolution supporting such a trial, Senator Chaudhry Shujaat Hussain of the Pakistan Muslim League (Q) party, which had been part of Musharraf's government, urged dropping of the word 'traitor' or 'Ghaddar' (in Urdu vernacular), from the Article, as it was inappropriate to describe a former Army Chief in this manner.

A new dimension developed due to Musharraf's sudden heart ailment (Jan 02, 2014), which occurred when he was going to appear before the special tribunal set up to try him. He was admitted to the Armed Forces Cardiology Institute, where he has remained ever since. His doctors there, senior Army Generals, issued a medical report indicating that he needed angiography, but added that the patient desired to have this done abroad, not in Pakistan. The medical report was placed before the Judges in the Special Court, but Musharraf had to finally appear before them , to be formally indicted. An unwritten understanding was reportedly arrived at between the Army leadership and the politicians that afterwards, Musharraf would be allowed to leave the country, ostensibly to visit his ailing mother in UAE. However, the PML (N) resiled from this 'deal', holding that only the superior Judiciary had the power to remove his name from the 'Exit Control List'.

Attack on Hamid Mir

Meanwhile, several Ministers in the Nawaz Sharif government joined the media debate to assert the correctness of the civilian political authority's position on trying Musharraf and allowing him to leave the country just yet.

Musharraf's defence, now led by the arch legal 'whiz kid', who defended many past military takeovers, veteran lawyer Sharifuddin Pirzada, is making the case that Musharraf acted on the advice of his team of administrators then, which included not only civilian politicians like then PM, Shaukat Aziz, but also Army Generals, like Kayani himself, then DG, ISI.

Worried on account of a serious security threat in his Islamabad farm house, Musharraf has since moved to Karachi, where the Army feels more comfortable tending to his security.

On April 19, 2014 Hamid Mir, Geo TV's popular media show anchor, who had been in the forefront of the media tirade against Musharraf, was attacked by unknown gunmen while on way to the city from Karachi airport. His brother, Amir Mir's accusation of the ISI's involvement, naming DG Lt Gen Zahirul Islam personally was promptly aired over Geo TV, causing a great sensation.

The Army and ISI took umbrage, getting Pakistan Electronic Media Regulatory Authority (PEMRA) officials to castigate the channel and forcing cable operators to take Go TV off the air. Other competitor channels were instigated to criticise Geo and the Jang group management for daring to take on the 'deep State'. Even as PM Nawaz Sharif visited the injured Hamid Mir in hospital, Army Chief Gen Raheel Sharif visited the ISI headquarters in Aabpara, Islamabad to show solidarity with the DG. Geo has since apologised to the Army and ISI, but has to seek remedy from the Courts against the ban on it.

Perhaps the behaviour of the current crop of civilian politicians elected to power in recent elections is conditioned by the awareness that the Army has been gradually discredited before civil society due to its actions and omissions, especially during Gen Musharraf's tenure, in the last seven or eight years. One of Kayani's first few decisions after he became Army Chief, to withdraw many junior level Army officers on deputation posts from civilian jobs was widely welcomed. The media, enjoying more freedom than ever before, (a situation ironically brought about by Musharraf) contributed substantially to this perception that democracy, even if imperfect or partial, may be the best antidote to prolonged or repeated Army interventions. The Army leadership is conscious of these changes in civil society perceptions and is possibly in the process of adjusting its responses to these realities.

Nevertheless, this issue could lead to unpredictable outcomes, with potential to destabilise civil-military relations in the future if the Army as an institution is dragged in beyond a point or needlessly brought into disrepute.

In South Asia, the political regimes in power have had rather lax standards of financial probity while judging themselves. Past regimes under Benazir Bhutto, Nawaz Sharif or Chaudhry Shujaat Hussain/Pervez Elahi availed of huge loans from State owned banks for ambitious privatisation schemes, never to be returned. Politically well-connected industrial empires like the Ittefaq group or the Brothers group (Chaudhry brothers – Shujaat and Pervez Elahi) thrived.[42]

So far, the emergence of these new entrepreneurs or business classes has not crossed the path of the Military's own ventures into economic and commercial activity, but in future, this could happen, if the Nawaz Sharif government makes some progress in normalizing trade relations with India and dissipates the 'bogey' of 'India as the traditional enemy'. The Military's appropriation of bulk resources from the national budget for the Defence sector could begin to be seriously questioned.

Recently, there have been reports about disproportionate clout given to sons and daughters of Nawaz and Shahbaz Sharif (Hamza, Salman, Hassan and Maryam) in handling mega development projects in Punjab funded from the State exchequer. As one perceptive commentator observed, "The more things change, the more fondly, and nostalgically, we remember the past. Impossible as it may sound, the "Dar inflation", the citadel of Islam is now experiencing lends, in retrospect, a kindly gloss to the banditry of the Zardari years. That was open banditry. This is a more closed shop, secrets shared among a narrow circle, and its effects are more insidious."[43]

Many complex factors confront the new civilian government in Pakistan and raise the more fundamental question as to whether the military and the civilians can at all work together to tackle them? This may require a change of old mindsets on both sides. As a leader with a substantial political mandate, Nawaz Sharif has an opportunity to establish civilian supremacy. However, he may have to contend with a strong Army, which may not quite be in the mood to give up its predominant position in society and the perks that go with it just yet.

NOTES

1. See Annexure, *Party positions in National Assembly & Provincial Assemblies*, Election Commission of Pakistan.
2. S. Akbar Zaidi, *Military, Civil Society and Democratisation in Pakistan*, (Lahore: Vanguard Books Pvt Ltd, 2011).
3. Hassan Abbas, *Pakistan's drift into Extremism: Allah, the Army and America's War on Terror,* (M. E. Sharpe. Inc., 2005), pp. 30-31.
4. Op cit, S. Akbar Zaidi, pp. 13-16;
5. Ayesha Siddiqa, *Military Inc. Inside Pakistan's Military Economy,* (London, Pluto Press, 2007), Chapters 3 and 4.
6. Frederic Grare, *Reforming the Intelligence Agencies in Pakistan's Transitional Democracy*, Carnegie Endowment for International Peace, 2009.
7. Op cit., S. Akbar Zaidi, pp. 19-20.
8. Shuja Nawaz, *Crossed Swords: Pakistan – Its Army, and the Wars Within,* (Oxford University Press, 2008), p. 450.
9. For chronological depiction of details, see author's article #3972, *Military & Nawaz Sharif,* @ www.ipcs.org: dated June 05, 2013.
10. The Hindu Business Line, *Lt Gen (retd) Shahid Aziz, then DDG (Analysis), ISI to Lt Gen Khwaja Ziauddin Butt, DG, ISI – as revealed in his Urdu book: Kab Tak Yeh Khamoshi ('For How Long This Silence')*, Feb 03, 2013.
11. Summary of *Kargil Review Committee findings*, www.fas.org/news/India; Feb 25, 2000.
12. Ayaz Amir, "Flight of the Spoons", *The News*, December 25, 2013.
13. Tikka Muhammad Iqbal case.
14. Khaled Ahmed, "Slippery Slope of Justice", *The Indian Express,* December 04, 2013.
15. Najam Sethi, "Civil-Military Ad-hocism", *The Friday Times*, July 19, 2013.
16. Huzaima Bukhari and Dr. Ikramul Haq, *The News,* December 07, 2013.
17. *ISPR Press Release* No. PR 241/2012 dated November 05, 2012.
18. Arif Nizami, "Lunch with Kayani", *Pakistan Today*, March 02, 2013.
19. Shaheen Sehbai, "General Kayani Spills the Beans", *The News, Pakistan*, April 15, 2013.
20. Ayesha Siddiqa, "Democracy Military Style", *Newsline*, March 20, 2013.
21. *Report of the Abbottabad Commission of Enquiry*, *Al Jazeera* website, July 08, 2013.
22. Babbar Sattar, "False Binaries", *The News,* July 20, 2013.
23. Wajahat S Khan, "The Ghosts that Haunt Kayani", *The Friday Times*, 28 October 2011.
24. "Such Gup", *The Friday Times*, July 12, 2013.
25. Imtiaz Gul, "Double Talk", *The Friday Times*, September 13-19, 2013.
26. Kamran Yousaf, "Rare Civil-Military Partnership: Ringing Endorsement for Dialogue with Taliban", *Express Tribune*, September 10, 2013; Amir Zia, "Inviting Catastrophe", *The News*, September 16, 2013; Ghazi Salahuddin, "Panel Discussion with Hamid Mir", *Capital Talk*: *Geo TV*, September 16, 2013.
27. Ayesha Siddiqa, "Countering Terrorism", *The Express Tribune*, July 31, 2013.
28. Hassan Askari Rizvi, "Countering Terrorism", *The Express Tribune*, July 15, 2013.
29. Col (retd) Muhd Ali Ehsan, "A New direction in Strategy?" *The Express Tribune*, December 27, 2013.
30. Najam Sethi, "Cut the Crap", *The Friday Times*, Jan 31, 2014.
31. Ayaz Amir, "The Times that Await Us", *The News, Pakistan*, July 26, 2013.

32. Lt Gen (retd) Abdul Qadir Baluch, "The Case of the Levies Force in Baluchistan", article in *The Baluch Hal*, 5 October, 2012.
33. Christine Fair and Shuja Nawaz, "The Changing Pakistan Army Officer Corps", *Journal of Strategic Studies*, UK, February 2011.
34. Hassan Abbas et al, "Police Reform in Pakistan", *Asia Society*, USA, June, 2012.
35. Malik Siraj Akbar, "Baluchistan-Point of no return?" *The Express Tribune*, 12 January, 2012.
36. Pakistan Institute of Peace Studies Report, *Conflict and Insecurity in Baluchistan*, October-December 2010.
37. Ashraf Jehangir Qazi, "*The Baluch Reality*", *The News*, 23 June 2010.
38. Najam Sethi, "Mengal's Six-point Agenda", *The News*, October 01, 2012.
39. Human Rights Commission of Pakistan, *The News*, July 16, 2013.
40. Maleeha Lodhi, "PPP – Rise and Fall", *The News*, August 13, 2013.
41. Interview given to Moeed Yusuf – as reported in the *Tribune* and the *News*, Dec 30, 2013.
42. Shahid-Ur-Rehman, *Who owns Pakistan?* (Islamabad: Aelia Communication, 1998).
43. Ayaz Amir, "A Raj Legacy We could have Done Without: Islamabad Diary", *The News*, October 25, 2013.

2

Pakistan's Military Build-up

Shalini Chawla

Pakistan's nuclear and conventional defence build up in the last two decades has been remarkable owing to consistent Chinese support and heavy flow of military aid from the United States. Despite its fragile economy, Pakistan has been maintaining a high defence expenditure of around 5.5 per cent of the GDP till recently, when it started to fall closer to 3.2 percent (on an average). The perceived threat perception from India and the dominant role of military in the country's power politics has led Pakistan to focus on arms acquisitions and building up it's military capability. The United States, China, France and some other European countries have been the main suppliers of military equipment. These suppliers have varied from time to time due to political and financial reasons.

The military leadership in Pakistan has focused primarily on defence build-up and modernisation highlighting the strategic threats in the region. Kashmir, since 1947 has been promoted by the military as the bone of contention between India and Pakistan, adding to the insecurity of the nation and building a legitimate basis for Pakistan's weapon modernisation. Pakistan has maintained a high defence budget, which does not include major weapon systems. The historical insecurity has been further deepened by the fragmentation of the Pakistani society, as the frequently changing regimes in Pakistan and fragile democratic structure have eroded a sense of oneness in the country. Islamic extremism and *Jihadi* terrorism have continued to prosper, creating a deep armament culture in the country.

Basic Objectives Shaping Pakistan's Military Capability

Pakistan has looked at arms procurement to satisfy its security concerns. The perceived threat perception from India, strategic developments on the border with Afghanistan and the emerging technologies, have been the dominant factors contributing to the sources and kind of arms procurement by the military. The basic objectives shaping arms acquisitions of Pakistan are:

Firstly, Pakistan's adversarial relationship with India has played a major role in the formation of its threat perception. The dominant military lobby in Pakistan has aggressively propagated the Indian threat within Pakistan to legitimise Pakistan's high defence spending, and on the international front to support the acquisition of high technology weaponry. This also interacts with and promotes the military's special and dominant role in the country's power structure.

Secondly, Pakistan's urge to match Indian's conventional military superiority. This has perpetually driven Pakistan into ways and means to acquire superior technology. In 2006, the then Chief of Air Staff, Air Chief Marshal Kaleem Saadat stated in an interview to *Janes Defence Weekly*, "When US sanctions were imposed in 1990, both the PAF and the Indian Air Force were second-generation air forces. No real-time surveillance capability, no air-to-air refuelling capability, no airborne early warning capability, no beyond-visual-range-capability, no stand-off weapon capability. However, after 13 years of sanctions, India had all the above and Pakistan had none until about three or four years ago. This is the gap.... We have to bridge this gap in the manner that we can deny the advantage that our neighbour has...."[1]

The strategic aims, as outlined by Ross Masood Husain are: "to strengthen national power; to prevent open aggression by India; to induce India to modify its goals, strategies, tactics and operations; to attain a position of security or, if possible, dominance, which would enhance the role of other (non-military) means of conflict; to promote and capitalise on advances in technology in order to reach parity or superiority in military power;"[2]

Thirdly, Pakistan's reliance on high technology weapons to seek competitive military advantage. The desire to acquire high technology weapons has been very strong in the Pakistan military and its alliance with the US has assisted Pakistan to procure high technology equipment.

Fourthly, Pakistan's belief in offensive aggressive strategies and its deep rooted belief that by going on the offensive, smaller size forces in history have won wars against bigger enemies. All the four wars which Pakistan has fought with India (in 1947-48, 1965, 1971 and 1999), have been initiated by Pakistan. The war in 1971 was caused by Pakistan's internal instability. But the actual war was initiated by Pakistan with a pre-emptive air strike against Indian Air Force bases on 3rd December. In addition, it adopted an offensive route for its covert war through terrorism in J&K since 1988 (besides that in Punjab in 1983-93). Pakistan has relied heavily on the strategy of offensive action and, thus, the acquisitions of high technology weapons are sought to support this strategy.

The defence build up in Pakistan has been facilitated by mainly three factors:

1. Pakistan's alliance with the United States.
2. Pakistan's consistently growing relationship with China.
3. Financial autonomy of the military within Pakistan.

Pakistan's Alliance with the United States – 1950s and early 1960s

During the early decades, Pakistan acquired arms mainly from the USA (for high technology systems) and China (for low cost but efficient systems) although a certain proportion was contributed by France. The US equipment which Pakistan received in the 1950s and later in the 1980's provided significant boost to its military modernisation. Pakistan joined the US sponsored military assistance pacts in 1950s and 1960s, SEATO and CENTO, and thus became a part of the frontline states, which were to deter the Soviet Union from any strategic and military moves.[3] It was the US arms embargo imposed during the 1965 conflict, which compelled Islamabad to diversify its sources of weapon supply.

The US arms supply has always been Pakistan's preferred option due to three reasons: "(i) as a symbol of strategic and political support and engagement by the United States; (ii) diversification of sources of weapon systems; and (iii) for higher end-technology weapons."[4]

In fact, the massive US arms aid to Pakistan in the late 1950s provided it with both the incentive to initiate the 1965 War as well as demonstrated the philosophy of high-technology weapons like the Patton tanks and state of the art fighter aircrafts, providing a competitive advantage against India, which in any case, was saddled at that time with obsolete systems being employed after the war in 1962. The classic case was the shooting down of the first four Vampire vintage aircraft by the combination of F-104 Starfighters and F-86 Sabres on the opening day of the war, forcing India to withdraw these and older fighters from combat, thus, reducing the quantitative advantage that India was supposed to enjoy.

Following this, in the same year, the US officials presented a secret aide-memoire boosting the military aid to $50 million with specific programme goals. The aide-memoire committed Washington to equip "4 army infantry and 1.5 armoured divisions, to provide modern aircraft for 6 air force squadrons, and to supply 12 vessels for the navy. The estimated cost of this programme was $171 million."[5]

America's interest in providing military aid to Pakistan was driven mainly by two factors:

> Firstly, the geographical location of Pakistan abutting the oil rich Persian Gulf region (where the US and the UK had extensive commercial interest) and the strategic location of the Strait of Hormuz offered Washington easy access to energy resources and also a monitoring point for the southern Soviet Union and western China. Pakistan's strategically important location, in fact, turned it into a convenient launching pad for the cold war strategies.[6] Secondly, fear of Soviet expansion into the Middle East.
>
> In the 1950s, the inflow from Washington included sophisticated Patton tanks (MBTs), modern artillery, howitzers, F-86 jet fighter squadrons, F-104 Starfighter supersonic interceptors, air-to-air missiles, submarine and state-of-the-art-radar, communication and transportation system. A further qualitative boast came from the military training by the US military teams and also in the US military schools to the Pakistan army.[7] The US military also provided assistance in setting up intelligence and special operations facilities creating the Special Services Group (SSG), which was used to unsuccessfully try and capture

Indian airfields in the 1965 war. While Pakistan failed to win the war in 1965, its military nevertheless projected it as a victory, especially in the air, and the thirst for high-technology systems intensified.

Affiliation with China

It was as early as 1959 when Pakistan signalled to Beijing its interest in demarcating the Sino-Pakistani border in northern Kashmir.[8]

Further boost to Sino-Pak relationship was post Sino-India border war in 1962. China displayed keen interest in extending support to Pakistan, despite its membership of the US alliance system against China and the Soviet Union. Pakistan received economic, military and strategic support from China and, in return, China was guaranteed a foothold in the subcontinent and also the possibilities of support from the Islamic world west of Pakistan.[9]

The informal Sino-Pak alliance grew and a border agreement was negotiated between the two nations in 1962. In March 1963, the two countries signed the boundary agreement on "China's Sinkiang and the contiguous areas the defence of which was under the actual control of Pakistan."[10]

The 1965 India-Pakistan war marked an important landmark in the Sino-Pakistan relations providing it a new dimension. China demonstrated support for Pakistan, which was a member of SEATO, basically constructed to counter communist expansion. China overtly threatened India and started firing on the border to apply pressure on India when Pakistan was losing the war. Post 1965, the Chinese military assistance and in the 1980, the nuclear assistance has been at an uninterrupted pace.

Chinese arms assistance to Pakistan began in 1965 following the imposition of the US arms embargo. While Pakistan turned towards Beijing as a trusted "all weather friend" in dealing with its "implacable" enemy, India; China, on the other hand, had in Pakistan a valuable proxy against India. China's added incentive has been to cater to its growing energy requirements from the Persian Gulf and Central Asia through Pakistan.

China is today Pakistan's biggest defence supplier, providing it with the largest variety and amount of defence equipment. In addition, China has enabled Pakistan to build up its indigenous defence capability. Chinese defence equipment turned out to be much cheaper as compared to equipment from the West and the Chinese sales were further facilitated by the availability of credit from China on easy repayment terms. In the 1960s, and later in the 1970s also, Pakistan received interest free economic aid and also a significant amount of free weapons from China and became the only non-Communist third World country to receive generous assistance from it.

Pakistan did manage to acquire high technology equipment from the US in the 1950s and early 1960s, which prompted it for its aggression in 1965 against India. It was mainly the US equipment, which was used by Pakistan in the 1965 war. In the 1960s and later in the 1970s also, Pakistan received interest free economic aid and also a significant amount of free weapons from China and became the only non-Communist Third World country to receive generous assistance from it.[11] The Chinese F-6 entered the PAF's inventory in 1966 followed by other systems. In the late 1960s, Pakistan received MiG-19 fighters from China, apart from the substantive infantry equipment. China supplied 115 F-6 fighters between 1971 and 1981. Chinese military assistance came in not only in the form of arms, but also for the development of infrastructure for repair and overhaul.

On the naval front, after the 1971 war, the Pakistan Navy opted for a modest acquisition programme in the form of new Chinese built missile/ torpedo attack crafty. Between 1972 and 1980, 12 Slaughter class attack FPBs, 4 Hunaim class attack craft and 4 Huchwan class hydrofoil craft were delivered to Pakistan.[12] Pakistan's naval acquisitions in the late 1970s focused on building surveillance and targeting capability and, thus, the deal for French Atlantiques was finalised.

Modernisation in the 1980s: Arms pipeline reopens

The Soviet invasion of Afghanistan in December 1979 led the Americans to review their South Asian policy, and consequently, Pakistan entered into a new engagement with the US. Pakistan was declared a "frontline state" and, in return, received massive military aid.[13] General Zia-ul-Haq managed to negotiate an elaborate military and security-related aid package of $3.2 billion. The US military assistance programme included the sale of 40 F-16 Falcon multi-role combat aircraft, one of the most advanced military aircrafts in the world at that time. Pakistan also received Harpoon anti-ship missiles, artillery, attack helicopters, and second-hand destroyers.[14] The second US package worth $4.02 billon commenced in 1987, but was suspended due to the US arms embargo in 1990 due to Pakistan crossing the nuclear "red line".

Notwithstanding the resumption of the US military sales to Pakistan, Chinese weapons continued to have a significant share in the Pakistani inventory. Chinese arms, though technologically inferior to those from the West, were capable systems, were affordable and provided a quantitative boost to Pakistan's military powers. In fact, by the early 1980s, China had provided Pakistan with roughly about 65 per cent of its aircrafts.[15]

During the 1980s, the focus of arms procurement was on strengthening the Pakistan Air Force (PAF). Pakistan had lost the last two wars and believed that effective air defence would give them leverage in future offensive operations against India. One of the lessons learnt from the last two wars was that an efficient air force would be important in providing close-battle support to the ground forces.[16] According to the strategic thinkers in Pakistan, the acquisition of the F-16s proved vital for the morale of not only the PAF, but also the nation as a whole. And the modern aircraft was viewed as a technological acquisition guarding the territorial integrity of Pakistan.[17] Thus, the Pakistan military leadership, in their second deal with Washington, sought 70 F-16s aiming to raise the inventory to 110 high performance multi-role combat aircraft. During the 1980s, Pakistan also made an unsuccessful attempt to acquire the Airborne Early Warning (AEW) from the US which, if successful, would have dramatically increased the Air Force combat capability.

China (besides France) continued to be a major source of PAF weapons and this increased after the US arms embargo in 1990. About 90 A-5s were obtained in 1983-84 for the price of $1 million per aircraft. Procurement of around 95 F-7 series aircraft was done adding to the quantitative element in the PAF.[18]

The defence expenditure in Zia's period was maintained at a high rate of approximately 6.5 percent of the GDP. During this period, Pakistan enjoyed considerable political and economic stability and this facilitated a higher level of arms acquisition. While the sources for acquiring arms in the 1980s came mostly from the US, the Arab states also provided funding for a significant portion of weapons procurement. Huge quantities of sophisticated small arms acquisitions (including the Stinger surface-to-air-missiles) came from many sources including the CIA pipeline for the Mujahedeen fighting the Soviets in Afghanistan.

In the 1970s and 1980s, their army inventory included significant numbers of Chinese equipment including the T-59 MBTs, T-60 Light Tanks and T-63 Light Tanks and Type 531 APC. By the early 1980s, China had provided Pakistan with roughly about 65 per cent of its aircraft and roughly 75 per cent of its tanks. Details of Pakistan's major arms acquisitions in the 1970s and 1980s are given in Table 1.

Table 1: Pakistan's Major Arms Acquisitions in the 1970s and 1980s

Supplier	*No. ordered / delivered*	*Weapon designation*	*Weapon description*	*Year(s) of delivery*
China	115	F-6	Fighter	1971-81
	142	Q-5 Fantan-A	fighter/grd attack	1983-86
	1044	T-59	MBT	1970-86
	50	T-60	LT	1981-82
	50 & 200	T-63 & Type 531 respectively	LT & APC respectively	1972-76
	4	Hainan Class	PC	1976-80
	4	Hegu Class	FAC	1981
	4	Huangfen Class	FAC	1984
	4	Huchuan Class	Hydrofoil FAC	1973
	12	Shanghai Class	PC	1972-73
France	3	Breguet Atlantique-1150	Maritime patrol/ ASW	1975-76
	4, 58 &10	Mirage-5DP, Mirage-5P & Mirage 5R, respectively	Fighter & Recce, respectively	1971-83
	36	Crotale SAMS	Mobile SAM system	1977-78
	432	R-440	Landmob SAM	1977-78
	2	Agosta Class	Submarine	1979-80
Iran	5	C-130E Hercules	Transport	1974
Jordan	10	F-104A	Fighter	1971
Portugal	1	Daphne Class	Submarine	1975
UK	6	SH-3D Sea King	Hel	1975
	1	County Class	Destroyer	1982

(Contd.)

Supplier	*No. ordered / delivered*	*Weapon designation*	*Weapon description*	*Year(s) of delivery*
USA	5	C-130B Hercules	Transport	1974-81
	34 & 6	F-16A & F-16B respectively	Multi-role combat aircraft	1981-84
	300	M-113	APC	1973
	135	M-48-A5	MBT	1982-85
	6	Gearing Class	Destroyer	1977-83

Source: Based on, Register of the trade in major conventional weapons with Third World countries, 1971-85, as cited in, Michael Brzoska and Thomas Ohlson, *Arms Transfers to the Third World, 1971-85,* (Sipri) (New York, Oxford University Press, 1987), pp. 230-233, cited in, Shalini Chawla, *Pakistan's Military and Its Strategy* (New Delhi, KW Publishers, 2009), p. 39.

Suspension of US Military Supplies in the 1990s and Enhancement of Chinese Supplies

American military and economic aid came to a halt following the sanctions in 1990. The sanctions were highly damaging in nature, as they not only suspended the US military aid and assistance, but also the procurement of spares was blocked. Intensive lobbying by Pakistan in the US resulted in some relief under the Brown Amendment, passed in 1995. The amendment permitted taking possession of the military equipment frozen in the United States, with the exception of nuclear capable F-16 combat aircraft.[19] Pakistan paid for 28 F16s, which were manufactured against the 1987 order of 110. But following the sanctions, the F-16s were not supplied. The US agreed to try and sell them to third country and return the money back to Pakistan. Thus, there were efforts to sell them to Indonesia, but the economic crisis stopped that plan. These sanctions actually impacted the PAF's capability and created confusion in the PAF planning and procurement regarding the replacement of this aircraft. The post nuclear test sanctions 1998 further hampered Pakistan's weapons supply as the United States persuaded the other G-7 countries to impose similar sanctions.

The decade of 1990s was a setback for PAF modernisation due to the American sanctions and also Pakistan's crippled economy. Economic growth recorded a steep decline and Pakistan was under severe pressure from the international financial institutions to cut down the spending on defence.

Despite the US sanctions, low GDP and a collapsed democratic structure, Pakistan tried hard to acquire the air force equipment. In 1990, fifty Mirage-3 (Table 2) were acquired from Australia for a paltry sum of $28 million along with engines and spares.[20]

Pakistan, with its nationalist ego boosted by the nuclear weapons tests (which it also believed would deter India from robust response), launched a war in the Kargil sector of J&K in early 1999. This misadventure not only led to its defeat, but also triggered the return of the army in control of the country, displacing the elected government in the coup of October 12, 1999. With the re-emergence of the military regime, another set of mandated democracy sanctions were imposed on Pakistan, with a pressure to return to democracy, reducing the possibility of acquiring high-technology weapons from the West.

Though the US supply routes remained closed for Pakistan in the 1990s, the nation continued to diversify its sources. Along with, which China remained a regular supplier of military hardware to Pakistan, France, Italy, United Kingdom and Ukraine provided the defence supplies.

Modernisation Post 9/11

By the late 1990s, Pakistan's economy was in shambles and its viability as a state was being questioned. Fears were raised about its prospects as a "failing state". But the September 11, 2001, terrorist attacks in the US led to a major strategic shift for Pakistan and, once again, it became a front line state for Washington and an ally in the global war on terror. The new US-Pakistan relationship helped Pakistan to move out of economic and military decline and it received substantive military assistance from the US and its Western allies. The immediate step from the Bush administration was the waiving of the US sanctions on Pakistan resulting from its 1998 nuclear tests and the "Democracy Sanctions".

Pakistan, in return, offered its complete military support to the US including use of its air space and agreed to the use of Pakistani air bases at Jacobabad, Pasni and Dalbandin by American forces for "search and rescue" missions. The US presence on the Pakistani bases led to substantial US investments for renovating the bases and in addition, Pakistan was paid for providing security for the bases. The Shahbaz air base Jacobabad, for example, went through extensive construction work to renovate the base, including, the installation of the radar equipment. Pakistan was able to obtain the US equipment and other support systems, including intelligence, which has been actively operating in the war against terrorism. In September 2003 alone, in order to enhance surveillance capability, the supply of the US air traffic control radars as well as associated equipment and services worth $110 million was authorised to Pakistan.[21]

In February 2002, Pakistan and the US signed a defence cooperation agreement, and Pakistan agreed for American forces to use its military equipment for training and other military exercises. Pakistan also agreed to provide other facilities like food, water, medical services and transportation against payment to the US forces operating in Afghanistan. Taking a step towards institutionalising the military relationship with Pakistan, the US, in an important strategic move, designated Pakistan as a "major non-NATO ally" (MNNA) in March 2004. Previously, only three Muslim countries had been accorded this status – Bahrain, Egypt and Jordan. Australia, Japan, Israel, Philippines and South Korea are the non-Muslim countries that fall in this category. The status of MNNA not only enhanced Pakistan's stature, but also enabled it to obtain state of the art military equipment and spares at rock bottom prices and on a priority basis. The modern US inventories and also the spare parts of the US equipment, which were being used in Pakistan, were made available to Pakistan. One of the most important advantages of this designation is that Islamabad would be able to obtain what is called the "Excess Defence Equipment (EDAs)". These are the weapons and equipment, which the US may not need anymore, and which may be transferred at nominal rates to the allies. Pakistan did receive the weaponry, which the US forces used during their operations at the Pakistani bases and facilities.

The last twelve years have witnessed exponential growth in Pakistan's defence modernisation. There has been rather limited acquisition of land equipment as compared to that of the Air Force and the Navy (Table 2). Army acquisitions include – Large Calibre artillery systems, Fire Control Radars. Bell-205/UH-1H, Bell-209/AH, BGM-71 TOW anti-tank missiles, ground based radars and the UAVs.

In 2006, Pakistan announced the development of Al Khalid II Main Battle Tank, the original agreement for which was signed in 1990 with

China North Industries Corporation (NORINCO). The first 15 pre-production Al Khalid MBTs were handed over to the Pakistan Army in July 2001. Subsequently, the MBTs have been handed over to the Army and, currently, the Pakistan Army possesses 355 MBT 2000 Al Khalid out of the total 2,501 MBTs in its inventory.[22] The Al Khalid II is reportedly a further improved variant of MBT 2000. Although, not much has been revealed about this new variant, but according to the Pakistani and Chinese sources, it's a major technological breakthrough for the Pakistan Army.

Post 2001, the Pakistan Air Force (PAF) has been on an acquisition spree and majority of the defence acquisitions have been on the Air Force front (Table 2). The US sanctions of the 1990s gave an impetus to Sino-Pakistan defence and, in the process, the two nations entered into deal for the co-development of a fourth generation fighter aircraft, the JF-17 (earlier called the FC-1), following the jointly produced K-8 jet trainer. The JF-17 is designated to be a low cost, multi-role combat aircraft to meet the tactical and strategic requirements of the Pakistan Air force. The JF-17 is co-developed by Pakistan and China and is being built by China's Chengdu Aircraft Industry Corporation (CAC) and Pakistan Aeronautical Complex (PAC) Kamra. According to the Pakistani official sources, currently, Pakistan Aeronautical Complex (PAC) possesses the exclusive rights of 58% of JF-17 airframe co-production work.[23]There have been reports that the design was developed by the MiG complex in Russia and transferred to China after the Russian Air Force cancelled procurements. JF-17 is fitted with RD-93 engine and has the combat radius of 378 n miles in the ground attack role (in the fighter role – 648 n miles). The initial batch of JF-17 delivered to Pakistan was fitted with the Chinese radar - KLJ-7 multirole pulse Droppler. There have been reports (in the past) suggesting that the forthcoming JF-17s might be equipped with the Italian Grifo-7. Pakistan has increased its initial target of buying 150 JF-17s to acquiring up to 250 aircraft.[24] This represents a quantum jump in Pakistan aircraft industry. With the production of JF-17, Pakistan has joined the exclusive club of a few nations manufacturing fighter aircraft.

Interestingly, beginning of May 2011, immediately after Osama bin Laden's killing in Pakistan's high security military compound of Abbottabad, China announced the decision to deliver 50 JF-17s free of cost to Pakistan, by the end of 2011. JF-17 is indeed a remarkable achievement for Pakistan, as it has now entered into the manufacturing of the fourth generation aircraft. Pakistan has been marketing the JF-17 quite aggressively and several countries including Algeria, Sri Lanka, Egypt, and Malaysia have shown keen interest in the acquisition of the aircraft.

In April, 2006, the PAF got the approval of the Pakistani leadership to go ahead with the negotiations for the acquisitions of J-10s from China, as part of its fighter force expansion plans. The J-10 has the combat radius of 250-300 n miles and the aircraft is configured with 1553B-standard databus and a helmet-mounted weapon sight. The agreement for the acquisitions of 36 J-10s (also called the FC-20s) was finalised in November 2009. But given the IMF restrictions and also financial limits, there has been no progress on acquisitions on this front.

Pakistan acquired the F-16A&B and also F-16C&D from the US, which has added enormous strength to the PAF capability (Table 1 and 2). Pakistan has been extremely keen to acquire the F-16s, partly because of political/psychological reasons, and partly, because it has been familiar with this multi-role combat aircraft since the early 1980s. The delivery of 18 new F-16D Block 525 was completed in 2012 and the US is assisting Islamabad in upgradation in Turkey through Foreign Military Assistance Programme.[25]

Pakistan signed in 2008 a deal for the purchase of Chinese AWACS (ZDK-03) for $278 million in 2008. Pakistan is the first country to buy the Chinese AWACS system, which China started to produce only in 2004. Pakistan has been focused on the acquisition of force multipliers and this deal with China is in addition to the Saab Turboprop 2000 (platform) equipped with Erieye, from Sweden. Pakistan has also acquired the IL-78 Midas refuellers from Ukraine (Table 2).

On the naval front, the focus has been on enhancing the maritime strike capabilities of the Navy. China has been the prime supplier for the Pakistan Navy. In 1984, four Huangfen Class missile attack crafts were transferred from Beijing for about $20 million per piece. It is interesting to note that the Chinese naval equipment, being inferior in quality was less desired, but Pakistan obtained the missile crafts mainly, with a longer term objective of striking a deal of technology transfer in the future, for indigenous production of the missile crafts.[26]

Pakistan's naval acquisitions from China in the decade of 2000 include 24 C-802/CSS-N-8 anti-ship missiles and four Jiangwei II class frigates. In 2006, the Pakistan Navy ordered four F-22P type frigates from China with the value of the deal at $600 million.[27] The first destroyer, PNS Zulfiqar, was delivered in 2009 and the second one in 2010. The F-22P, which is a modification of a Chinese frigate that uses a Russian-designed main gun rather than a Chinese model, is armed with eight C-802 anti-ship warfare missiles, eight FM-90 surface-to-air missiles (SAM), one AK-176M main gun and two Chinese 30 mm close-in weapon systems (CIWS). The frigates can be loaded with one Z-9EC helicopter.[28] Fourth F-22P PNS ASLAT was inducted in the PN in September 2013. PNS ASLAT is the first Frigate of the Navy, which has been indigenously built at the Karachi Shipyard and Engineering Works (KS&EW). The production was done in collaboration with the China Shipbuilding and Trading Company.[29] This was to fulfil a pledge to transfer Chinese shipbuilding technology that was part of the April 2005 agreement to build the frigates.

Other defence production plans on the naval front include four modern corvettes, which are planned to be built alongside with F-22P in Karachi Shipyard and Engineering Works. The Navy also plans to manufacture and procure additional mine hunters, tankers, missiles and patrol boats.[30] China has also confirmed the sale of six ship-based medium sized Z 9C helicopters to the Pakistan Navy.[31] Main naval acquisitions from the US include P-3C Orion Maritime Patrol Aircraft, USS Mc Inenary–frigate and Harpoon Anti-ship missiles.

Development of the Gwadar Port

Gwadar has been developed with the Chinese assistance and the primary objective has been the construction of deep sea port to expand its maritime role and allow the trade to and from the land locked Central Asia. More importantly, the port would have the conversion facilities to allow the movement of natural gas for the Turkmenistan-Afghanistan-Pakistan natural gas pipe-line when constructed. Gwadar offers the geo-economic and geo-strategic pivot to China and Pakistan. It is strategically located on the south-western coast of Pakistan, between three increasingly important regions of the world; South Asia, Central Asia and oil-rich Middle East. Gwadar, overlooking the Gulf of Oman and being the entrance to the Persian Gulf region, is just 180 nautical miles from the Straits of Hormuz. Thus, Gwadar would eventually emerge as the key shipping hub providing mass trade to Central Asian Republics through Pakistan and China, and important naval base. China's involvement in Gwadar is undoubtedly a response to China's emerging energy requirements, China being world's second largest oil importer. Approximately, 70 per cent of Chinese oil supply comes from the Middle East and Africa through sea. China is expanding its energy procurement efforts and is following the strategy of establishing a series of ports along the oil shipment routes, which would allow it to safeguard and monitor energy flows. Gwadar, being built in the Baluchistan coast, would enable Pakistan take control over the world energy jugular and interdiction of Indian tankers.

From the military point of view, Gwadar is a decongestion point to the Pakistan Navy and it will provide it a berthing point for its submarines and surface warships. Gwadar port area has been designated as the "sensitive defence zone" by the Government of Pakistan.[32] Although, there has been no official Chinese announcement on the subject, but various reports are indicative of Gwadar being a future berthing point for the PLA-Navy fleet of the Indian Ocean, facilitating China's military presence in the region. This would add to the deterrent against the Indian Navy.

The development of deep sea port has strategic implications for India, which were pointed out by the former Indian Naval Chief, Admiral Suresh Mehta in a lecture in Chennai:

"1. Being only 180 nautical miles from the exit of Straits of Hormuz, Gwadar being built in Baluchistan coast, would enable Pakistan take control over the world energy jugular and interdiction of Indian tankers.
2. The pressure for countries to cooperate in the maritime military domain to ensure smooth flow of energy and commerce on the high sea ill grow even further.
3. A highway is under construction joining Gwadar with Karachi and there are plans to connect the port with the Karakoram Highway, thus providing China a gateway to the Arabian Sea."[33]

Table 2: Pakistan's Major Arms Acquisitions during 1990-2013

Supplier/ Licenser	*No. ordered / delivered*	*Weapon designation*	*Weapon description*	*Year(s) of delivery*
Australia	50	Mirage 3	Fighter	1990-92
Britain	3	3 Lynx HAS- 3	ASW helicopters	1994-96
China	40	F-7P	Combat aircraft	1993
	6	K-8	Trainer aircraft	1994
	20	Armoured combat vehicles		1995
	75-100	K-8	Fighter/trainer aircraft	2000-08
	40	F-7 MG	Fighter aircraft	2001
	44	F-7 PG Aircraft	Combat Aircraft	2001-02
	3	Type-347G	Fire control Radar	1997-2001
	250 (33 delivered)	FC-1/JF-17	Multirole Combat Aircraft	China-Pakistan joint venture, delivery possibly starting 2006
	6	A-5	Combat aircraft	2003
	2	Type-347G PL-12/SD-10	Fire Control Radar BVR AAM	2004 Year of order – 2004
	64	FM-80/HQ-7 PL-12/SD-10	SAM BVR AAM	Year of order – 2005 Year of order – 2004
	4	F-22P type	Frigates	Year of order – 2006
	4-6	Z 9EC	Helicopter	Year of order – 2006
	4 (2 delivered)	ZDK-03	AEW	Year of order – 2008
	40	J-10	Multirole Combat Aircraft	Year of order – 2009
France	4	SA316 Alouette III	Helicopters	1994
	3	Breguet Atlantique-1	MPA and strike aircraft	1996
	8	Upgraded Mirage-IIID/V	Combat aircraft	1999
	48	Mirage IIID/5	Combat Aircraft	1998-2000
	11	Mirage V	Combat aircraft	2000-02
	96	F-17P	AS torpedo	1999-2004
Italy	192	Grifo radar	Combat ac fire control radar (for Mirage and F-17/7 combat aircraft)	2000-2004

Supplier/ Licenser	*No. ordered / delivered*	*Weapon designation*	*Weapon description*	*Year(s) of delivery*
	4	Galileo Falco	UAV	2006
Netherlands	5	Fokker F27-200	Aircraft	1994-96
Sweden	7 (3 delivered)	Saab-2000 AEW	AEW&C ac	Year of order – 2006
USA	3	P-3C (update 2.75)	Orion maritime reconnaissance and strike aircraft	1996-97
	28	Harpoon	Anti-ship missiles for the P-3C Orions	1996-97
	10	Bell-209/AH-IS	Helicopters	1997
	6	S-70/UH-60 Blackhawk	Helicopter	2003-04
	26	Bell-412EP	Helicopters	2004
	6	C-130E Hercules*	Transport aircraft	2004
	40	Bell-205/UH-1 H	Helicopter	2004
	40	Bell-209/AH-1F*	Combat Helicopter	2004
	19	T-37 B*	Aircraft	2003
	8 (7 delivered)	P-3C	MP and Strike Aircraft	Year of order – 2005
	2	F-16 A*	Multirole Combat Air craft	2005
	7	C-130E Hercules	Transport ac Ex-RAAF	2005
	100 (all delivered)	Harpoon	Anti-ship missiles	2006 (order)
	54 (18 F-16 C/D Block 50/ 52 delivered)	F-16 (36 F-16 A &B+18 F-16 C&D)	Multirole Combat Air craft	2007
	6	AN/TPS-77	Air surveillance radar	Year of order – 2005
	6	L-88 LASS	Air surveillance radar	Year of order – 2003
	121	Refurbished Missile Launchers		
	115	M-109	Self Propelled Howitzers	
	500	Sidewinder	Air to Air Missile	
	20	AH-IF Cobra	Attack Helicopters	
Ukraine	4	IL-78	Aerial Refueller	Year of Order – 2008

*US Excess Defence Equipment which is normally transferred at price of less than 10 per cent of the original. For example, the cost of each F-16 is a little over $6 million.

Source: Based on, *Stockholm International Peace Research Institute*, *Yearbook* (issues of various years) (New York, Oxford University Press) and Pakistan's major arms imports, as cited in Jasjit Singh, "Trends in Defence Expenditure," *Asian Strategic Review*, 1998-99, (New Delhi, Institute for Defence Studies and Analyses, 1999), *SIPRI 2002, 2004, 2005, United Nations Register of Conventional Arms* for various years and Defence Security Cooperation Agency at, http://www.dsca.mil; "Update on Pakistan C-130E Acquisitions," *Air Forces*, January 2006, p.22, *The Military Balance 2007, IISS* (London, Routledge, 2007), *The Military Balance 2014, IISS.*
The previous version of the table cited in Shalini Chawla, *Pakistan's Military and Its Strategy,* (New Delhi: KW Publishers, 2009), pp. 42-44.

The Nuclear Build-up, Doctrine and Strategy

Pakistan's deep desire to possess nuclear weapons and hence its nuclear strategy cannot be viewed in isolation, and, has to be studied and analysed in the context of its overall "grand strategy". Pakistan's acquisition of nuclear weapons has been rationalised as a deterrent to the Indian conventional military superiority and to provide an umbrella under which to pursue a proxy war through terrorism.

The basic objectives behind acquiring the nuclear capability by Pakistan are:

Neutralise India's conventional superiority

India's conventional military superiority and Pakistan's desire to neutralise India's superiority has shaped the latter's defence build-up (including the build up of its nuclear arsenal).

The central assumption on which Pakistan has progressed and built up its nuclear arsenal is that a credible nuclear deterrent would compensate for the inferiority in conventional weapons. The ruling elites in Pakistan consistently felt that Pakistan is deficient of adequately equipped and numerically sufficient armed forces as compared to India.

Former Foreign Minister Agha Shahi referred to India's conventional force stating the objectives of Pakistan's nuclear weapons. He said:

> "The rationale of the (nuclear) programme is linked to the sovereignty, independence and the security of Pakistan. It is grounded on the security imperatives of Pakistan to equalise, to compensate our military imbalance that hangs like a sword of damocles over the heads of the nation....*Agha Shahi*."[34]

In this respect, Pakistan adopted a doctrine and strategy not very different from that pursued by the North Atlantic Treaty Organisation (NATO) against the USSR. Pakistan visualised nuclear weapons as the main guarantor of national survival, and thus, started to seek Chinese assistance for its nuclear weapon programme in the late 1960s itself.

To be visualised as the leader of the Islamic World

Pakistan's nuclear build up cannot ignore its deep desire to emerge as a formidable country of the Muslim world and to be visualised as the *leader of the Islamic world.* In its pursuit of nuclear power status, Pakistan did have financial support from Saudi Arabia and Libya and eventually, it did share nuclear data and expertise with Iran, Libya and Iraq. Pakistan believed that once it was able to achieve nuclear weapons capability, demand for Pakistani skilled manpower and technology would go up in the oil-rich Muslim countries. In return, Pakistan would have easier access to the oil wealth of West Asian nations to fulfil its needs for technological development.[35]

Pakistan's appeal for financial assistance for the acquisition of nuclear bomb for the 'sake of Islam' struck a strong emotional appeal in the Muslim world. Pakistan started receiving significant financial support from the Arab world by mid 1970s. By 1976, five Arab countries and Iran had provided grants and loans worth nearly, US$ 1,000 million. In a matter of three years (between 1973-74 and 1976-77), the Muslim countries were at top of the list of aid donors to Pakistan.[36] After Pakistan attained the nuclear status, it obviously feels technologically superior and positions itself as the leader of the Islamic world.

Possession of nuclear weapons to facilitate Pakistan's covert war through terrorism

Pakistan, since its very inception, has been resorting to the use of terror and adopted the route of covert war against India. The strategy of covert war has been a part of the grand strategy from the very beginning, when in 1947, General Akbar Khan wrote the plan for the first aggression under the title of "Armed Revolt inside Kashmir".[37] The *aggression,* which is often termed as 'revolt', did not break out of major dissatisfaction with the ruling class or the will of the Muslim population to seek Kashmir's accession to Pakistan. The aggression was a well thought out planned conspiracy by the Pakistani political leaders, Pakistan Army and the ex-servicemen of the erstwhile Indian Army and the Indian National Army, which, with the help of the local tribes, led to the outbreak of 1947 war between the two newly independent nations.

In 1965 war, the strategy of covert war was developed around Operation Gibraltar as a covert component. Since then, Pakistan has been not only using covert war through terrorism, but has eventually intensified its proxy war through the adoption of new tactics and means learnt by its war in Afghanistan during the 1980s as the 'frontline' state of the US. In the late 1980s and 1990s, Pakistan became much more active in sponsoring terrorism and has persistently carried on terrorism in various parts of India with deadly legacy. The possession of nuclear weapons and the announcement of the doctrine 'first use', undoubtedly, in the minds of Pakistani leadership provides a shield, which would deter any military retaliation from the Indian side in response to its terrorist activities. Pakistan's resort to nuclear blackmail has strengthened in the last two decades with the expansion of its arsenal.

Pakistan's Nuclear Programme

Pakistan has consistently claimed that it developed its nuclear programme in response to security threats from India, more specifically, Pakistan traces the genesis of its programme to India's peaceful experiment in Pokhran, in 1974. But the fact is that Bhutto was seriously pressing for nuclear weapons much before India's peaceful experiment, which became an immediate excuse for Islamabad. Pakistan's nuclear weapons are certainly not in response to India's nuclear weapons programme, but, because Pakistan's ruling elites believed that nuclear weapons were the only means to match India's conventional military superiority. Zulfiqar Ali Bhutto had openly announced Pakistan's ambition for the nuclear bomb in January 1972 (well before July 1974).

Bhutto was very determined to develop Pakistan's nuclear capability and in this context, he asserted:

> "All wars of our age have become total wars; all European strategy is based on the concept of total war; and it will have to be assumed that a war waged against Pakistan is capable of becoming a total war. It would be dangerous to plan for less and our plans should, therefore, include the nuclear deterrent.... It is vital for Pakistan to give the greatest possible attention to nuclear technology, rather than allow herself to be deceived by an international treaty limiting this deterrent to the present nuclear Powers."[38]

Bhutto called for a secret meeting of top Pakistani scientists in Multan on 20 January 1972, overtly adopted the nuclear weapon programme, motivated the Pakistani scientists and announced total support for nuclear weapons. Soon after the Multan meeting, Bhutto started seeking external support to finance the nuclear weapon programme. He visited the Middle Eastern countries which included Iran, Saudi Arabia, Libya, Egypt, United Arab Emirates and Syria. Various reports in the past suggest that the Arab world had been keen to develop the nuclear option.

Unlike his predecessor Bhutto, who adopted a confrontationist attitude, Zia was relatively subdued in his approach and did not formally declare his intention to acquire the nuclear bomb. He created a posture of nuclear ambiguity for Pakistan and mounted a peace offensive to join the NPT on the condition of India signing it.[39] The military regime in Pakistan further highlighted the Indian threat perception in order to acquire domestic legitimacy for the acquisition of the nuclear capability. The efforts for building the bomb continued and towards this end, a sustained and clandestine campaign was undertaken.

China proved to be Pakistan's crucial partner in its nuclear programme and in the 1970s and 1980s, there were definitely state-to-state deal and Pakistan's former top Pakistani nuclear scientist and proliferator Abdul Qadeer Khan, was the key intermediary.[40] Pakistan received help with the reactor, weapon design and nuclear material. A Q Khan visited China on a regular basis and the Chinese scientists were present at Kahuta, possibly helping the Pakistani scientist.[41] In 1986, China also concluded a comprehensive nuclear cooperation agreement with Pakistan and in the same year, reportedly, the Chinese scientists began assisting Pakistan with the enrichment of weapon grade uranium. Pakistan also received tritium gas from China that could be used to achieve fusion in hydrogen bombs and boost the yield of atomic bombs. The amount of gas transferred to Pakistan was apparently sufficient for making ten nuclear weapons.[42]

By 1984, General Zia announced that Pakistan has acquired the capability of producing small quantities of low enriched uranium. In 1981, 1,000 centrifuges were being assembled and they could produce uranium for one nuclear weapon every two years. In the following couple of years, Pakistan had acquired up to 10,000 centrifuges, which could produce 150 kg of enriched uranium per year and which would amount to seven nuclear bombs every year.[43] According to a former senior Pakistani official, Pakistan had acquired complete nuclear capability by 1983. Zahid Hussain, in his book, claims that Dr Khan openly announced in an interview with him that his organisation had conducted several cold tests in 1983 and 1984. Dr Khan apparently also claimed that General Zia was aware of the fact that Pakistan is ready for a nuclear test in a week's notice.[44] By 1986, Pakistan thought to have produced enough fissile material for the weapon and by 1987, it is believed that Pakistan could carry out a full nuclear explosion. Reports suggest that Pakistan conducted cold tests of a nuclear implosion device at Chagai.

Pakistan conducted its nuclear tests on May 28 and May 30 1998, two weeks after the Indian nuclear tests, at the Chagai Hills test site in western Pakistan.

Pakistan has subsequently endeavoured to use the nuclear weapons to carry on and intensify its proxy war in Kashmir claiming the valley to be the "nuclear flashpoint". Pakistan's grand strategy of 'bleeding India through thousand cuts" has been carried out under the nuclear umbrella.

Nuclear Doctrine

In the pre-nuclear test period, Pakistan's doctrine was that of ambiguity. Although, Pakistan even today does not have an officially announced doctrine, statements made by responsible policy makers in Pakistan have outlined the basic elements of its nuclear doctrine, which is solely Indo centric. There is an unofficial code adopted by the Pakistani leadership, based on *Indo-centricity, credible minimum deterrence* and *first use.* Very interestingly and rather ironically, the code asserts on the principles of peaceful programme revolving more around maintaining a balance against the Indian force build up, but it includes making a first strike in response to not only a conventional attack by India, but also a posed threat from India.

Minimum Nuclear Deterrence

This is one of the basic tenets of Pakistan's nuclear doctrine. The concept of credible minimum deterrence is not based specifically on the numbers, but it is the weapon arsenal including the nuclear weapons, delivery systems, command and control, and the doctrine and strategy, based on the perceived threat perception from India. Credible minimum deterrent force intends to build a minimum force capable of inflicting assured destruction on India. Prime Minister Nawaz Sharif very distinctly talked about it in May 1999 when he highlighted the key elements of Pakistan's nuclear policy at the National Defence College:

> "Nuclear restraint, stabilisation and minimum credible deterrence constitute the basic elements of Pakistan's nuclear policy."[45]

Pakistan Foreign Minister, Abdul Sattar repeated the doctrine in November, 1999: "Minimum nuclear deterrence will remain the guiding principle of our nuclear strategy."[46]

A perceptive Pakistani commentator had stated that Pakistan "has to copy the qualities outlined in the Indian doctrine".[47] Therefore, Pakistan has projected its nuclear doctrine as credible minimum deterrent, but, the one which is India specific and more manageable.[48] The reasons for Pakistan's adoption of credible minimum deterrence are obvious. Pakistan desires for a financially viable nuclear arsenal as the whole logic of going nuclear was Pakistan's inability to cope with India's conventional build-up, primarily due to the financial constraints.

The term 'minimum' begs definition and can be interpreted differently by the states. It's unclear that Pakistan has actually quantified deterrence and minimum for Pakistan would be based on the calculation of threat owing to the number of the nuclear weapons and missile systems with India. Pakistan's minimum deterrence appears to be based on the capability to inflict unacceptable damage or assured destruction.

First Use

Pakistan's long held belief that being the weaker state, it can compensate that weakness by taking a bold initiative, preferably with strategic surprise, to attack Indian military capability and thus, reduce the adverse margin of capabilities. This was the military strategy it practiced in all the wars waged against India including the last one, which was a regular war in Kargil in 1999 and more important war through terrorism across the border for quarter century. The specific concentration of terrorism in the border districts in Punjab, west of River Beas, was clearly aimed at similar goals. Seen in the context of this strategic mind set, it is not surprising that it has adopted a nuclear doctrine of "First Use". In fact, it has often claimed (in the past) that it would/could use nuclear weapon at the very beginning of the war with India if the Indian military even crossed the international border.

Pakistan's first use doctrine has been clearly stated in Lt General (Retd) Sardar F.S. Lodhi's writing in the Pakistan Defence Journal:

> "The political will to use nuclear weapons is essential to prevent a conventional armed conflict, which would later on escalate into a nuclear war… Pakistan's Nuclear Doctrine would, therefore, essentially revolve around the first-strike option. In other words, we will use nuclear weapons if attacked by India even if the attack is with conventional weapons. With his American experience of a graduated nuclear response, Professor Stephen P. Cohen feels that Pakistan would use what he calls an 'option-enhancing policy' for a possible use of nuclear weapons. This would entail a stage-by-stage approach in which the nuclear threat is increased at each step to deter India from attack. The first step could be a public or private warning, the second a demonstration explosion of a small nuclear weapon on its own soil, the third step would be the use of a few nuclear weapons on its own soil against Indian attacking forces. The fourth stage would be used against critical, but purely military targets in India across the border from Pakistan. Probably in the thinly populated areas in the desert or semi-desert, causing least collateral damage. This may prevent Indian retaliation against cities in Pakistan. Some weapon systems would be in reserve for the counter-value role."[49]

Rejecting India's proposal for a joint no first-use pledge in the aftermath of the nuclear tests, Pakistan took the stand that it will be the first to use the nuclear weapons to counter India's conventional capability.

Pakistan's argument has been, that in case of the likelihood of a conventional attack, or in a situation when India has breached the defence line causing major setback to the defence and security arsenal of Pakistan, then, due to the fear of being defeated in a conventional war against India, Pakistan has resorted to the first use option. Pakistan will go for the nuclear weapons first even if the attack from the Indian side is with the conventional weapons. Thus, a first use policy, according to the Pakistani leadership, provided credible security guarantees to their national sovereignty.

The need for Pakistan to maintain this position of first use is further exacerbated with India's assertion that the possibility of the conventional confrontation is not ruled out even in the nuclear environment. This obviously creates disturbances within Pakistan because it stands in contrast to Pakistan's rationale for the nuclear weapons, which is to deter India from using conventional force against them.[50] To deter India from using the conventional force, Pakistan holds the position of first use, in case, it "feels" the need.

Possibility of Pre-emption

Pakistan's obsessive reliance on the doctrine of first use policy seems to be emerging from two factors. First, Pakistan wants to keep an option open for "Pre-emptive nuclear strikes" against India and it is convinced that its pre-emptive strikes would lead to the destruction of India's second strike retaliatory capabilities. Secondly, Pakistan has failed to consider the consequences of the Indian retaliation. Pakistan seems to assume that India would not use nuclear weapons against it even after getting hit.

The scenarios in which Pakistan would opt for nuclear weapons have been spelled out by Pakistani elites, who have cultivated the posture of irrational rationality to try and enhance the effect of this posture. Lt Gen. Khalid Kidwai, the head of the Strategic Planning Division in Pakistan's Nuclear Command and Control system, in 2002, in an interview to the Italian journalists, claimed that "nuclear weapons would be used only "if the very existence of Pakistan as a state is at stake". He said that Pakistan would definitely use nuclear weapons in case the deterrence fails and:

1. If India attacks Pakistan and conquers a large part of its territory (space threshold);
2. If India destroys a large part either of Pakistan's land or air forces (military threshold);
3. If India proceeds to the economic strangling of Pakistan (economic strangling);
4. If India pushes Pakistan into political destabilisation or creates large-scale internal subversion in Pakistan (domestic destabilisation).[51]

The last two elements based on economic strangulation and domestic destabilisation cannot be seen in isolation and it would not be incorrect to say that these vaguely drawn vast parameters can potentially include various steps taken up by the Indian government in the wake of acute tension or conventional confrontation.

Weapon of last resort

Most of the Pakistani writings pre 1998 pointed towards build up of the nuclear capability against the Indian conventional forces and, thus, implied its first use. But there seems to be a shift in the Pakistani thinking regarding the use of nuclear weapons and adoption of a relatively moderate stand by claiming nuclear weapons as the "weapon of last resort".

President Pervez Musharraf, in May 2002, said that if it came to war between the nuclear-armed rivals, he would "respond with full might." These statements were interpreted to mean that if pressed by an overwhelming conventional attack from India, which has superior conventional forces, Pakistan might use its nuclear weapons. Similar interpretation can be drawn from Pakistan's defence Minister, Rao Sikander's statement when he said: "The country's ultimate security lies in the use of atom bomb; it is not a mere show piece."

Pakistan perceives nuclear weapons as the ultimate guarantee of its security and national survival, but it has not been very clear in defining the red lines and the scenarios, which could lead to its first use. Abdul Sattar (former Pakistan Foreign Minister), Agha Shahi and Zulfiqar Ali Khan jointly authored an article in *Dawn* on October 5, 1999, which stated:

"The exigency under which Pakistan army may use nuclear weapons is spelt out as: 'Although the precise contingencies in which Pakistan may use nuclear weapons have not been articulated or even defined by the government, the assumption has been that if the enemy launches a war and undertakes a piercing attack to occupy large territories or communication junctions, the *weapon of last resort* would have to be invoked."

Weapon of last resort can be logically interpreted towards the scenario where no other means are left with the nation to defend itself. In case of a conventional war between India and Pakistan, if Pakistan's military reserves are destroyed, then it may not have the capacity to defend itself and rather than losing war, it would opt to use nuclear weapons against India. Pakistan's use of nuclear weapon even if it is as a last resort would face Indian retaliation, which talks about "unacceptable damage". Although, the option of weapon of last resort stands in contradiction of Pakistan's earlier statements and appears moderate, but on the other hand, it also projects a mind set for self destruction, where complete destruction of the nation is preferred over all other possible options.[52]

Nuclear Policy based on Restraint and Responsibility

In the last few years, Pakistan's endeavour has been to project itself as a *responsible* nuclear power. The need to do so was exacerbated with India and the US signing the nuclear deal. Pakistan has been keen for a similar nuclear agreement with the US and, thus, the projection of a responsible nuclear posture became inevitable. In 2006, Lt Gen. Khalid Kidwai, in his address to the Naval Postgraduate School, Monterey, said that Pakistan has dealt with formidable challenges by developing a nuclear policy based on 'restraint and responsibility' with four silent features:

> "(1) Deterrence of all forms of external aggression; (2) ability to deter a counter strike against strategic assets; (3) stabilisation of strategic deterrence in South Asia; and (4) conventional and strategic deterrence methods."

The evolving nuclear strategy of Pakistan is of "flexible response" with the recent developments. In 2011, Pakistan tested its short range surface-to-surface multi-tube ballistic missile NASR (Hatf-9) a 60 km range missile, which belongs to the category of Tactical Nuclear Weapons. Pakistani leadership claims that the NASR is in response to India's Cold Start Doctrine. Despite the widespread attention and debate that the Cold Start

Doctrine attracted, the fact of the matter is that is has never been adopted by the Indian military. The adoption of TNWs obviously, projects an extremely low nuclear threshold for Pakistan and is aimed to deny any space in conventional war to India. There have been pervasive concerns not only about the destabilising impact the TNWs would potentially have, but also about the safety and security of these weapons. The safety of TNWs becomes extremely critical, especially in the case of Pakistan, given its volatile security environment with raging insurgency and terrorism.

Reportedly, Pakistan is also advancing towards sea based missile capability, which, according to the Pakistani leadership, would provide it *second strike capability* and *survivability*. But again, there are international concerns about vulnerability of these weapons. Islamabad, reportedly, intends using sea based missiles from the diesel operated submarines and, thus, the survivability of these weapons remains a concern.

Pakistan is certainly enhancing its options with increased number of platforms and varying ranges. Looking into Pakistan's stance on nuclear weapons, numerous contradictions can be seen. It talks about the use of nuclear weapons as last resort, with restrain and responsibility. Obviously, last resort has not been defined by Pakistan and, thus, creates uncertainty, which enhances deterrence and, thus, serves the Pakistani objectives. TNWs, on the other hand, project an extremely low nuclear threshold and raise different set of issues. It would not be incorrect to state that *Pakistan has very rationally adopted the posture of irrationality.*[53]

Arsenal and the Delivery Systems

Current Status of Nuclear Power

After the overt nuclear tests, Pakistan has continued to expand its nuclear arsenal, both the number of warheads as well as the delivery systems, including the ballistic missiles, cruise missiles and nuclear capable aircraft.[54]

According to the *World Association of Nuclear Operators*, the current status of Nuclear Power in Pakistan is as follows.[55]

- Pakistan's first nuclear reactor – KNAUPP, supplied by Canada, is a small 137 Mwe (125 Mwe net), pressurised heavy water reactor

(PHWR). The reactor was started in 1971 near Karachi and is operated at reduced power.

- The second reactor is Chashma-1 (also known as CHASNUPP-1) in Punjab, supplied by China under safeguards, which was started in 2000. Chashma-1 is a 325 Mwe (300 Mwe net) 2-loop pressurised water reactor (PWR) (Table 1). The main part of the reactor was designed by the Shanghai Nuclear Engineering Research and Design Institute (SNERDI) based on Qinshan-1. Construction for Chashma-2 commenced in 2005 with the Chinese technical and financial assistance. The enriched fuel for the PWRs is imported from China.
- In 2008, Pakistan announced the plans for the construction of two new reactors - Chashma-3 and 4 with the Chinese assistance. China has agreed to provide 82 per cent of the total cost at an extremely low interest rate. The construction agreement between China and Pakistan was signed in 2010 for the two 340 Mwe (315 Mwe net) units and are scheduled to be completed in eight years (Table 4).
- Reportedly, in 2010, PAEC has signed a construction agreement with China National Nuclear Corporation (CNNC) for the fifth unit at Chashma.
- As far as the fuel cycle is concerned – A uranium centrifuge plant at Kahuta has been under operation since 1984. The Kahuta project was launched in 1972 after the India-Pakistan war in 1971. Reportedly, there is also a new plant at Gadwal.
- In 2006, PAEC announced that it is preparing to set up a new civil conversation, enrichment and fabrication plant – Pakistan Nuclear Power Fuel Complex (NPFC) for PWR reactors.
- PARR-1 is a 10 MW pool-type research reactor (of 1965 vintage), supplied by the US under the Atoms for Peace Programme. In 1991, the reactor was converted to use low-enriched uranium fuel. PARR -2, operational since 1974, is based on the Chinese design and is using high enriched fuel. Both PARR-1 and 2 are located at the PINSTECH Laboratory, Nilore near Islamabad.
- In 1998, a larger multipurpose reactor started operating near Khushab. The reactor is reportedly producing weapons grade plutonium. Another large heavy water reactor is under

construction at Khushab since 2002 and it is supposed to be operational in 2009. In 2006 and 2011, (supposedly), the construction of the third and fourth reactors has commenced. These would certainly add to substantive plutonium production in Pakistan, which would compensate for the laxity in uranium resources.

Table 3: Operating Nuclear Power Reactors in Pakistan

Reactor	*Type*	*MWe net*	*Construction start*	*Commercial operation*	*Planned close*
KANUPP	PHWR	125	1966	12/72	
Chashma 1	PWR	300	1993	June 2000	2040
Chashma 2	PWR	300	2005	May 2011	2051
Total (3)		725			

Source: "Nuclear Power in Pakistan" at http://www.world-nuclear.org/info/inf108.html

Table 4: Nuclear Power Reactors under Construction and Planned

Reactor	*Province*	*Type*	*MWe gross*	*Construction Start*	*Planned Commercial Operation*
Chashma 3	Punjab	CNP-300	340	May 2011	Dec 2016
Chashma 4	Punjab	CNP-300	340	Dec 2011	October 2017
Karachi Coastal 1	Sindh	ACP1000	1100	late 2014	
Karachi coastal 2	Sindh	ACP1000	1100	late 2015?	
Total (4)				2880	

Karachi Coastal is also known as KANUPP 2&3.

Source: *Nuclear Power in Pakistan,* World Nuclear Association, at http://www.world-nuclear.org/info/Country-Profiles/Countries-O-S/Pakistan/

Since the time of its overt nuclearisation, Pakistan has been expanding its nuclear arsenal, which includes the building of two new plutonium reactors and new reprocessing facility, which would enable Pakistan to fabricate more nuclear weapons fuel.[56] There has been a significant increase in the number of nuclear delivery systems including the ballistic missiles, cruise missiles and the nuclear capable combat aircraft. It is estimated that Pakistan has a nuclear weapons stockpile of 90-110 nuclear warheads.[57]

The estimated figure according to the SIPRI 2013 Yearbook is between 100-110.

According to Internal Panel on Fissile Materials (2013), at the end of 2012, Pakistan had an accumulated stockpile of about 0.15 ± 0.05 tonnes of plutonium. Pakistan's current production of plutonium, which is from the two operation plutonium production reactors Khushab I and Khushab II, is at the rate of 12-24 kg per year, sufficient for 2-6 plutonium weapons.[58] Two additional production reactors with similar capacity are under construction at the similar site. Pakistan also produces highly-enriched uranium (HEU) sufficient for 10-15 warheads per year. As of end of 2012, it had an estimated stockpile of about 3± 1.2 tonnes of HEU.[59]

Delivery Systems

Pakistan's nuclear delivery systems can be put under three categories:

1. Land-based missiles.
2. Aircraft.
3. Cruise missiles

Pakistan's missile development programme has been primarily carried out with China's assistance and, to some extent, North Korea's, after the United States imposed sanctions on China.[60] China had been willing to transfer nuclear weapons to Pakistan as early as 1965 itself, shortly after it became a nuclear power.[61] Bhutto had been arguing for the nuclear weapons in the late 1960s, but Ayub had turned down the proposal as it was not deemed necessary or affordable at that point of time for Pakistan. Since 1972, Pakistan sought Chinese assistance for its nuclear development programme and China has been Pakistan's predominant source of foreign technological support for its missile development efforts. Chinese missile assistance to Pakistan ranges from providing equipment and training to transferring the complete missiles. In 1989, Lt Gen Talat Masood, Chairman of Pakistan's Ordnance Factories (POF) Board (1981-1988) acknowledged China's active role in Pakistan's missile programme in an interview.[62] The US Assistant Secretary of State, Winston Lord was not wrong when he wrote a letter to Senator Robert F. Bennett stating, "The entire strategic weapons program should be stamped 'Made in China'."[63]

The Chinese M series of SRBMs commenced development in the early

1980s and the three versions are known as, the M-9, M-11 and M-18. These designations were apparently used for the export versions.[64] Information from various sources indicates that Pakistan had negotiated the deal for the M-11 during Zia's regime. According to the US officials, Pakistan agreed to pay China $15 million as a partial payment on its 1988 contract with the state-owned China Precision Machinery Import-Export Corporation (CPMIEC) for an undetermined number of M-11 missiles, launchers, and support equipment.[65]

M-11 is a single stage, solid fuelled missile with a reported range of 300 km and payload of 800 kg. In 1989, Pakistan test-fired a 150 kg multi stage rocket at an altitude of 640 km. This was followed by the testing of short range, solid propellant, *Hatf-I and Hatf II* missiles, for which China provided vital assistance. Pakistan went in for the longer range missiles, as these missiles were unable to target Pakistan's prime objective, New Delhi.[66]

The technology for the M-11 was used to develop future missiles by Pakistan. Technical evaluation of the missile *Hatf-3 (Ghaznavi),* tested for the first time in 2002, suggests that *Hatf-3* is a version of M-11 or may be even a repainted M-11. Reportedly, the production facilities of these missiles have been set up with Chinese assistance.[67]

Hatf-4 or Shaheen-1 is believed to be a scaled up version of M-11 missiles supplied to Pakistan in 1993. Shaheen is a single stage, solid propellant missile with an inertial guided system and has a maximum range of 750 km.[68]

Ghauri missile (*Hatf*-5) was developed with North Korean assistance. Ghauri missile, which resembles the shape of the Russian 'Scud B', is an outcome of coordinated inputs from both North Korea and China. There were reports regarding an arrangement made between Pakistan, China and North Korea, whereby China would provide with soft technology and engineering for Ghauri, North Korea would act as an agent for the transfer of Chinese technology and would provide hardware and components from its Nodong missile programme.[69] The first flight test for Ghauri, single stage, liquid propellant missile was in April 1998 with a range of 800-1200 km.

Hatf 6, test fired in 2004, has maximum range of up to 2500 km and is believed to be based upon the earlier Chinese two-stage solid propellant missile M-18, which was demonstrated in 1998.

On April 19, 2011, Pakistan tested its short range surface to surface multi tube ballistic missile *Hatf* 9 (NASR). The official press release for NASR said:

> "The missile has been developed to add deterrence value to Pakistan's Strategic Weapons Development programme at shorter ranges. NASR with a range of 60 km, carries nuclear warheads of appropriate yield with high accuracy, shoot and scoot attributes. This quick response system addresses the need to deter evolving threats."[70]

Although, a missile of 60 km range is more likely to be a free flying rocket, Pakistan has claimed the missile to be nuclear capable, which is possible. NASR falls under the category of Tactical Nuclear Weapons and has generated ample debate in the Indian defence and strategic community.

Pakistan conducted a test-firing of its latest domestically manufactured (as it claims) cruise missile, known as *Babur (or Babar, Hatf-7),* exactly at the time when President Asif Zardari was in Washington and due to meet US President Barack Obama, in May 2009.[71] Babur is an air, ground, ship and submarine launched short range, turbojet powered, single warhead cruise missile, and does have Chinese technical input.

In May 8, 2008, Pakistan tested a nuclear-capable, air launched cruise missile, the Hatf-8 – Ra'ad, with a range of 350 km. The first test-launch for the Ra'ad was carried on in 2007. The Hatf-8 missile has been developed exclusively for launch from aerial platforms, enabling Pakistan to achieve greater strategic capability on land and at sea.[72]

In the 1980s, Pakistan was in full swing with its nuclear development programme, and saw aircraft as the chief means of delivering nuclear weapons. The main sources of its aircraft have been the United States, France and China. The aircraft, which will be used as the delivery systems in the nuclear programme, are the F-16s, J-10s, J-11, Mirages and the A-5.

Financing the Defence Budget

Pakistan has consistently spent a high portion of its national income on defence. It's defence spending has always been a matter of concern for the

Fig. 1. Pakistan's Ballistic Missiles (Ranges)

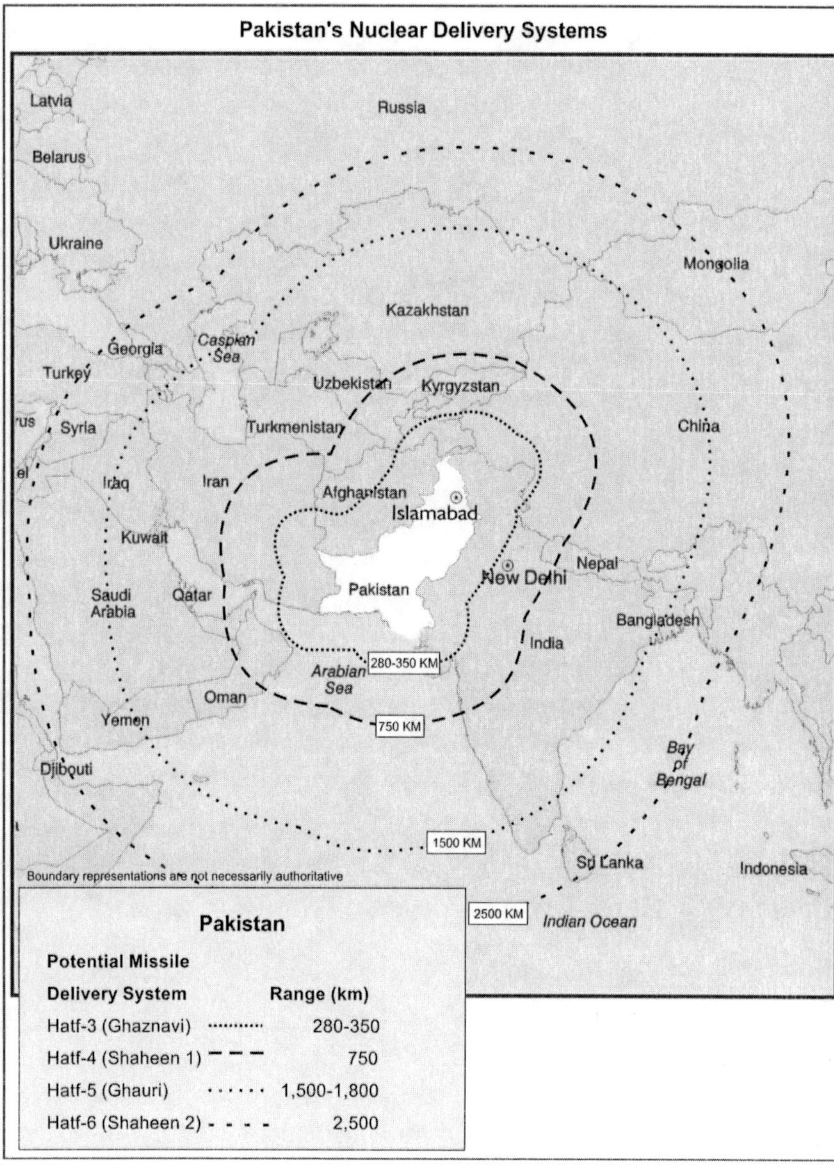

Boundary representation is not necessarily authoritative

Source: Dr Shalini Chawla, *Nuclear Pakistan* (New Delhi: KW Publishers, 2012), p. 107.

Fig. 2: Pakistan's Cruise Missiles

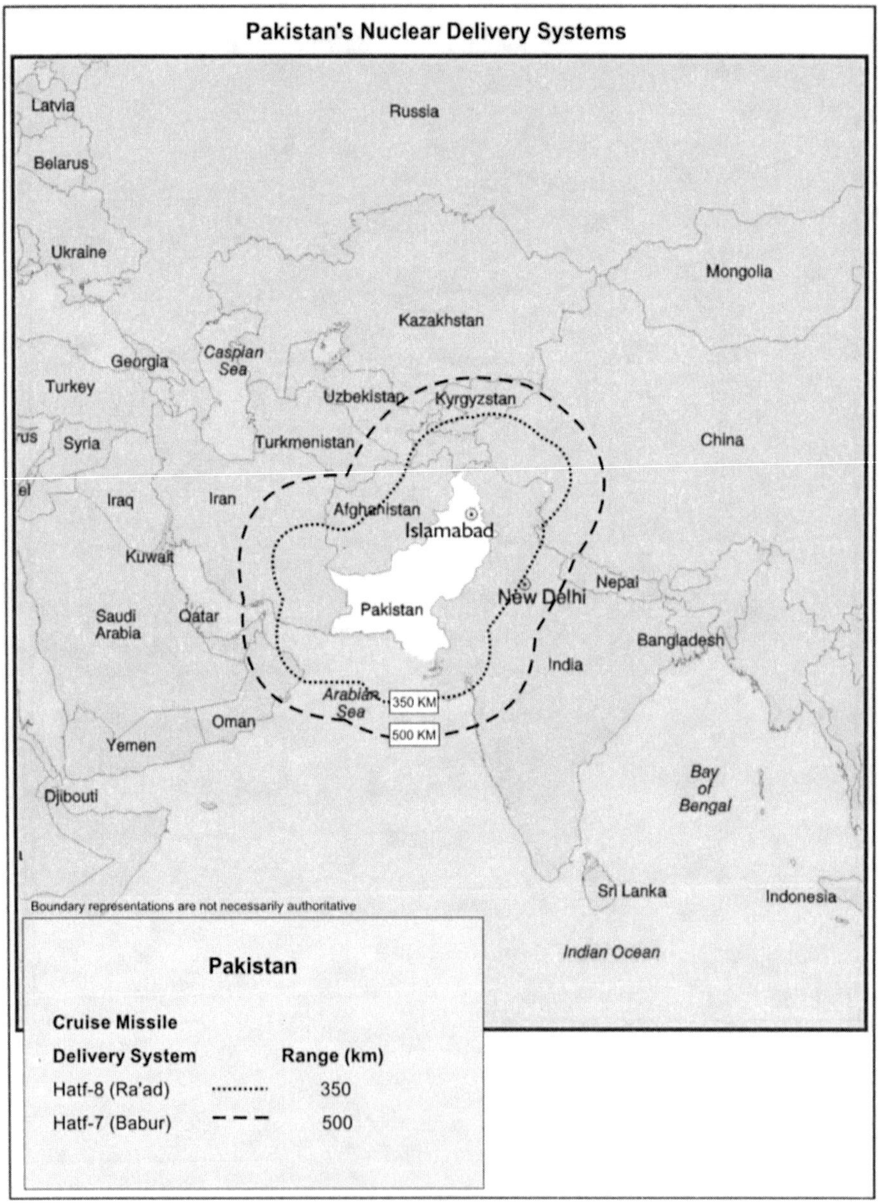

Boundary representation is not necessarily authoritative
Source: Dr Shalini Chawla, *Nuclear Pakistan*, p. 110

Table 5: Pakistan's Nuclear Delivery Systems

Type	*Range (km)*	*Payload (kg)*
Ballistic Missiles		
M-9	600 km	
M-11	300 km	800 kg
Hatf-3 (Ghaznavi)	280-350 km	700 kg
Hatf-4 (Shaheen 1)	750 km	
Hatf-5 (Ghauri)	1,500-1,800 km	
Hatf-6 (Shaheen 2)	2,500 km	
Hatf 9 (NASR)	60 km	
Cruise Missiles		
Hatf-7 (Babur)	500 km	450 kg
Hatf-8 (Ra'ad)	350 km	
Aircraft		
F-16A/B	1,600 km	1 bomb
F-16C/D		
Mirage V	2,100 km	1 bomb
A-5		
JF-17		

Source: Jane's Strategic Weapon Systems, Issue 48, 2008; *Jane's All the World's Aircraft*, various issues.

economists and academicians within Pakistan and the financial institutions abroad. Pakistan has maintained defence spending at the rate of 6 per cent of the GDP till the late 1990s. In the last six years, the *official* defence spending figures have been kept low owing to massive international pressure in the past and strong debate in Pakistan blaming the defence spending for the country's economic woes in the 1990's. In the previous decade, the official defence spending has been maintained on an average of about 3.2 per cent of the GDP.

Every successive regime, civil or military, has been spending a significant portion of its national resources on defence and military requirements. Thus, in the last two decades, the defence budget of Pakistan has been constantly under pressure by the international monetary organisations and strategic thinkers. Pakistan, in the 1990s, experienced deplorable state of social sector, which stood in a complete contrast to the grandeur of the military elites in Pakistan.

Pakistan's defence budget, unlike India or even China, is not transparent and no details about the breakdown of defence expenditure are available. Only an overall defence budget figure is provided by the government. Estimated military spending is significantly higher as external military assistance in various forms is not included in the official figures of the defence expenditure. Also, several military related expenditures are covered under the civil and public administration.

Estimated Defence Expenditure

The defence budget provided by the government of Pakistan is just the total figure without indicating any details regarding the distribution of funds under various heads. It is a normal practice to get the defence budget passed by the parliament as a one line item on the agenda. According to reliable Pakistani sources, the defence expenditure figures do not include the costs of acquisitions of major weapon systems.[73] The major weapon acquisition in Pakistan takes place from the military and economic assistance provided by the United States, the Arab world and other nations. For example, the initial payment of US$ 1.4 billion of the first 40 F-16 aircrafts in 1980-81 was reportedly funded by the Saudi money.[74] Pakistan is believed to partly finance its defence expenditure out of the budget sources obtained through secret allocations by the Gulf countries or Army controlled private organisations, such as the Fauji Foundation or ISI procured drug money. These are reported facts which would be difficult to prove or disprove, but revenues from these clandestine sources can be assumed to be a regular source of funding Pakistan defence budget.

Pakistan did separate the military pensions, which amount to approximately 11 per cent of the budget in the year 2000 from the defence budget and placed them under the civil administration expenditure, to project decline in the defence budget. The money spent on providing various perks and facilities to serving, as well as retired defence personnel is also absorbed under various other heads. The estimated military spending including the entire military power is much higher than projected in the official defence budget of Pakistan.[75]

The actual defence spending is higher due to multiple factors. The foreign aid, which Pakistan has been receiving, specifically, the US aid in the last 12 years, has been for military purposes, but is not a part of the defence budget. The Foreign Military Financing (FMF) component of the aid stood at US$ 2751 million for the years 2002-2013. Also, Pakistan being a Non-NATO ally has been receiving the Excess Defence Articles from the US, at very low cost or even free of cost. The Coalition Support Funds have also been an added investment in Pakistan's military infrastructure.

The Chinese equipment, on the other hand, is received at a very low cost with easy instalments. Pakistan does enjoy exceptional leverages with respect to its weapons dealing with China. For example, immediately after the killing of Osama bin Laden in 2011, China announced 50 JF-17s for Pakistan free of cost.

Conclusion

The Pakistani elites, over the decades, have convinced themselves and recycled this belief that India is Pakistan's prime enemy, which, in turn, facilitated the military's assumption of preeminent and pervasive position in the national power structure for most of Pakistan's existence. In turn, this also made arms acquisitions unanswerable to public or political influences. In specific, they have sought to build military power on the basis of this fundamental strategy and, hence, pursued:

1. Acquisition of high-end military technology to neutralise what it perceived as India's conventional superiority.
2. External political support for its policies and supply of sophisticated arms (essentially from the US and China)
3. Building indigenous arms production capabilities to reduce dependence on outside sources. China has provided substantive support in this process.

The current trends in the defence build up are as follows:

1. Pakistan has accorded high priority to the acquisitions of the Air Force and Maritime strike capabilities of the Navy. The impact of the modernisation can be seen in Table 6:

2. Pakistan Air Force is engaged in massive modernisation since 1990 (boosted after 9/11) both qualitatively and quantitatively. The thinking, writing and arms procurement in Pakistan indicates the historical consistency of approach to military capability – the desire and efforts to acquire high technology arms to take the initiative to compensate for asymmetry in numbers and increase options for offensive strategy.

Table 6: Modernisation Effect

	1990	*2018*
Combat*	380	420
AEW&C	Nil	8
Air-to-Air Refuelling	Nil	4
Maritime Ptl & Air Strike Ac	3	18
Attack helicopters	**10**	**60+**

*It is interesting to note that the combat number in the table does not give the true picture. Out of the total combat aircraft in 1990, just around ten per cent were fourth generation. *But by 2020, more than 90 per cent would be fourth generation aircraft in the PAF inventory.*
Source: Dr Shalini Chawla, *Nuclear Pakistan*, p.74.

3. Pakistan is making significant efforts to add force multipliers in the PAF inventory.
4. Consistent demands for high technology weapons clearly indicate the modernisation of the Pakistan Air Force and Naval Air Force, even more than the Army and Navy, which implies that they expect the Air Force to play a major role in any future conflict.
5. Nuclear arsenal has been expanded enormously to continue the doctrine of "offensive defence". Pakistan's grand strategy has been to use the nuclear card for aggressive militancy in Kashmir in the 1990s and eventually terrorism in other parts of the Indian territory. In 1989, the then Army Chief, General Aslam asserted that Pakistan lost the previous wars with India due to "lack of clear strategic vision". He announced that Pakistan had a coherent strategy now. "One aspect of the strategy was launching of the militant proxy war in J&K from July 31, 1988; and the other was the achievement of nuclear deterrence (to provide "defence"

in the offensive-defence strategic doctrine, while irregular war was used for the "offensive" component) by 1987". [76]

6. Pakistan believes in enhanced deterrence and thus, has been aggressively expanding its missile base with extended range (Figure 1 and 2). Pakistan's reliance on nuclear weapons would increase in the near future with the deterioration of the internal security situation within Pakistan.[77]

NOTES

1. Robert Karniol, "Pakistan Plugging the Gaps," *Jane's Defence Weekly,* March 20, 2006.
2. Ross Masood Husain, "Threat Perception and Military Planning in Pakistan: The Impact of Technology, Doctrine and Arms Control", Eric Arnett, ed. *Threat Perception in Pakistan,* (Oxford: Oxford University Press, 1997), p. 130.
3. Ayesha Siddiqa-Agha, *Pakistan's Arms Procurement and Military Buildup, 1979-99: In Search of a Policy,* (New York: Palgrave, 2001), p. 91.
4. Dennis Kux, *The United States and Pakistan, 1947-2000: Disenchanted Allies,* (New York: Oxford University Press, 2001), p. 249.
5. Ibid, p. 69.
6. Pran Chopra, "Pakistan Squanders A Strategic Advantage", in Ajay Darshan Behra and Mathew Joseph, ed., *Pakistan in a Changing Strategic Context* (New Delhi: Knowledge World, 2004) p. 90.
7. Dennis Kux, n 4, pp-86-87.
8. Ibid, p. 113.
9. Samina Yasmeen, "China and Pakistan in a Changing World", ed. K Santhanam and Srikanth Kondapalli, *Asian Security Review 2003, Asian Security and China 2000-2010,* (New Delhi: Shipra Publications, 2004) p. 310.
10. *The Boundary Agreement between China and Pakistan, 1963.*
11. Ayesha Siddiqa-Agha, n 3, p. 105.
12. "Pakistan Navy" at http://www.globalsecurity.org/military/world/pakistan/navy-intro.htm
13. Immediately after this development, President Carter unveiled his doctrine, which included, "assembly of a Rapid Deployment Force (RDF), increase of naval presence in the Indian Ocean, a collective security framework in the region and commitment to the defense of Pakistan by transfer of significant amount of weapons and dollars." *The New York Times,* January 25, 1980, as cited by Hamid Hussain, "Tale of a Love Affair that Never was: United States-Pakistan Defence Relations", at http://www.defencejournal.com/2002/june/loveaffair.htm
14. Rodney W. Jones, "The Military and Security in Pakistan", in Craig Baxter, ed. *Zia's Pakistan: Politics and Stability in a Frontline State,* (Lahore: Vanguard, 1985), p. 83.
15. Pervez Iqbal Cheema, *The Armed Forces of Pakistan,* (Oxford: Oxford University Press, 2002) p. 164.
16. Ayesha Siddiqua-Agha, n 3, p.139. The largest share of the American military aid (the first package) was used for the Air Force. Out of the military component of $1.6 billion, $1.2 billion was spent on the acquisition of 40 F-16 aircraft.

17. Ayesha Siddiqua Agha, n 3, p 161.
18. Ibid, p. 144.
19. For details, see, Dennis Kux, n. 4
20. Ayesha Siddiqua Agha, n 3, p.145. These aircrafts were retired from the RAAF and most of them had about a hundred flying hours remaining on their airframes.
21. US Defence Security Cooperation Agency at http:www.dsca.mil.
22. *The Military Balance 2014*, IISS, p. 270.
23. "JF-17 Aircraft", *Pakistan Aeronautical Complex , Kamra,* at http://www.pac.org.pk/jf-17
24. Interview, Air Chief Marshal, Tanvir Mahmood Ahmed, Pakistan's Chief of Air Staff, 4 April, 2007, *Jane's Defence Weekly*, p.34
25. *The Military Balance 2014,* p. 218
26. Ayesha, n 3, p. 159.
27. Bilal H. Khan, "Pakistan Navy Modernization Program", Pakistan Military Consortium, at http://www.pakdef.info/pakmilitary/navy/pn_,odernization.html
28. Ibid.
29. "Navy gets fourth F-22 Frigate", *The Nation,* September 4, 2013, at http://www.nation.com.pk/karachi/04-Sep-2013/navy-gets-fourth-f-22-frigate
30. "Pakistan Navy" *Pakistan Defence*, at, http://www.defence.pk/pakistan-navy/
31. *The Military Balance 2005-2006, IISS* (London, Taylor and Francis, 2005) p.230
32. "PNS Gwadar" at, http://www.globalsecurity.org/military/world/pakistan/pns-gwadar.htm
33. http://intellibriefs.blogspot.in/2008/01/gwadar-port-has-strategic-implications.html
34. Address by Agha Shahi, in Fasahat H. Syed, ed. *Nuclear Disarmament and Conventional Arms Control including Light Weapons*, (Islamabad: FRIENDS, 1997), p. 421.
35. Maj Gen D K Palit and P K S Namboodari, *Pakistan's Islamic Bomb*, (New Delhi: Vikas Publishing House Pvt Ltd, 1979), p. 17.
36. Ibid, p. 36.
37. See, Maj Gen Akbar Khan, *Raiders in Kashmir*, (Delhi: Army Publishers) p. 14.
38. Zulfikar Ali Bhutto, *The Myth of Independence*, (London: Oxford University Press, 1969) p. 153.
39. Ashok Kapur, *Pakistan's Nuclear Development,* (London: Croom Helm, 1987) p.185.
40. Gordon Corera interview with Gary Malhollin, Eashington, D.C., December 14, 2005, as cited in Gordon Corera, *Shopping for Bombs*, (New Delhi: Foundation Books, 2006), p. 45.
41. Ibid.
42. "Incidental Intelligence: China Emerging As Third World Weapons Supplier," *Asia-Pacific Defence Reporter*, September 1991, p. 19; Gary Milhollin and Gerard White, "Bombs From Beijing: A Report On China's Nuclear And Missile Exports," May 1991, p. 17; *The Risk Report*, May 1995, p. 8; Gary Milhollin and Gerard White, "A New China Syndrome: Beijing's Atomic Bazaar," *Washington Post*, 12 May 1991, pp. C1, C4. As cited in, "China's Nuclear Exports and Assistance to Pakistan", *NTI*, at http://www.nti.org/db/china/npakpos.htm.
43. Israeli letter, UN General Assembly, A/36/298, p. 3, as cited in Ashok Kapur, n 39, p. 210.
44. Zahid Hussain, *Frontline Pakistan: the Path to Catastrophe and The Killing of Benazir Bhutto,* (New Delhi: Penguin Books, 2008) p. 159.

45. 'Remarks of the Prime Minister of Pakistan, Nawaz Sharif, on Nuclear Policies and the CTBT", National Defence College, Islamabad, 20 May 1999.
46. Address to the "Pakistan Response to the Indian Nuclear Doctrine" Seminar, Foreign Minister Abdus Sattar, November 25, 1999, in "Pakistan Responds to India's Nuclear Doctrine", *Disarmament Diplomacy*, Issue No.14, November 1999.
47. M.B. Naqvi, *Defence Journal,* (Karachi) February 2000, p. 15, as cited in Jasjit Singh, "Pakistan's Nuclear Strategy: An Assessment", *Aakrosh,* October 2001, Vol. 4, No. 13.
48. Ibid.
49. Lt Gen (Retd) Sardar F. S Lodhi, "Pakistan's Nuclear Doctrine", *Defence Journal,* Volume 3, Number 4, April 1999, at http://www.defencejournal.com/apr99/pak-nuclear-doctrine.htm
50. Manpreeth Sethi, *Nuclear Strategy: India's March towards Credible Deterrence,* (New Delhi: Knowledge World, 2009), p. 61.
51. As cited in Paolo Cotta-Ramusino and Maurizio Martellini, *Nuclear Safety, Nuclear Stability and Nuclear Strategy in Pakistan,* Landau Network – Centro Volta Report.
52. See, Dr Shalini Chawla, *Nuclear Pakistan* (New Delhi: KW Publishers, 2012).
53. For details, see Ibid.
54. For details, see Ibid.
55. The details for the status of Nuclear Power in Pakistan are taken from "Nuclear Power in Pakistan" at http://www.world-nuclear.org/info/inf108.html.
56. Hans M. Kristensen and Robert S. Noris, "Pakistan's Nuclear Forces, 2011", *Bulletin of the Atomic Scientists,* at http://bos.sagepub.com/content/67/4/91.full.pdf+html.
57. Ibid.
58. International Panel on Fissile Materials, Countries Pakistan, at http://fissilematerials.org/countries/pakistan.html.
59. Ibid.
60. For details see, Dr Shalini Chawla, "China-Pakistan Strategic Nexus: Probability of a Two Front War, in Air Commodore Jasjit Singh, ed. *China's India War 1962: Looking Back to See the Future,* (New Delhi: KW Publisher, 2013)
61. There is no doubt that this would have created a major rift between the US and Pakistan, which may have been Mao's real motive.
62. Roger Frost, "Pakistan's Procurement Chief on New Programs", *International Defence Review,* June 1989, p. 765.
63. Bill Gertz, "China Plays a Major Role in Expanding the Nuclear Club", *Washington Times,* May 29, 1998
64. "Nuclear Weapons Database: Pakistan's Possible Nuclear Delivery Systems", at http://www.cdi.org/nuclear/database/panukes.html
65. Bill Gertz, *Washington Times,* 4 October 1994, p. A8; Barbara Starr, *Jane's Defence Weekly,* 15 October 1994, p. 6 as cited in "China's Missile Exports and Assistance to Pakistan – Statements and Developments" at http://cns.miis.edu/archive/country_india/china/mpakchr.htm.
66. Bhumika Chakma, *Pakistan's Nuclear Weapons,* (London: Routledge, 2009), p. 69.
67. S. Chandrashekar, Arvind Kumar and Rajaram Nagappa. "An Assessment of Pakistan's Ballistic Missile Programme: Technical and Strategic Capability", *NIAS* Study - 2006, p 10.
68. *Jane's Strategic Weapon Systems* Issue 48-2008, p. 112.

69. Joseph Bermudez, "A Salient Partner", *Jane's Defence Weekly* (Coulsdon Surrey), 20 May 1998.
70. *ISPR*, Press Release, No PR94/2011-ISPR, April 19, 2011, at https://www.ispr.gov.pk/front/main.asp?o=t-press_release&id=1721.
71. "Pakistan Test-fires Babur Cruise Missile" at http://forum.pakistanidefence.com/lofiversion/index.php/t82549.html.
72. Iftikhar A. Khan, "Cruise Missile Fired from Aerial Platform", *Dawn*, May 9, 2008, at http://www.dawn.com/2008/05/09/top4.htm.
73. Air Marshal A. Rashid Shaikh, PAF (retd), "Security and Development: Hobson's Choice", *Defence Journal*, vol. XXI, May-June 1996, p.13, as cited in Jasjit Singh, "Trends in Defence Expenditure", *Asian Strategic Review 1998-99*, (Delhi: Knowledge World, 1999), p. 75.
74. Jasjit Singh, Ibid, p. 75.
75. For details see, Shalini Chawla, *Pakistan's Military and its Strategy*, (New Delhi: KW Publishers, 2009).
76. General Mirza Aslam Beg, *The Nation*, December 13, 1993, as cited in, " The Army in Pakistan", ed. Air Commodore Jasjit Singh, *Kargil 1999: Pakistan's Fourth War for Kashmir*, (New Delhi: Knowledge World, 1999), p. 47
77. For details, see Dr Shalini Chawla, n 52.

3

Pakistan's Economy: An Unviable State?

Sushant Sareen

1. Introduction

Nine months after the Nawaz Sharif government took office, Finance Minister Ishaq Dar has been confidently asserting that the economy was well on the path of recovery. Rattling off numbers, Mr Dar claimed that almost all the crucial economic indicators were moving in the right direction: GDP growth was expected to be around 4.5 per cent, inflation had been contained at around 8.5 per cent, tax collections were up around 18 per cent, budget deficit had not been allowed to balloon, foreign remittances were up by 11 per cent, nearly 2500 new companies had been registered and private sector credit off-take had picked up, which was a clear sign of growing business confidence, the Karachi Stock Exchange index had touched new heights, foreign reserves were rising and the Pakistani Rupee (PKR) had not only recovered its value from a low of around 110 to a dollar to the level of 98.[1] On the back of these encouraging numbers, Dar expressed confidence that Pakistan would not only meet all the benchmarks set by the IMF in the $ 6.7 billion EFF programme it had given, but also that Pakistan would meet the medium-term goals (by 2017) set by the Nawaz Sharif government, i.e., GDP growth of 6-7 per cent (currently around 3%), investment/GDP ratio of 20 per cent (currently 13%), Tax-GDP ratio of 13% (currently 8.5%), foreign exchange reserves of around $ 20 billion (currently around $ 9 billion), fiscal deficit of four per cent (in 2012-13, it was around 8.5%) and Public Debt-GDP ratio below 60 per cent (currently it has breached this benchmark for a number of years though some dodgy accounting and figure fudging has tried to portray otherwise).[2]

Mr Dar's optimism notwithstanding, senior economists in Pakistan have punched holes in the figures he had been presenting. Although Mr Dar has managed to 'talk up' the economy and infuse some amount of business confidence, the upward trend that he is presenting is neither reliable nor sustainable.[3] For instance, the revaluation of the PKR is not so much on the inherent strength of the economy as it is because of a 'gift', or 'grant' by Saudi Arabia of $ 1.5 billion for what some allege are 'services promised' by Pakistan. Other reasons for the upturn in the value of the PKR is the weakening of the US$, inflows from IMF, expected inflows from World Bank and ADB, release of Coalition Support Funds (CSF) by the US, market interventions by the State Bank of Pakistan (SBP), and a bit of playing the foreign exchange markets through signalling by Mr Dar, which led to an off-loading of dollars by exporters and last, but not the least, a shifting of the oil trade from the government account to a short-term deferred payment arrangement with foreign banks, thereby temporarily easing the pressure on the foreign exchange reserves with the SBP. Economists have also questioned the data on GDP growth, Fiscal Deficit (FD) and the Public Debt (Ishaq Dar boasted that the revaluation has reduced the debt by PKR 800 billion).[44]

The simple fact of the matter is that until now the Nawaz Sharif government has done nothing substantial to address the fundamental structural issues that have made Pakistan something of a basket case economy over the last couple of decades. Although Nawaz Sharif has acquired a reputation for being business friendly and there is a general belief that the economy does well under his watch, the reality is quite different. The truth is that his 'business friendly' policies are really a euphemism for 'crony capitalism' and the last time he was in power, Pakistan's economy was in even deeper trouble than it arguably is at present. If anything, when Nawaz Sharif was overthrown by a military coup in 1999, the Pakistan economy was bankrupt and in technical default of its international obligations.

The current economic crisis is not something that has come about all of a sudden. It has been years in the making. Over the last quarter of a century, Pakistan's economy has lurched from one crisis to another. In fact, since the country came into existence, it has had a very erratic growth record. There have been periods of feverish economic growth followed by a period of slump, the cycle being repeated a number of time. Interspersed in this boom-bust cycle have been periods of indifferent or anaemic growth (see Fig. 1 below).

Broadly, Pakistan's growth record can be broken down into three or four distinct periods: 1958-59 to 1964-65 when the economy boomed, which ended with the 1965 war with India. By 1968-69, the economy picked up once again before the 1971 war, once again, brought it crashing down. Growth in the 1970s was not anything to write home about. Nationalisation programme of ZA Bhutto, the oil shocks and the reduction in foreign assistance were the dampening factors. The Afghan war, which started in the late 1979, opened up the tap for Western assistance and the economy boomed in the 1980s when a military dictator, Gen Zia-ul Haq was running the show.

The return of democracy in 1988 was followed by a lost decade of the 1990s. By the time Pakistan's fourth military dictator, Gen Pervez Musharraf, took the reins of power in 1999, the economy was virtually on the ropes. Musharraf remained an international pariah until the 9/11 terror attacks came to his rescue. The second Afghan war, which started in 2001, once again opened the floodgates of Western aid for Pakistan. But by around 2006-07, the boom seemed to have run its course. Since then, it's been one steep downslide for the economy.

Like every other country, Pakistan has suffered its share of some big internal and external shocks – wars (all of them self-inflicted), oil shocks in 1973, 1979 and 2007, US sanctions imposed after the nuclear explosions in 1998, a massive earthquake in 2005, floods of biblical proportions in 2010, terrorism (also self-inflicted), political instability, poor governance, etc. But Pakistan has also benefited from externalities that more than compensated for some of these shocks – for instance, remittances from the oil rich Middle East, successful leveraging of its geographical location in the late 1950s, 1980s and then post 9/11, which led to billions of dollars in aid.

Fig. 1: GDP Growth

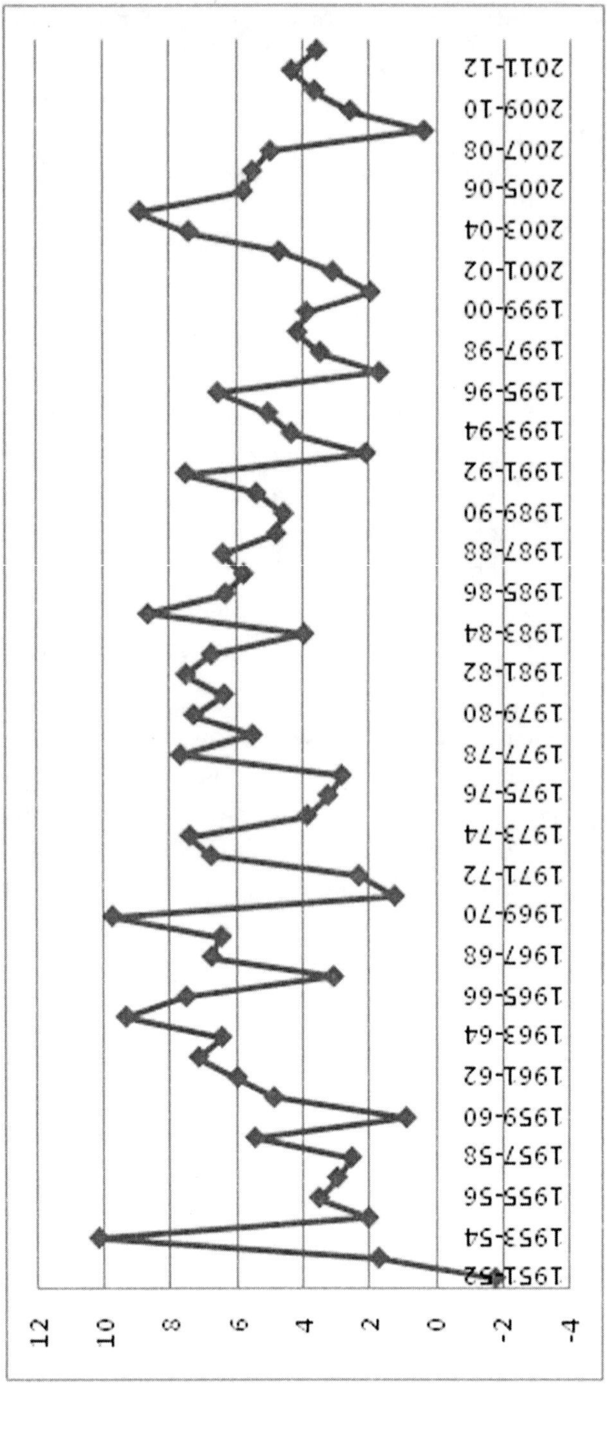

Source: Pakistan Bureau of Statistics.

Although Pakistan likes to wallow in the difficulties imposed by the shocks and blame someone else for its economic problems, the simple truth is that it itself is to blame for almost all of its economic difficulties. Pakistan failed to build its economic sinews so that it could weather out the inevitable storms that would come its way. In other words, it remained a fragile economy, which thrived every time the aid tap opened and which slumped every time the aid tap either dried out or became a drip. Remarkably, in the last about 20 years, except for a few years, the Official Development Assistance (ODA) that Pakistan received has remained below three per cent of Gross National Income (GNI) (see Fig. 2). But this is enough for perking up the economy because with official aid comes deeper engagement with the West, which, in turn, helps the economy. This is an indicator of a) Pakistan's economic dependence on the West and b) How much Pakistan's economy operates on the margin where the boom and bust cycle depends not so much on market conditions as it does on whether or not Pakistan has access to 'other people's money' and munificence.

The critical importance of and dependence on foreign assistance and engagement is in large part an outcome of the deep structural problems that forever seem to dog the economy. When the aid tap opens, these structural problems get glossed over, but when the aid starts to dry up, these problems manifest themselves. What has compounded the current crisis in Pakistan is that the downturn since 2006-07 has happened despite foreign aid and engagement not drying up. Indeed, the structure problems in the economy, which in earlier years got brushed under the carpet of foreign aid, have now acquired proportions that even foreign assistance alone cannot manage. Pakistan needs serious structural reform if it wants to come out of the woods. But on top of the ever present problem of political will and vision to undertake rescuing reform, have come serious problems like ever rising terrorism, an abysmal law and order situation, growing civic unrest, which is manifesting itself in violence on the streets, separatism, sectarianism, and what have you. And if all this isn't enough, there are the other structural problems like a crippling energy crisis, debilitating governance crisis, and a developing crisis in the social sector. Worse, all these various crises are feeding on each other, making the problem even more difficult to manage, without ever increasing amount of foreign

Fig. 2: Role of Foreign Aid

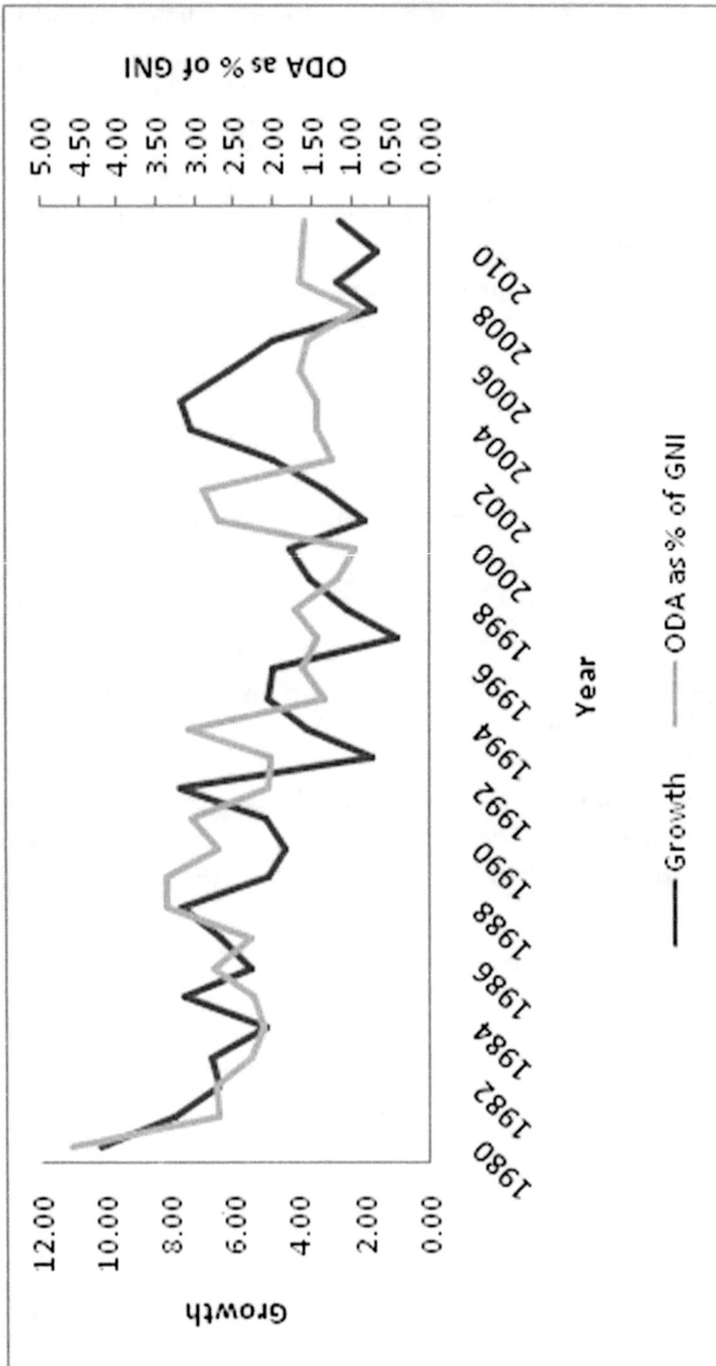

Source: World Development Indicators, World Bank.

assistance, investment and engagement (through concessional market access, among other things).

2. Current Economic Situation

The SBP annual report 2012-13 has warned that "Pakistan is approaching the situation of a debt trap where the government is meeting its debt servicing requirement by borrowing more."[5] The Central Bank's warning was perhaps directed at the finance minister, who has tried to justify the $6.7 billion Enhanced Financing Facility (EFF) from the IMF by maintaining that the new IMF package would not increase the public debt because the fresh loan was being taken to repay the loans taken by the previous government![6] This state of affairs should not come as any surprise in a country where the effectiveness of a finance minister is increasingly judged by his ability to contract loans from foreign lenders (bilateral and multilateral).

Undoubtedly, the Nawaz Sharif government inherited a virtually ravaged economy. The five years of the PPP-led coalition saw growth plummet, public debt double, investment (domestic and foreign) and savings collapse to historic lows, crippling energy shortages, and revenue generation reduced to unsustainable levels. But while the economic mismanagement of the PPP government was legendary, it too had inherited a very weak economy from the Gen. Musharraf-led PMLQ government in 2008. At that time, Ishaq Dar was the finance minister for a couple of weeks, within which time he 'talked down' the economy by exposing the data fudging by the ancien regime.[7] In the process, Dar shattered whatever little confidence remained in the economy, within and without Pakistan.

Dar's negative signalling was, however, not the only problem that the PPP government faced. The coalition it led prevented it from undertaking any major economic reform. For instance, it was forced by its coalition partners like MQM to back down on the issue of imposing the Reformed GST (RGST). The judiciary was forever breathing down its neck and interfering with policy decisions. The uncertain security and law and order situation – the Islamist insurgency in the North West, the Baloch insurgency in Balochistan, rampant lawlessness in the commercial capital Karachi, and the terrorist violence (targeted killings and bombings) in other parts of the country – was another major inhibiting factor. Although the

Americans came up with the $7.5 billion Kerry-Lugar-Berman aid package, much of this money did not come into the government coffers. Other traditional donors like Saudi Arabia had a cold relationship with the Asif Zardari regime and did not open the purse strings. Add to all this, the unsavoury reputation of corruption and crony capitalism, which severely undermined business confidence.

As a result, almost all the economic indicators moved south during the five years of the PPP government. The GDP growth remained extremely weak and averaged around 2.5 per cent. Fiscal deficits remained consistently high and except for one year, the deficit number was over six per cent and in the last two years, it was well above eight per cent. This is having an impact on inflation, which touched a high of around 21 per cent in 2008, but has since come down to around ten per cent in 2012. But food inflation remains high and was around 18 per cent in 2011. Anecdotal evidence suggests that inflation and economic distress levels remain fairly high and the government has juggled data by changing the base year and also the weightage given to some items to show a fall in inflation.[8] The tax-GDP ratio steadily fell and in the last two years, it has been around the 8.5 per cent mark. Public debt ballooned from around PKR 6.5 Trillion in 2008 to around PKR 16 Trillion. The bulk of this debt was domestic, which tripled from PKR 3.4 trillion to PKR 9.8 trillion. Worse, short term debt in total domestic debt has been rising at an alarming pace and constitutes around 55 per cent of the domestic debt.[9] External debt almost doubled from PKR three trillion to PKR 5.9 trillion. Not surprisingly, the public debt breached the legal limit of 60 per cent of GDP and in 2013, it was around 68 per cent of the GDP. The implication of this on the fiscal situation was quite severe. Total debt servicing was close to 60 per cent of tax, 52 per cent of revenue and 34 per cent of the total government expenditure. In 2012, almost the entire revenue of the government (99%) was eaten up by just three things: defence, interest payments and subsidies.

While Pakistan has always been a laggard in terms of generating savings (and this is one of the main reasons for its dependence on foreign aids, loans and capital), the national savings rate has fallen to around 13.5 per cent of the GDP in 2013. The investment rate in the economy was an abysmal 12.6 per cent in the last fiscal. Given that Pakistan has claimed a growth rate of around 3.6 per cent, this means that the Incremental Capital

Output Ratio (ICOR) is around 3.5, which is clearly unrealistic because such an ICOR signifies a very efficient use of capital resources. Given the state of the economy, development, technology and a host of other factors, not the least of which is the energy crisis, it clearly means that Pakistan has been window dressing its economic performance. In other words, the growth figures are, in all likelihood, fudged and artificially hiked to show a better performance than is actually the case. Quite aside the fact that if a growth of 3.5 per cent is being presented to portray a respectable growth, then the actual situation is even worse than what the fudged numbers show, dodgy data has for long been a huge problem in Pakistan.

The latest instance of this has been the claim of 5.1 per cent growth in the first quarter of 2013-14, which has been busted by some top economists, who point out that according to the Pakistan Bureau of Statistics (PBS), large scale manufacturing in the first half of the year grew by 6.8 per cent in which "production of diesel was up by 94 per cent, sugar production registered a growth of 78 per cent, deep freezers and air conditioners grew by 115 per cent and 116 percent, respectively…"[10] In an earlier article, the same writer disclosed that "such an impressive recovery in large-scale manufacturing is based on fictitious growth in the production of several components of this sector, for example, vegetable ghee registered a growth of 131 per cent, footwear (46.1 per cent), paints and varnishes (36.2 per cent), air-conditioners (106.7 per cent), electric bulbs (43.4 per cent), TV sets (86.4 per cent), diesel (132.7 per cent), billets (32.5 per cent) and so on."[11] Innovative accounting (hardly surprising given that the Finance Minister is an ace chartered accountant) has been used in the current year to show to the IMF that the government has got a handle over the deficit situation.[12]

In the external sector, except for the one bright spot of remittances that have steadily gone up from around $ 6.4 billion in 2007-08 to around $ 14 billion in 2012-13, Pakistan has had to contend with deficit in the current account, which has led to the PKR falling from around 60 to a dollar in 2008 to around 108 in November 2013 before recovering to around 98 today. For the last three to four years, exports have been stagnant at around $24 billion, while imports have risen to over $ 44 billion. Foreign Direct Investment (FDI) has fallen from a high of $ 5.5 billion in 2007 to just around $ 850 million in 2012. Portfolio investment has also fallen. A number of MNCs, including banks, airlines, and other companies have wound up operations in Pakistan and the government is having a tough time attracting new investors. The Chinese have been promising investments in a range of fields, but apart from a raft of MoU's that have been signed, there is very little investment that has flowed in. The pressure on Balance of Payments (BOP) has been exacerbated by the debt repayments that became due in 2012-13. Matters became worse when the SBP tried to artificially prop up the PKR by off-loading dollars in the market. As a result, the foreign exchange reserves fell to dangerously low levels of under $ 3 billion earlier this year. By the end of March, the foreign exchange reserves are expected to touch $ 10 billion, but this includes around $ 5 billion held by private banks as well as the $ 1.5 billion 'gift' given by the Saudis and the IMF loan. Even when the foreign exchange reserves were a healthy $ 18 billion in 2009-10, most of the reserve was borrowed money.

In the energy sector, the Nawaz Sharif government decided to bite the bullet and clear in a shot the 'circular debt' that had hobbled the sector. The nearly PKR 500 billion payment made a big hole in the government finances, but gave temporary relief from the average 14-18 hour power cuts. The government also revised tariffs and withdrew some subsidies. But within months, the circular debt has again raised its head and is currently around PKR 250 billion. The energy sector requires deep structural reform because the methods used by the Nawaz Sharif government to give relief had been done in the past by the PPP government as well only to be pulled back to square one. Indeed, it is not just the energy sector, but practically the entire economy that needs massive structural reform if Pakistan has to remain a viable state.

3. Structural Problems

The Pakistan economy suffers from the problem of living beyond its means or, to put it another way, consuming far more than it produces. This manifests itself in three deficits or gaps: a) saving-investment, b) revenue-expenditure and c) current account.

Much of the growth that the economy clocks is consumption driven as can be seen from Table 1. What is more, in the last decade, this consumption component of growth has been rising and is now reaching an unsustainable level if it is accompanied by a fall in the investment level in the economy.[13]

Table 1

Year	*Final consumption expenditure, etc. (% of GDP)*
2003	82.65
2004	82.39
2005	84.79
2006	88.08
2007	87.77
2008	91.62
2009	89.73
2010	90.03
2011	90.89
2012	93.01

Source: World Development Indicators and Economic Survey 2012-13, *Express Tribune.*

Fig. 3: Final Consumption Expenditure, etc. (% of GDP)

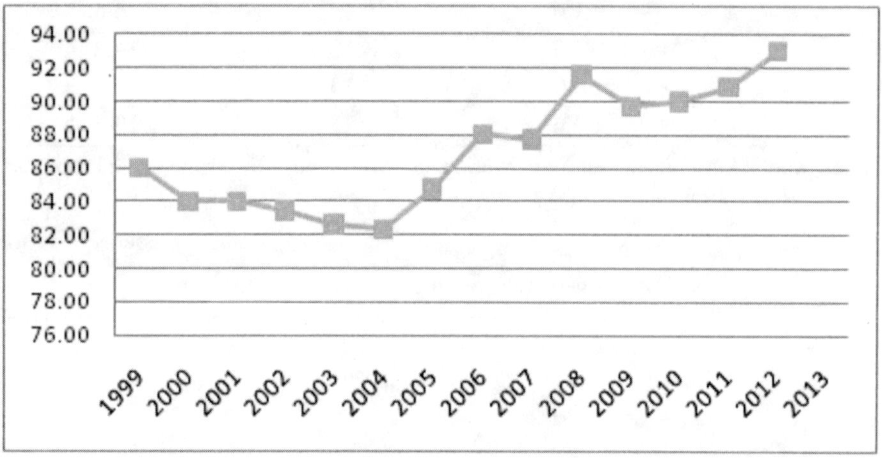

The consumption driven growth is being reflected in not just the falling level of investment and stagnant savings rate, but also the fact that growth appears to be either independent or only marginally affected by the rate of savings and investment in the economy (see Table 2 and Fig. 4).

Perhaps, the breakdown of the linkage between saving, investment and growth is reflected in the wildly fluctuating estimates of ICOR, which appears to be worked more as a residual rather than on the basis of how productively capital is used (Table 3).

Table 2

Year	*GDP growth (annual %)*	*Gross fixed capital formation (% of GDP)*	*National Savings (% of GDP)*
1999	3.7	13.9	11.7
2000	4.3	15.9	14.1
2001	2.0	15.7	16.5
2002	3.2	15.3	18.6
2003	4.8	15.1	20.8
2004	7.4	15.0	17.9
2005	7.7	17.5	17.5
2006	6.2	17.7	15.2
2007	4.8	17.2	14.0
2008	1.7	17.6	11.0
2009	2.8	15.9	12.0
2010	1.6	14.2	13.6
2011	2.8	12.5	14.2
2012	4.0	13.3	12.8
2013	3.6	12.6	13.5

Source: World Development Indicators, World Bank; SBP Annual Reports (various); Economic Survey (various).

Fig. 4: Growth, Saving and Investment

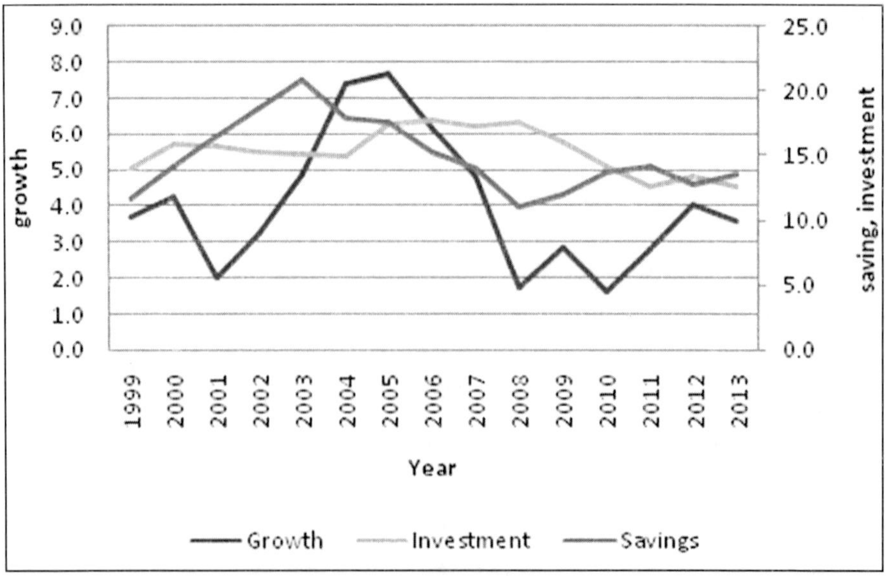

Table 3

Year	*ICOR*
2000-01	9.05
2001-02	5.59
2002-03	3.72
2003-04	2.1
2004-05	1.86
2005-06	3.15
2006-07	2.94
2007-08	5.38
2008-09	9.42
2009-10	4.88
2010-11	4.49
2011-12	3.24
Average	4.63

Source: State of the Economy Reports 2011 and 2013 of Institute of Public Policy, Beaconhouse National University, Lahore.

Fig. 5: ICOR

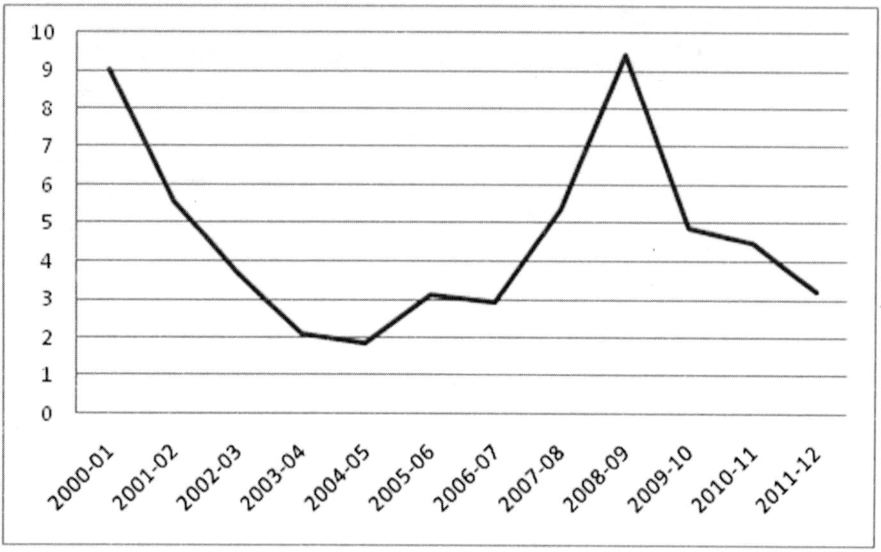

Over the years, the structure of the Pakistan economy has changed significantly in terms of the shares contributed by different sectors of the economy to the GDP. Until the 1960s, agriculture was the dominant sector contribution close to 50 per cent of the GDP. Services contributed around 38 per cent and industry came in third with around 15 per cent. In the next couple of decades, services became the largest contributor, industry has remained stagnant at around 22-23 per cent, around the same level as agriculture (Table 4.)

Table 4

	Agriculture, value added (% of GDP)	*Industry, value added (% of GDP)*	*Services, etc., value added (% of GDP)*
1960	46.2	15.6	38.2
1970	36.8	22.3	40.8
1980	29.5	24.9	45.6
1990	26	25.2	48.8
2000	25.9	23.3	50.7
2012	24.4	22	53.6

Source: World Development Indicators

The shifting contribution of the various sectors to GDP is nothing out of the ordinary. The problem, however, is that when it comes to contributing to the revenue of the state, the bulk of the burden falls on the industrial sector, which is practically reeling under this burden (Table 5).

Table 5: Sectoral Contribution to Tax (in %)

	2009-10		*2012-13*	
	Share in GDP	*Share in Tax*	*Share in GDP*	*Share in Tax*
Agriculture	22.0	1.0	21.4	2.5
Industry	25.0	63.0	20.9	60.8
Services	53.0	26.0	57.7	36.7

Source: "Taxing the Agriculture Income in Pakistan", PILDAT Briefing Paper, November 2011 and Economic Survey 2012-13.

The fact that neither agriculture nor the services sectors is contributing to the tax revenues in accordance with their contribution to the GDP, is one of the reasons for the constantly falling tax-GDP ratio, which has gone below nine per cent (Table 6). If the GDP growth was high, then even if the tax-GDP ratio was low, the government would have been able to garner resources to meet its ever increasing expenses and obligations. But the anaemic growth rate coupled with poor tax revenue has resulted in heavy reliance on deficit financing with fiscal deficits not only reaching unsustainable levels, but also contributing to inflationary pressure on the economy.

Table 6

Year	*GDP growth (annual %)*	*Fiscal deficit (% of GDP)*	*Tax revenue (% of GDP)*
1999	3.7	6.1	13.2
2000	4.3	5.4	10.1
2001	2.0	4.3	10.0
2002	3.2	5.5	10.3
2003	4.8	3.6	10.8
2004	7.4	2.3	10.3
2005	7.7	3.3	9.6
2006	6.2	4.0	8.7
2007	4.8	4.1	9.2
2008	1.7	7.3	9.5
2009	2.8	5.2	8.9
2010	1.6	6.2	10.0
2011	2.8	6.5	9.2
2012	4.0	8.2	9.7
2013	3.6	8.6	8.9

Source: World Development Indicators and Fiscal Policy Statement 2013-14 (Pg 5), Ministry of Finance, GOP, SBP Annual Report 2012-13.

Complicating the situation further and making it even more unsustainable is the fact that the entire revenue of the government is consumed by just three items: interest, defence expenditure and subsidies (Table 7).

Table 7

Year	*Expense (current LCU)*	*Revenue, excluding grants (current LCU)*	*Military expenditure (current LCU)*	*Interest payments (current LCU)*	*Subsidies and other transfers (current LCU)*	*Total of interest, military, subsidy*	*I+M+S as % of revenue*
1999	558.12	464.37	147.00	199.87	11.84	358.71	77.25
2000	657.60	531.30	154.00	236.59	21.19	411.78	77.50
2001	684.29	535.09	170.00	312.72	200.13	682.85	127.61
2002	753.62	619.07	188.00	318.75	238.57	745.32	120.39
2003	820.53	701.58	207.00	257.43	348.97	813.41	115.94

(Contd.)

Year	*Expense (current LCU)*	*Revenue, excluding grants (current LCU)*	*Military expenditure (current LCU)*	*Interest payments (current LCU)*	*Subsidies and other transfers (current LCU)*	*Total of interest, military, subsidy*	*I+M+S as % of revenue*
2004	814.19	760.98	232.00	317.72	207.32	757.04	99.48
2005	950.52	844.88	263.00	274.72	287.90	825.61	97.72
2006	1162.33	1021.41	287.00	361.61	325.28	973.89	95.35
2007	1415.58	1254.97	310.00	373.64	434.22	1117.86	89.07
2008	1908.67	1375.35	351.00	489.68	521.73	1362.41	99.06
2009	2137.42	1783.60	412.00	751.59	459.39	1622.99	90.99
2010	2601.78	2051.94	482.00	814.60	662.25	1958.85	95.46
2011	3219.22	2235.89	565.00	855.46	798.66	2219.13	99.25
2012	3768.56	2536.75	628.00	980.73	912.64	2521.37	99.39

Source: World Development Indicators, World Bank. All figures in PKR billions

From the above Table, it is clear that the government has to borrow money even to run own day to day affairs. Worse, the dependence on loans has led to rising public debt whose servicing requirements are pushing the country into a debt trap situation (Table 8a and 8b).

Table 8a

Year	*Total Public Debt*	*Domestic Debt*	*External Debt*	*Debt Servicing (Total)*	*Interest Paid*	*Principal repaid*
1999	3135.4	1375.9	1695.9	343.1	220.1	123.0
2000	3416.2	1559.9	1788.4	353.9	256.8	97.1
2001	4003.3	1708.5	2223.8	325.0	237.1	87.9
2002	3783.0	1717.9	2005.6	444.1	279.2	164.9
2003	3824.0	1853.7	1927.7	305.1	241.7	63.4
2004	3949.9	1979.5	1937.5	337.2	226.0	111.3
2005	4288.9	2149.9	2031.7	358.8	236.2	122.6
2006	4564.2	2321.7	2146.9	424.4	294.0	130.4
2007	5023.6	2597.0	2337.7	538.5	425.6	112.9
2008	6475.6	3412.0	3063.6	641.8	521.6	120.2
2009	8306.7	4151.0	4155.7	947.0	669.4	277.6
2010	9685.9	5027.6	4658.3	1044.9	668.6	376.3
2011	12131.0	6424.0	5707.0	1017.0	807.0	210.0
2012	14115.0	7919.0	6196.0	1266.0	972.0	294.0
2013	15758.0	9833.0	5925.0	1542.0	1053.0	489.0

Table 8b

Year	*Debt as % of GDP*	*Debt servicing as % of tax*	*Debt Servicing as % of revenue*	*Debt Servicing as % of Expenditure*
1999	106.7	87.8	73.2	53.0
2000	107.3	87.2	65.9	47.6
2001	115.3	68.9	57.0	49.5
2002	85.9	92.9	71.2	53.8
2003	79.3	55.1	42.5	33.8
2004	71.4	55.2	42.2	34.7
2005	64.3	56.7	39.9	28.0
2006	58.8	56.4	39.4	22.7
2007	56.7	60.5	32.8	21.4
2008	63.2	64.7	37.2	29.9
2009	65.2	68.4	46.6	38.6
2010	66.0	61.5	40.4	30.3
2011	66.3	49.5	45.1	25.8
2012	70.2	57.6	49.3	26.3
2013	68.7	59.7	51.7	34.4

Source: 1999-2001 from SBP Annual report 2000-01; 2002-04 from SBP Annual Report 2004-05 (explicit liabilities like $ bonds etc form the difference between total and sum of external and domestic debt); 2005-07 data from SBP Annual Report 2006-07 (total debt includes explicit liabilities, i.e., all foreign liabilities owned by the Government 2008-10 data from SBP Annual Report 2009-10 (Domestic debt includes PSE domestic debt); Debt service as % of revenue from Debt Policy Statement 2010-11; Debt service as % of tax and expenditure for 2008/09 from SBP Annual Report 2008-09 and for 2010 calculated from Fiscal Policy Statement 2012-13; 2011-13 data from SBP Annual Report 2012-13; Public debt includes PSE debt, privaye sector external and intercompany debt, but not domestic liabilities; 2011-13 all percentages calculated from data taken from debt and fiscal policy statements 2013-14 of Ministry of Finance; GDP calculated from SBP Annual Report 2012-13.

Economists often argue that it isn't so much the quantum or stock of debt as the ability to service it that is important. A look at the debt sustainability indicators suggests that more than the external debt, it is the internal debt, which is primarily responsible for strangulating the fiscal space available to the government. Considering that Internal Debt (and within this, short term debt) as a proportion of Total Debt has been outstripping external debt in recent years, this should come as no surprise (Table 9). The following two Tables (10a and 10b) deal with the domestic and external debt sustainability indicators.

Table 9: Domestic Debt (DD) as a % of Total Debt (TD)

Year	*DD/TD (%)*
2000	47
2001	44.3
2002	48.9
2003	51.2
2004	52.3
2005	52.7
2006	53.2
2007	54
2008	54.4
2009	50.7
2010	52.1
2011	56.2
2012	60.3
2013	66.2

Source: Debt Policy Statements, Economic Survey, SBP Annual Report, Statistical Supplement (all various years).

From the Table 10a below, it comes out clearly how the domestic interest payments are eating into the government finances. In 2012, it accounted for 66 per cent of the net revenue of the federal government (i.e. after the provinces share was taken out from total revenue, which included both tax and non-tax revenues). There was marginal improvement in the last fiscal, but domestic interest payments were still accounting for over 60 per cent of the net revenue. Interestingly, the ratio of domestic interest payments to total tax revenue (before sharing it with provinces) has been steadily rising in the last few years. This shows the growing importance of non-tax revenues because of the inability of the government to raise tax revenues.

The issue of the state's failure to collect taxes, reflected in the tax-GDP ratio is one that is becoming a sort of a test case to judge the sincerity of successive governments in putting the economic house in order. But there are a number of issues involved. The first is, of course, a debate on whether the tax-GDP ratio is falling not so much because of the government's inability to collect taxes or because of widespread evasion, but because of the GDP being artificially hiked up. If indeed this is the case, then it would follow that the tax-GDP ratio is much higher and might well have been at a level where revenue can be increased only at the margins. This is so because even now, the tax structure is seriously distorted and regressive (this issue is dealt with later in the paper).

Table 10a

Year	*Total Tax*	*Net Revenue*	*Domestic Interest (DI)*	*DI/Net Revenue*	*DI/Tax*
2000	386	387.7	218.7	56.4	56.7
2001	422.8	371.9	195.4	52.5	46.2
2002	459.1	447.6	212.5	47.5	46.3
2003	525.7	508.8	189	37.1	36.0
2004	580.1	549.6	182	33.1	31.4
2005	626.3	630	181.9	28.9	29.0
2006	715.7	721.3	237.1	32.9	33.1
2007	839.6	823.1	358.6	43.6	42.7
2008	1005.6	941.7	473	50.2	47.0
2009	1252	1111	597	53.7	47.7
2010	1483	1396.7	630	45.1	42.5
2011	1679.4	1238.2	715	57.7	42.6
2012	1945.7	1334.3	881	66.0	45.3
2013	2048.6	1560.4	963	61.7	47.0

Source: DI from SBP Annual Report 2003-04, chap 6; Tax and net revenue from SBP Statistical Annexure, chap 4, table 4.1; SBP Statistical Annexure 2000-01; SBP Annual Report 2007-08, chap 4; SBP Annual Report 2011-12, 2012-13

Insofar as the debt sustainability indicators for external debt are concerned, although there is no standard benchmark or yardstick to measure safe threshold limits of external debt, the Pakistan authorities are of the view that External Debt and Liabilities (EDL) to Foreign Exchange Earnings (FEE) ratio of <2 and a below 20 per cent ratio of External Debt and Liabilities Servicing (EDLS) to FEE are safe.

From Table 10b some clear trends are available. The first is that steep fall in EDL/GDP ratio from a high of 52 in 2001 (on the eve of 9/11) to a much more manageable 25 per cent in 2013. This was one of the windfalls of the 9/11 attacks in the USA. Before the 9/11 attacks, the EDL was over 17 times the FER. This was after the nuclear tests of 1998 when US sanctions kicked in. Pakistan had at that time approached the IMF, successfully leveraging its 'too dangerous to fail' strategy to get a bail out. The IMF package helped to bring the EDL/FER ratio to 11 times. But the real change came after 9/11 when a massive aid package of over $ 13 billion was put in place by the West to recruit an ever willing Pakistan as a partner in the War on Terror (Table 11).

Table 10b

Year	*EDL/GDP (%)*	*EDL/FER (%)*	*EDL/FEE (%)*	*EDLS/FEE (%)*	*EDLS/XE*
2000	51.7	1750.3	297.2	11.9	31.6
2001	52.1	1146.7	259.5	13.7	32.7
2002	50.9	571	236.8	7.8	36.7
2003	43.1	329.6	181.2	6.5	22.8
2004	36.7	286.4	164.7	13.5	32.5
2005	32.6	283.8	134.3	5.4	14.9
2006	28.9	286.8	120.6	13.2	13.3
2007	28.1	266.3	124.2	12.6	11.4
2008	27.6	406.3	125.9	11.8	15.6
2009	31.7	425.7	148.9	17.9	24.8
2010	34.7	370	160	19.3	21
2011	31.1	360	140	11.4	13.9
2012	29.1	430	120	12.5	23.5
2013	25.3	540	120	14.3	24

Source: Debt Policy Statements, Economic Survey, SBP Annual Report, Statistical Supplement (all various years); FER is Foreign Exchange Reserves; XE is Export Earnings

Table 11

Year	*Debt forgiveness or reduction*	*Debt stock reduction*	*Debt stock rescheduled*	*Interest rescheduled (capitalised)*	*Principal rescheduled*	*Total amount of debt rescheduled*
1998	0.00	0.00	0.00	0.00	0.00	0.00
1999	0.00	0.00	614.80	625.30	2157.98	3420.73
2000	0.00	0.00	29.30	236.34	652.64	917.76
2001	0.00	0.00	11334.34	128.95	1324.76	13302.47
2002	-300.00	300.00	0.00	145.67	0.00	157.21
2003	-708.38	701.71	0.00	6.87	0.50	26.12
2004	-481.66	481.66	0.00	0.17	0.00	0.04

Source: World Development Indicators; All figures in millions of US$.

The debt relief package coupled with the opening of floodgates of aid and inflow of foreign investment in the mid 2000s led to the EDL/FER ratio falling to under three by 2007. But since then, this ratio has been rising and is once again acquiring ominous proportions. In terms of flows, however, the ratios of EDLS to FEE and XE are still within tolerable limits. But since the mid 2000s, these ratios have deteriorated and have started putting pressure on the availability of foreign exchange. By 2017, when repayments of a lot of the debt that was rescheduled in 2001 will start, the pressure on the external balances will increase, unless of course Pakistan is able to raise its foreign exchange earnings and reduce the outflow to a level that it can meet these obligations.

To return to the issue of tax revenues falling to dangerously low levels when measured against the GDP, there have been, for some time now, the usual noises demanding taxes on agricultural incomes. Aside of the political difficulties in taxing agricultural incomes, the math of such taxes doesn't really enthuse. In fact, many of those raising this demand admit that taxing agriculture has more symbolic value rather than any major revenue impact. Estimates of the revenue that can be generated by taxing agricultural incomes range from a conservative estimate of around PKR 80 billion to an optimistic estimate of PKR 160 billion.[14] This amount is clearly not going to serve as a panacea for the tax problems of Pakistan. According to former SBP Governor Ishrat Husain, only about three per cent of farm families have holdings that will cross the threshold of taxable income and, therefore, it is unrealistic to expect more than one to two per cent increase in total tax revenue from agricultural incomes.[15] Husain argues that without a structural transformation of the economy in which the formal sector expands significantly, the burden of taxation will continue to fall on the poor and the salaried middle-class. In fact, the way the taxation system is currently structured, there is an incentive to evade and avoid tax. Not surprisingly, the Federal Bureau of Revenue had estimated a tax gap (the difference between potential and actual tax collection) to be around 79 per cent in 2011-12. Another study in 2008 had estimated the gap in direct taxes to be around 143 per cent and indirect taxes 36 per cent.[16] An FBR study has estimated that that from around the mid-1990s onwards, the tax gap has been between 80-90 per cent.[17]

Efforts by the government to broaden the tax base and crack down on evasion have so far come a cropper. In 2011, with much fanfare, the tax authorities issued around 450,000 notices as part of a plan to bring some 700,000 people into the tax net and raise PKR 70-80 billion in revenue. But all that they had to show for their labour a year later was a measly PKR 700 million. Worse, the number of people, who filed their tax returns, fell from about two million to 1.2 million, i.e. by 40 per cent.[18] Since then, the situation has only worsened and in 2012-13, only 25 per cent of the people with National Tax Numbers (890,000) filed their income tax returns.[19] Clearly, these numbers indicate one of two things: either the deteriorating economic condition is causing immiserisation to a level that people are falling off the tax grid; or else, the state's writ and ability to collect taxes is deteriorating precipitously and an informal or parallel or black economy is growing to a level that the formal economy is becoming less and less important. Studies, using a variety of techniques and methods, have estimated that the size of the informal/parallel economy is anything from a moderate and manageable 30 per cent to an astounding 90 per cent of the formal economy.[20]

The inability of the government to raise the tax-GDP ratio has worsened the fiscal imbalance of the federal government even more because of the 7th National Finance Commission (NFC) award in 2009. While this award was widely welcomed by the political class because it transferred more funds to the provinces and went a long way in addressing the grievances of the smaller provinces, it has proved to be quite disastrous for the federal government. At least in terms of distribution of resources or the share of the national cake, the 7th NFC shifted the balance of power in favour of the provinces and against the centre. Out of the total divisible pool, the provinces got 57.5 per cent leaving the centre with just 42.5 per cent as opposed to the previous award in 2006, which gave 45 per cent to provinces and 55 per cent to the centre. What is more, the 7th NFC included many taxes, which were absent from the divisible pool in previous NFC awards (see Table 12).

As a result of the 7th NFC, the provincial finances got a massive boost (Table 13). According to one calculation, in 2010-11, the federal government would get around PKR 235 billion less under the 7th NFC than what it would have received under the 2006 interim award.[21]

Table 12: Evolution of Divisible Pool in Various Awards

	Divisible Pool	*Shared Revenue Sources*[a]			
		NFC 1991	*NFC 1996*	*Presidential Order 2006*[c]	*NFC 2009*
A.	Income Tax[b]				
	Personal	80%	37.50%	45%-50%	56%-57.5%
	Corporate	80%	37.50%	45%-50%	56%-57.5%
	Wealth Tax		87.50%	45%-50%	56%-57.5%
B.	Sales Tax	80%	37.50%	45%-50%[d]	56%-57½%[e]
C.	Excise Duties				
	Tea	-	37.5	45%-50%	56%-57.5%
	Tobacco	80%	37.50%	45%-50%	56%-57.5%
	Sugar	80%	37.50%	45%-50%	56%-57.5%
	Betel nut	-	37.50%	45%-50%	56%-57.5%
	All excise duties (excluding GST)	-	37.50%	45%-50%	56%-57.5%
D.	Export Duties				
	Cotton	80%	37.50%	45%-50%	-
	Jute	-	-	45%-50%	-
E.	Estate & Succession Duties	-	-	-	-
F.	Capital Value Tax on Immovable Properties	-	37.50%	45%-50%	devolved to provinces

Notes:
a Share of the provinces combined.
b Excluding taxes on income consisting of remuneration paid out of federal consolidated fund.
c Provincial share was decided to be 45% for 1st Financial year and would reach 50% with subsequent increase of 1% per annum.
d Other than 1/5th of sales tax collected in lieu of zila/octroi transfer to be transfered to the province of origin.
e Sales Tax on services devolved to provinces.

Source: State of the Economy: Devolution in Pakistan, Fourth Annual Report 2011, Institute of Public Policy, BNU, Lahore.

Although the provinces got extra money, it didn't necessarily strengthen the provinces, which were neither able to utilise the extra money productively nor were able to discharge the extra responsibilities devolved to them under the 18th Constitutional Amendment, which abolished the concurrent list. The federal government continues to remain saddled with much of the staff and many of the responsibilities that the provinces should

Table 13: Composition of Transfers from Federal to Provincial Governments (PKR Billion)

	Divisible Pool Transfers	*Straight Transfers*	*Special Grants*	*Total Transfers*
1990-91	32.1	1.7	0	33.8
% of Total Transfers	95	5	0	
1991-92	47.5	16.3	2	65.8
% of Total Transfers	72.2	24.8	3	
1996-97	119.2	18.2	2	139.4
% of Total Transfers	85.5	13.1	3	
1997-98	104	20.3	7.4	131.7
% of Total Transfers	79	15.4	5.6	
2005-06	244.6	62.8	8.7	316
% of Total Transfers	77.4	19.9	2.7	
2007-08	403.1	70.6	33	506.7
% of Total Transfers	79.6	13.9	6.5	
2009-10	574.1	87.2	57.8	689
% of Total Transfers	80	12.1	7.9	
2010-11	865.8	197	6	1068.7
% of Total Transfers	81	18.4	0.6	

Source: State of the Economy: Devolution in Pakistan, Fourth Annual Report 2011, Institute of Public Policy, BNU, Lahore.

have taken over, but no longer has the funds that it earlier had.[22] The rather generous resource sharing formula agreed in the 7th NFC was predicated on the tax-GDP rising by about one per cent point every year to reach 15 per cent by 2014-15, the terminal year of the NFC award.[23] But this basic assumption has collapsed because the tax-GDP ratio, instead of rising, has actually fallen.

By 2012, the PPP-led government, which had been patting itself for empowering the provinces financially through the NFC award, started to appreciate the financial mess that this had created for the federal government. Presenting the Economic Survey for 2011-12, the then finance minister Abdul Hafeez Shaikh admitted that the NFC award had financial constraints for the federal government. According to Shaikh, apart from the 57.5 per cent of the divisible pool, the provinces were also given their share in the Gas Development Surcharge and Net Hydel profit. In addition, resources were transferred by the federal government to FATA and Pakistan occupied Kashmir (both 'Azad' Jammu and Kashmir and Gilgit-Baltistan). The federal government was, therefore, left with only 30 per cent of the resources, which were consumed by debt servicing, defence and running of the civilian administration.[24] Later that year, the government pleaded helplessness in meeting the ever increasing electricity subsidy Bill because with 70 per cent of resources being transferred to the provinces and other territories, it was in no position to address the crippling energy crisis by throwing more money in the bottomless pit of energy subsidies.[25]

Clearly, this is not a sustainable state of affairs, even less so given the inability of the federal government to either raise revenue or cut costs. In order to meet its expenses, the federal government is ever more dependent on deficit financing, which is not just raising the national debt, but is also inflationary. There has been talk of resolving the imbalance created by the 7th NFC in the next award, something that the IMF has also recommended. The problem, however, is that after the 18th Amendment, making any change in the revenue sharing formula between the federation and the provinces will require another constitutional amendment.[26] Given the split mandate thrown up by the 2013 general elections – two provinces run by opposition parties and the PMLN government in Islamabad in no position to muster a 2/3rd majority required for a constitutional amendment – this will not be easy, especially because no province would like any change, which leads to less money in its coffers. From a time when the federal government had fixed a system which made provinces totally dependent on federal transfers[27] to now when the federal government desperately pleads with the provinces to ensure surplus budgets in order to rein in the fiscal deficit so that the government can meet its obligations to multilateral institutions and also is trying to convince the provinces to share in the federal government's expenditures on defence and law and order, the fiscal federalism structure in Pakistan has undergone a huge transformation.[28]

The problem of low revenues, made worse by the resource distribution formula of the 7th NFC, has left the federal government with no fiscal space to address the crippling energy shortages that the country has been facing for close to a decade now (Table 14). Power outages and load-shedding in large parts of the country average 6-8 hours and, at times, even 20-22 hours in rural areas. According to some estimates, Pakistan is losing anything between 2-4 per cent of GDP because of the electricity and gas crisis.[29]

Table 14: Generation Capacity, Demand and Shortfall

Year	*Installed Capacity (MW)*	*Generation Capability (MW)*	*Peak Demand*
2008	20,232	14,707	19,281
2009	20,556	16,040	20,314
2010	21,614	15,144	21,029
2011	23,327	15,430	21,086
2012	23,538	16,104	22,622

Source: State of Industry Report 2012, NEPRA (Table 27 & 28)

The energy crisis is really the result of wrong policy choices (in terms of energy mix), ineffective governance (in terms of collecting bills, managing subsidy and the inevitable corruption in running of the power sector), poor management (in terms of maintenance and upgradation of infrastructure to reduce transmission and distribution losses and proper pricing of electricity). The problem can really be traced back to the 1990s when Pakistan went in for thermal (gas and oil) based power projects. Pakistan was at that time well-endowed with natural gas, which was priced much below the international price. Alternate energy like wind and solar was still not a very viable technology. Hydropower was an option, but partly because of long gestation, partly because of the initial costs involved and partly because of domestic political disputes, it was neglected in favour of oil based power plants (Table 15).

Table 15: Pakistan Energy Mix

Year	*Electricity production from oil, gas and coal sources (% of total)*	*Electricity production from hydroelectric sources (% of total)*	*Electricity production from nuclear sources (% of total)*
1985	45.3	53.2	1.5
1990	54.3	44.9	0.8
1995	58.4	40.7	0.8
2000	71.8	25.2	2.9
2005	64.5	32.9	2.6
2010	62.7	33.7	3.6
2011	64.5	29.9	5.5

Source: World Development Indicators, World Bank.

In the mid 1990's, with oil prices reaching around $10 per barrel, it made a lot of sense to go in for thermal power projects, and a spate of Independent Power Projects were set up. The installed capacity at that time was much more than what Pakistan required and there was even talk of exporting electricity to India. But by the mid 2000s, things started going wrong. Domestic gas production started falling even as demand was growing because of, inter alia, massive expansion in the domestic consumer section and allocation to the transport sector (CNG stations).

The real trouble started in 2006-07 when international oil prices went through the ceiling, at one point touching almost $150 per barrel. Suddenly, the electricity economics in Pakistan went haywire because the price at which electricity was being sold was lower than the price at which it was being generated and distributed – for instance, in June 2013, the average price of generation was PKR 14.5, while the average price the consumer was paying was PKR 8.87 leading to a gap of PKR 5.63 out of which the government was paying PKR 3.02 as subsidy.[30] The uncovered gap of PKR 2.61 did not take into account some of the losses in terms of transmission and distribution and arrears by both public and private sector consumers.

Table 16: Average Cost of Energy Units (PKR/KwH)

	2010-11	*2011-12*
Hydro	0.27	0.16
Coal	2.95	3.12
HSD	14.79	18.89
RFO	12.01	15.94
Gas	3.42	4.24
Nuclear	0.98	1.13
Import	4.62	8.99
Mixed	11.21	12.78
Wind	9.5	9.12

Source: State of Industry Report 2011-12, NEPRA.

This basic mismatch gave rise to the phenomenon of 'circular debt', which has been defined as "the amount of cash shortfall within the Central Power Purchasing Agency (CPPA), which it cannot pay to power supply companies. The overdue amount is a result of: (a) the difference between the actual cost and the tariff determined by National Electric Power Regulatory Authority (NEPRA), which is the Distribution Company's loss over and collections under that allowed by NEPRA, (b) the delayed or non-payment of subsidies by the government, and (c) delayed determination and notification of tariffs."[31] The political compulsions of the quasi-military regime in 2007 (an election year) prevented it from biting the bullet of rising energy costs and passing these on to the consumers. This started the spiral of circular debt, which has continued to this day.

The Nawaz Sharif government tried to take the bull by the horn and in one fell swoop cleared around $ 5 billion (PKR 480 billion) of accumulated circular debt. In addition, it raised tariffs by 40-172 per cent for different consumers.[32] This did provide relief, albeit temporarily. A few months down the line, the monster of 'circular debt' once again started haunting the government with the consequent power outages. In a sense, Nawaz Sharif did what his much maligned predecessor regime had done – try to buy yourself out of trouble by throwing money at the problem by clearing the 'circular debt', raising tariffs and announcing new projects aimed at changing the energy mix from expensive oil and gas to cheaper coal and competitively priced solar, wind and other alternate energy sources. But like his predecessors, he too remained either unwilling or unable to undertake the necessary reform in infrastructure and management of the power sector. Although during the election campaign in 2013, Nawaz Sharif made tall promises about solving the energy crisis within months if not weeks. As soon as he assumed power, he changed track and admitted that it will take at least five years before power outages can be reduced significantly. Until then, Pakistan will have to bear 6-10 hours of load-shedding. Some energy sector professionals, including from the national regulator NEPRA, have admitted that the earliest that Pakistan will become outage-free will be in the next decade.

The energy crisis is only partly an outcome of supply constraints. The demand side of the problem and even more important the management side of the problem has just not received the same amount of attention as the supply side or power generation. This is partly because setting up new power projects is easier than reforming the system. Also, it is politically more profitable to set up new plants than administer the pain of reform to the consumers. But with no fiscal space available with the government to set up new plants, it is dependent on private sector and foreign investment. Both come with their own problems, but the Nawaz Sharif government has put that all aside and has put in place plans to double the electricity generation in the next five years.

This rather ambitious plan is very heavily dependent on foreign investment, most of it coming from China, partly under the $40 billion Economic Corridor project. But a lot will depend on the law and order situation in Pakistan. The wave of terrorism and extremism that is sweeping through the country has spooked both domestic and foreign investors. The disturbed conditions in the country's commercial and financial capital, Karachi, where in 2013 around 2700 people were killed, most of them in political, ethnic, sectarian and terrorist violence, doesn't invoke much confidence in either the domestic or foreign investor.[33] Incidents of kidnapping and extortion are also on the rise and have become another factor to dissuade investors. In fact, there are reports that despite their 'higher than mountains and deeper than oceans' friendship with Pakistan, the Chinese have made it clear that their investment plans will depend on the security situation in Pakistan. Upcountry, in Punjab, the law and order situation is also nothing to write home about, even though incidents of terrorism in the province were a fraction of what occurred in the other three provinces.

While law and order and economy have a direct correlation, in 2011, the Pakistan government, for the first time, attempted to put a number to the impact that terrorism has had on the Pakistan economy. A special Chapter was included in the Economic Survey 2010-11 quantifying the cost (direct and indirect) incurred by Pakistan in the years since it joined the War on Terror (Table 17).

Table 17: Cost of War 2001-2011

Year	*$ billion*	*PKR billion*	*% Change*
2001-02	2.669	163.9	-
2002-03	2.749	160.8	3
2003-04	2.932	168.8	6.7
2004-05	3.41	202.4	16.3
2005-06	3.986	238.6	16.9
2006-07	4.67	283.2	17.2
2007-08	6.94	434.1	48.6
2008-09	9.18	720.6	32.3
2009-10	13.56	1136.4	47.7
2010-11*	17.83	1528	31.5
Total	67.926	5036.8	

Source: Economic Survey 2010-11, p. 220.

Given the proclivity of Pakistani authorities to fudge figures to serve their purpose, the estimates worked out above are very debatable because they have been jacked up in order to extract more aid and assistance from the rest of the world. By the time of the Economic Survey 2011-12, the Pakistan government stopped giving out estimates of costs of terrorism in official publications because, according to one report, the Finance Ministry officials admitted that the $ 68 billion figure was wrong and revising the figure downward would "raise the issue of credibility of the country's statistics."[34] By the time the Nawaz Sharif government came into office just two years later, the Pakistani officials had given wings to their flights of fancy and using some undisclosed, but very imaginative arithmetic, came up with a figure of $ 125 billion as the cumulative cost of War on Terror. However, even the Finance Minister Ishaq Dar found this figure so bizarre – his own estimate was around $ 80-85 billion – that he decided to exclude it from the Economic Survey 2012-13.[35]

Be that as it may, the Economic Survey 2010-11 did try to justify its estimate by pointing out how the War on Terror impacted Pakistan. According to the Survey, "The events that transpired after 9/11 in Afghanistan worsened the security environment in the country. As a result, the western countries including the United States continued to impose travel ban for their citizen *(investor, importers, etc.)* to visit Pakistan. This has affected Pakistan's exports, prevented the inflows of foreign investment, affected the pace of privatisation programme, slowed the overall economic activity, reduced import demand, reduced tax collection, expenditure over-run on additional security spending, domestic tourism industry suffered badly; hundreds and thousands of jobs could have been created had the economic activity not slowed as well as thousands of jobs were lost because of the destruction of domestic/foreign tourism industry; destruction of physical infrastructure (military and civil); massive surge in security related spending; migration of thousands of people from war affected areas and the associated rise in expenditure to support internally displaced persons."[36] The Survey even puts numbers of each of these things (Table 18).

Imaginative number crunching has not been restricted to just the cost of war on terror estimates, but even more on poverty data. From around the 1990s, when the Pakistan economy started on its secular downslide, poverty levels started to rise. By 2002, official estimates put the poverty

Table 18: Cost of War Estimate ($ billion)

	2001-02	*2010-11*
Exports	1.4	2.9
Compensation to affectees	0	0.8
Physical Infrastructure	0	1.72
Foreign Investment	0.15	2.1
Privatisation	0.5	1.1
Industrial output	0.11	1.7
Tax collection	0.25	2.1
Cost of uncertainty	0.1	2.9
Expenditure over-run	0.11	1.6
Others	0.1	0.9
Total	2.72	17.82

Source: Economic Survey 2010-11, p. 220.

headcount ratio at around 35 per cent. But then something dramatic happened, not so much in the real economy, but more in the statistics division of the Government of Pakistan, which magically led to an astounding 11 per cent drop in the poverty headcount ratio in just under three years. Subsequently, the enthusiasm of the number crunchers to reduce the poverty ratio went in an overdrive and by 2008, this number had been brought down to 17 per cent and by 2011 to just over 12 per cent (Table 19).

From tables 19 and 20, it is clear that with growth rates falling, inequality remaining high, inflation in double digits, and population growth much higher than what official statistics claim – according to the 1998 Census, the annual population growth rate was 2.69 per cent and with no major change in either the economic structure or the social structure (which has only regressed) in the ten years since 1998, it boggles the mind as to how there has been a close to one per cent drop in population growth rate by 2008 – to expect poverty rates to fall requires both a leap of blind faith and a touch of voodoo economics.[38] Punching a hole in the claims on poverty rates of the Pakistan government are the estimates of the remarkable welfare programme called Benazir Income Support Programme (BISP), which was started by the PPP-led government. The BISP estimated that 45.7 per cent of the people were living below the poverty line and 36.5 per cent were living in chronic poverty.[39] Another estimate by the distinguished

Table 19

Year	*GINI index*	*Poverty headcount ratio at national poverty line (% of population)*	*Population growth (annual %)*	*Income share held by fourth 20%*	*Income share held by lowest 20%*	*GDP growth (annual %)*	*Inflation, consumer prices (annual %)*	*Food Inflation (annual %)*
1991	33.23		2.79	21.68	8.08	5.06		
1997	28.65		2.67	21.09	9.97	1.01		
1999	33.02	30.6	2.48	20.84	8.73	3.66	4.14	
2002	30.39	34.5	1.91	21.17	9.39	3.22	3.29	2.50
2003						4.85	2.91	2.83
2004						7.37	7.44	6.01
2005	31.18	23.9	1.80	21.13	9.16	7.67	9.06	12.49
2006	32.74	22.3	1.84	20.69	9.01	6.18	7.92	6.92
2008	30.02	17.2*	1.86	21.12	9.6	1.70	20.29	17.64
2009							13.65	23.70
2010							13.88	12.47
2011		12.4*					11.92	17.95

Source: World Development Indicators, Statistical Supplement 2011-12 Ministry of Finance, (*figures worked out by official agencies but not released officially)[37]

economist, Dr Akmal Hussain, puts poverty at around 43 per cent in 2011-12 because of the high food inflation.[40]

Table 20: Poverty Line (in PKR Per Adult equivalent Per Month)

Year	*Poverty Line*
2001-02	723.4
2004-05	878.64
2005-06	944.47

Source: PRSP-II accessed at http://www.imf.org/external/pubs/ft/scr/2010/cr10183.pdf

Another chronic structural problem that the Pakistan economy faces is on the external payments front. For the last four years, exports have been stuck at around the $ 24 billion mark, while imports have been steady at over $ 40 billion. Even more worrisome is the fact that the composition of the export basket has remained more or less static and bulk of the exports are accounted for by three commodity groups viz. textiles (cotton and cotton manufactures), leather and leather products and rice (table 21).

Table 21: Exports (%)

Commodity	*1999-2000*	*2005-06*	*2010-11*	*2012-13*[a]
Cotton	61	59.4	52.9	51.4
Leather	6.3	6.9	4.4	4.5
Rice	6.3	7	8.7	7.8
Sports	3.3	2.1		
Synthetic Textiles	5.3	1.2		

(a) nine month from Jul-Mar.
Source: Economic Survey (various).

While the export basket hasn't changed much – the direction of exports has, not so much in terms of region as in terms of individual countries. Over the last five years, while the US remains the largest export destination for Pakistan, China and Afghanistan have gained in importance. In 2008-09, the US accounted for 18.9 per cent of Pakistani exports, followed by the UAE with 8.2 per cent.[41] By 2012-13, the US share had fallen to 13.3 per cent and China with 10.9 per cent, UAE with 8.6 per cent and Afghanistan with 8.5 per cent were the other major export destinations.[42] As far as imports are concerned, the biggest share (over 20%) is accounted for by petroleum and petroleum products. Other major imports are edible oils, machinery, chemical products, metals and transport equipment. In the five years between 2006 and 2011, China's share in Pakistan's imports has gone up from 10.3 per cent to 15.2 per cent. The UAE has also increased its share from 10.2 per cent to 14.3 per cent, while Saudi Arabia's share has remained almost static at around 9.8 per cent. The US share fell from over six per cent to just over three per cent of Pakistan's imports. Kuwait has, however, increased its share from around 5.6 per cent to 8.2 per cent.[43]

The imbalance on the trade front has been met to a great extent by the appreciable rise in remittances, which have grown by almost 60 per cent in the five years since 2009-10. But the current account deficit remains a problem, especially because of a drop in both foreign aid and investment. And with repayments of previous loans having to be made, the pressure on the balance of payments forced the government to once again approach the IMF in 2013 with liquid reserves with the SBP being reduced to under $ 3 billion, enough to cover just over three weeks of imports (Table 21). Even during the PPP-led government, the foreign reserves position wasn't very healthy. The then government was never tired of crowing about the 'record' reserves, which at one point crossed $ 18 billion. But most of this was made up by loans (including from the IMF) and nearly $ 4-5 billion was accounted for by foreign exchange held by private banks, which technically the government could not count upon. Although in recent weeks the reserves position has improved because of the $ 6.7 billion EFF arrangement with the IMF, which in turn has opened the tap of funds from other multilateral institutions, like the World Bank and ADB, the balance of payments crisis has just been pushed forward and not solved.

The persistent foreign exchange crisis, low level of domestic savings, foreign direct investment and portfolio investment not really coming in a significant way, and high fiscal deficits have made Pakistan critically dependent on foreign assistance and hand-outs. The initial spike in growth was largely on the back of foreign aid with Overseas Development Assistance (ODA) constituting almost 60 per cent of gross capital formation in 1960-61. Since then, the ODA as a percentage of gross capital formation has steadily come down, but so has growth shown a downward trend.

Table 22: Foreign Trade and Current Account

Year	*Exports*	*Imports*	*Remittances*	*Trade Balance*	*Current Account Balance*	*Foreign Reserves in weeks Import Cover*
1998-1999	7,779	9,432	1,060.19	-1,653	-2,429	8
1999-2000	8,569	10,309	983.73	-1,740	-1,143	7
2000-2001	9,202	10,729	1,086.57	-1,527	-513	16
2001-2002	9,135	10,340	2,389.05	-1,205	1,338	34
2002-2003	11,160	12,220	4,236.85	-1,060	3,165	37
2003-2004	12,313	15,592	3,871.58	-3,279	1,314	-
2004-2005	14,391	20,598	4,168.79	-6,207	-1,753	16
2005-2006	16,451	28,581	4,600.12	-12,130	-5,624	16
2006-2007	16,976	30,540	5,493.65	-13,564	-7,361	16
2007-2008	19,052	39,966	6,451.24	-20,914	-13,874	8
2008-2009	17,688	34,822	7,811.43	-17,134	-9,260	16
2009-2010	19,290	34,710	8,905.90	-15,420	-3,946	20
2010-2011	24,810	40,414	11,200.97	-15,604	214	16
2011-2012	23,624	44,912	13,186.58	-21,288	-4,658	12
2012-2013	24,460	44,950	13,920.16	-20,490	-2,466	3[a]

Source: Pakistan Bureau of Statistics; Statistical bulletin 2011-12 (Ministry of Finance), SBP Annual Report 2012-13.

Note: (*) World Development Indicators and "Foreign Currency Deposits and International Liquidity Shortages in Pakistan by Abbas Mirakhor and Iqbal Zaidi IMF Working Paper, http://www.imf.org/external/pubs/ft/wp/2004/wp04167.pdf

(a) http://www.thenews.com.pk/Todays-News-9-217812-Declining-forex-reserves

Except for a brief spike in foreign investment in 2006-07 when telecom companies made big investments, the general trend has been that of falling FDI and portfolio investments. This has meant that Pakistan continues to remain dependent on official assistance and concessional aid from donor countries.

Table 22 gives a good idea of the role that foreign aid plays in keeping the Pakistan economy afloat.

Fig. 6: Role of ODA in Capital Formation and Economic Growth

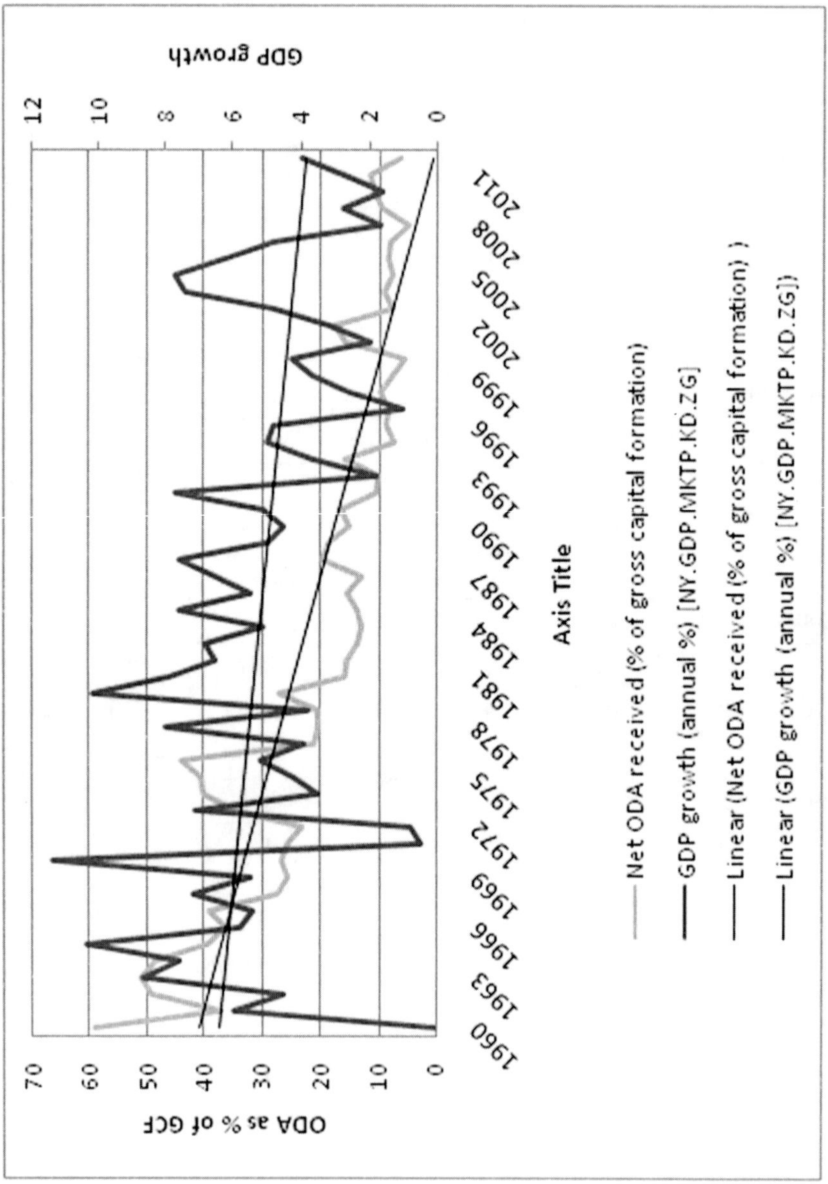

Fig. 7

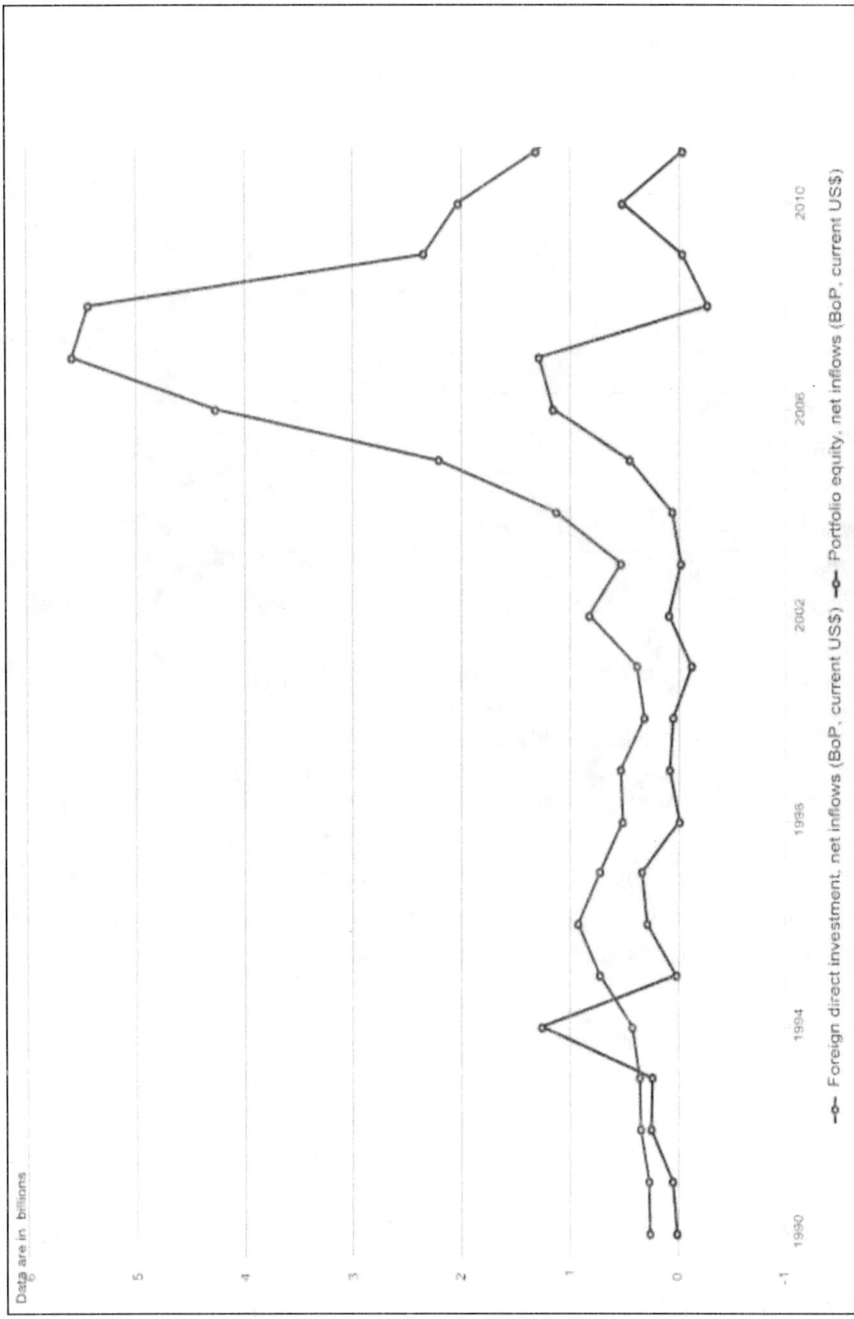
Data are in billions
6
5
4
3
2
1
0
-1
1990
1994
1998
2002
2006
2010
Foreign direct investment, net inflows (BoP, current US$)
Portfolio equity, net inflows (BoP, current US$)

Table 23

Year	*Net ODA received (% of GNI)*	*Net ODA received (% of central government expense)*	*Net ODA received (% of gross capital formation)*	*Net bilateral aid flows from DAC donors, Total (current US$)*	*Net bilateral aid flows from U.S. (current US$)*	*Net ODA received (current US$)*
1999	1.19	6.20	7.56	455.5	74.97	741.29
2000	0.96	5.53	5.52	508.53	88.46	702.69
2001	2.72	16.53	15.81	1164.47	775.64	1942.9
2002	2.90	17.20	17.56	745.49	208.98	2105.44
2003	1.25	7.65	7.68	570.66	102.28	1072.01
2004	1.44	10.18	8.86	426.4	76.91	1439.79
2005	1.44	10.07	7.72	836.86	323.07	1614.61
2006	1.68	11.22	7.72	1207.5	477.72	2180.44
2007	1.56	9.71	7.03	1047.8	433.57	2269.57
2008	0.93	5.07	4.29	981.28	350.63	1549.71
2009	1.67	10.19	9.39	1428.83	613.04	2769.06
2010	1.64	9.71	10.97	2590.19	1196.76	3013.03
2011	1.59	9.33	12.73	2892.28	1273.85	3508.56

Source: World Development Indicators.

From the above Table, it is clear that since 2001, around ten per cent of the central government's expenses are met through foreign assistance programmes. In the initial years of this period, an astounding 16-17 per cent of government expenses depended on foreign aid. What is even more remarkable is that much of the foreign aid to Pakistan rides on the back of the US.

Although on its own, the correlation between US aid and economic growth in Pakistan is somewhat tenuous – US aid is at best a necessary condition and not a sufficient one for boosting growth in the Pakistan economy – what makes the US so critical to Pakistan is the fact that when the US opens the floodgates of aid, other Western countries follow and the money that flows in creates an artificial boom. Interestingly, even though this money is just a fraction of the GDP of Pakistan, yet this is enough to perk up the economy. This is partly because of the fiscal space that is created for the government, partly because of the engagement with the rest of the

Fig. 8: US aid and Growth

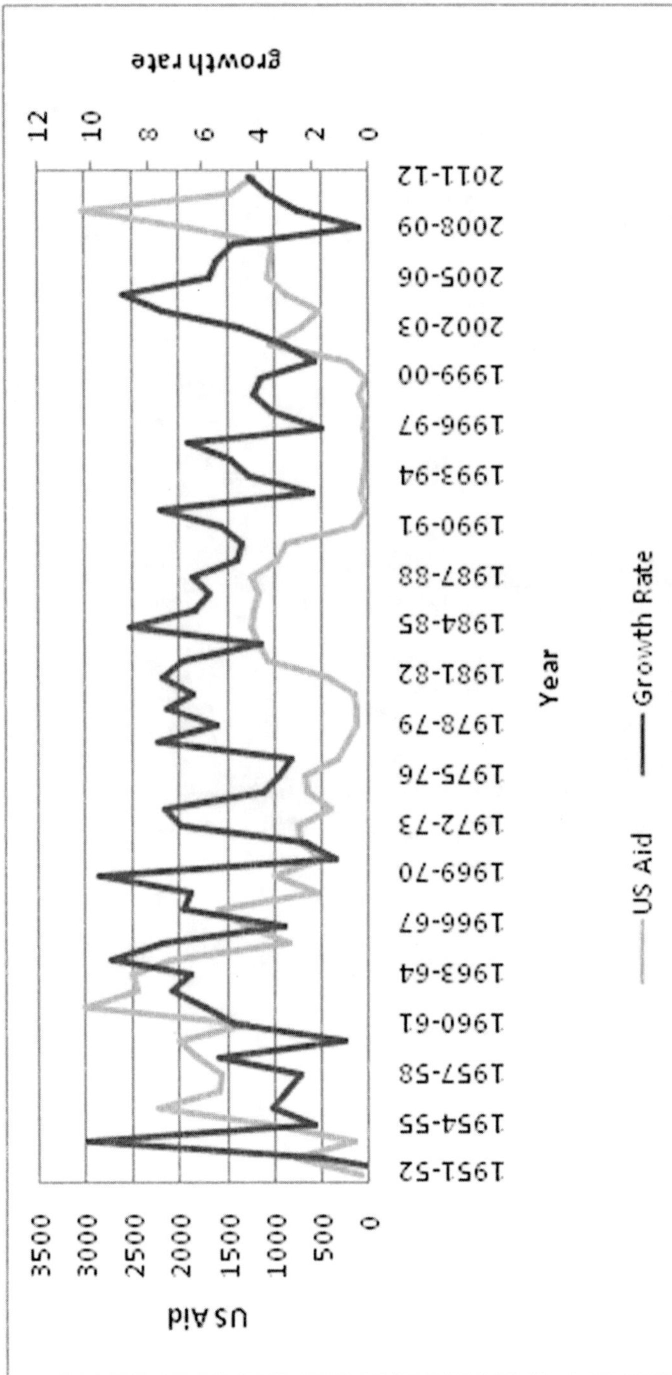

Source: World Development Indicators.

Fig. 9

world (including concessions in trade and the military assistance that flows in) and partly because of the excess money that comes into the economy.

Since Pakistan came into existence, the US has given close to $60 billion (in constant 2012 US$) in both military and economic assistance (Table 23).

Table 24: Program or Account

	Economic Assistance, Total	*Military Assistance, Total*	*Economic and Military Assistance, Total*	*Non-Concessional U.S. Loans, Total*
1948	0.81	.	0.81	.
1951	3.02	.	3.02	.
1952	77.74	.	77.74	.
1953	783.47	.	783.47	.
1954	164.43	.	164.43	.
1955	768.1	278.68	1,046.78	.
1956	1,116.49	1,138.32	2,254.81	.
1957	1,130.52	458.21	1,588.73	.
1958	1,013.87	558.27	1,572.14	20.43
1959	1,433.24	384.32	1,817.56	.
1960	1,770.53	241.39	2,011.92	21.76
1961	1,036.24	272.77	1,309.01	37.99
1962	2,444.87	574.95	3,019.82	138.18
1963	2,164.37	306.11	2,470.48	.
1964	2,327.66	196.4	2,524.06	.
1965	2,021.07	81.08	2,102.14	.
1966	854.87	8.8	863.67	27.32
1967	1,270.76	27.58	1,298.34	50.74
1968	1,572.77	27.21	1,599.99	293.03
1969	567.68	0.52	568.2	6.62
1970	1,014.25	0.91	1,015.16	24.66
1971	496.76	0.76	497.52	58.01
1972	725.79	0.44	726.22	.
1973	749.37	1.26	750.63	118.79
1974	400.02	0.91	400.93	0.79
1975	643.43	0.92	644.34	.
1976	674.64	1.33	675.97	48.78
1976TQ	207.18	0.32	207.5	21.55
1977	334.31	0.96	335.26	.
1978	225.14	1.58	226.72	73.76

(Contd.)

	Economic Assistance, Total	*Military Assistance, Total*	*Economic and Military Assistance, Total*	*Non-Concessional U.S. Loans, Total*
1979	134.91	1.24	136.15	69.4
1980	144.05	.	144.05	.
1981	171.96	.	171.96	.
1982	419.65	1.2	420.85	.
1983	559.59	523.54	1,083.13	.
1984	595	582.25	1,177.24	129.47
1985	636.08	611.22	1,247.31	.
1986	653.17	571.71	1,224.87	.
1987	627.43	559.69	1,187.13	.
1988	805.58	451.12	1,256.70	.
1989	586.26	384.47	970.73	.
1990	574.07	296.89	870.96	.
1991	156.67	.	156.67	53.23
1992	28.43	3.85	32.27	.
1993	77.72	.	77.72	.
1994	71.68	.	71.68	.
1995	24.22	.	24.22	53.08
1996	23.87	.	23.87	134.63
1997	59.88	.	59.88	.
1998	38.04	.	38.04	.
1999	108.47	2.73	111.2	.
2000	29.73	1.22	30.95	.
2001	225.95	0.18	226.13	.
2002	966.39	95.72	1,062.11	257.56
2003	395.12	328.63	723.74	.
2004	417.6	103.59	521.19	.
2005	503.38	374.3	877.67	18.83
2006	705.34	366.63	1,071.97	.
2007	670.68	379.88	1,050.57	37.01
2008	566.05	457.36	1,023.41	5.32
2009	1,406.62	505.23	1,911.85	.
2010	2,081.96	964.23	3,046.19	10.18
2011	772.7	690.53	1,463.23	42.26
2012	1,137.65	82.1	1,219.75	76.7
Total	44,369.30	12,903.51	57,272.76	1,830.08

Source: US Overseas Loans & Grants [Greenbook]

All figures in constant 2012 US $ million

Fig. 10: US Aid

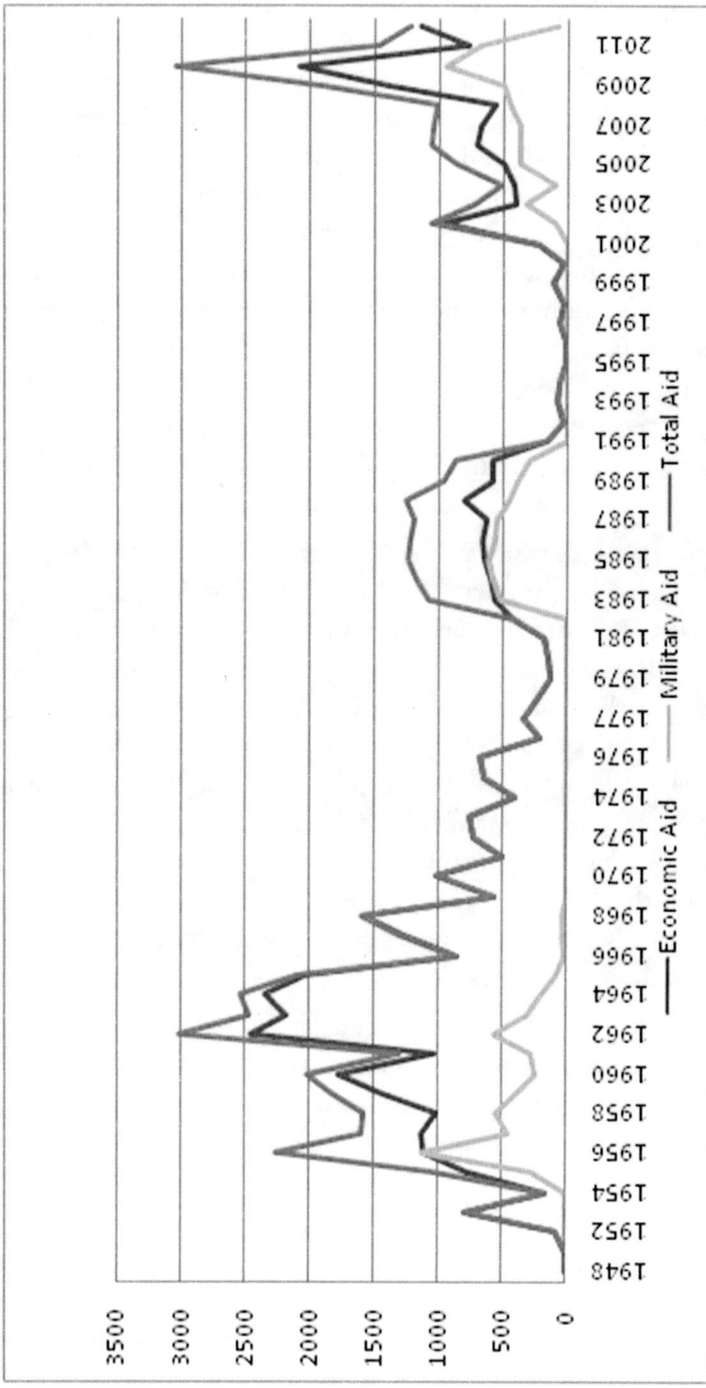
3500
3000
2500
2000
1500
1000
500
0
1948
1952
1954
1956
1958
1960
1962
1964
1966
1968
1970
1972
1974
1976
1977
1979
1981
1983
1985
1987
1989
1991
1993
1995
1997
1999
2001
2003
2005
2007
2009
2011
Economic Aid
Military Aid
Total Aid

4. Conclusion

The Nawaz Sharif government has come into office promising to put the economy back on the rails. But apart from initiating some grandiose projects (many of which are still MoUs) and tinkering with some of the deep structural problems, one year later, it has still shown no signs of undertaking rescuing reform. What Pakistan needs is surgical intervention; what it seems to be getting is cosmetic surgery. The latter might give some temporary relief, but without addressing the structural issues, it is simply a matter of time before the next crisis hits Pakistan's ailing economy. The failure to reform means that the pressures being built by the structural problems of the economy become worse when the next crisis erupts, making it even more difficult to address them. But political compulsions and constraints are likely to hold the Nawaz Sharif government down.

As things stand, the Nawaz Sharif government is patting itself on the back for being able to contract more loans. This is being showcased as the confidence that the international community is reposing in the PMLN government and is seen as a great achievement. The trouble with loans in Pakistan is that these are treated as disposable income, something that invariably creates a crisis when the time comes to pay them back. Unfortunately, Pakistan continues to bank upon the belief that it is too important, or more appropriately, too dangerous, to be allowed to fail and, therefore, every time it reaches the brink, the rest of the world will come to its rescue. It is this belief that also prevents Pakistan from undertaking the structural reforms that are so necessary for putting the economy on a sustainable path.

The fact that foreign loans have once again started flowing – the PMLN government has managed to get around $10 billion in aid and loans over the last one year – has meant that the urgency and compulsion to undertake reform is no longer there. This despite the conditionalities that the IMF has imposed and the clear message from the World Bank that its $ 11 billion Country Support Programme will depend on the Pakistan government living up to its commitment to undertake structural reforms. There are also massive investment proposals, including nearly $ 50 billion of Chinese investments, which are expected to become operational over the next couple of months and years. But for the government to bank on these alone and avoid the reforms could easily lead to a situation where

Pakistan gets the worst of both worlds, i.e., neither the investments take place nor is there any reform.

Among the most critical things that Pakistan needs to address is the problem of extremism and terrorism. With the drawdown of foreign forces from Afghanistan likely to be completed by the end of 2014, new pressures and challenges – both economic and security – are likely to dog Pakistan. The power and energy crisis is another very urgent issue that needs to be addressed. None of the new projects that are being set up are going to become operational immediately. Even if that were to happen, unless the issue of power infrastructure and management (including pricing) is addressed, the new projects will only add to the problem. There is also the problem of the parlous state of finances of the government. While plugging leakages in revenue collection and broadening the tax base will be useful, there are reasons to believe that Pakistan is already a very heavily taxed country and there isn't much scope for increasing revenue to a level where the fiscal problems of the government become a thing of the past. This means that the government and the state will need to downsize, something that is not possible if Pakistan continues along its delusional strategic orientation and continues to have hostile relations with its neighbours, especially India.

It is no longer enough for Pakistan to move on one thing at a time. The problems are acquiring dimensions that even the restarting of aid and assistance from foreign donors will no longer be enough to pull Pakistan's chestnuts out of the fire. There are some signs that Nawaz Sharif understands what needs to be done, but as yet there are few signs of his government doing what needs to be done. The longer the government delays taking the tough decisions and actions, the more difficult it will become for it to bit the bullet of reforms. In fact, it might already have become late.

NOTES

1. "Pakistan Debt Down by Rs 800 Billion", *The News International* 13/3/2014.
2. "Medium Term Roadmap Projects 7 pc Growth" in *Dawn* 15/3/2014.
3. http://www.thenews.com.pk/Todays-News-2-238154-How-did-the-finance-minister-do-it.
4. http://www.thenews.com.pk/Todays-News-9-236143-Living-on-illusion; http://www.thenews.com.pk/Todays-News-9-238951-Irrational-exuberance
5. SBP Annual Report 2012-13, p. 91.

6. "IMF Loan not to Raise Public Debt Volume: Dar, *The Nation,* 6 July 2013.
7. "Inflation will Soar to 10 pc", *The Nation*, 10 April 2008.
8. "Gradual Slowdown: Inflation Dips to Year Low Despite Govt Borrowing", *Express Tribune*, 3 May 2013.
9. SBP Annual Report 2012-13, pp 92.
10. Ashfaque H Khan, "Living on illusion", *The News International*, 4 March 2014.
11. Ashfaque H Khan, "Statistical Issues", *The News International*, 10 December 2013.
12. "Government Shifts Numbers to Show Impressive Performance", *Express Tribune*, 11 February 2014.
13. SBP Annual Report 2011-12, pp 2.
14. *Daily Times*, 24 February 2013.
15. Ishrat Husain, "Stubborn Tax Regime", *Dawn*, 11 March 2014.
16. "Tax Evasion Hits 79 pc, FBR Admits", *Dawn,* 7 June 2011.
17. "Informal Economy in Pakistan", accessed at http://www.dgtrdt.gov.pk/Research/fol%2036.pdf
18. "Number of Tax Dodgers Grossly Overstated: FBR", Express Tribune, 23 February 2012; Also see "Tax Return Filing Drops 42 pc in 2011", *Dawn*, 31 January 2012.
19. http://tribune.com.pk/story/687674/move-backfires-fbr-under-scrutiny-for-tax-collection/
20. M. Ali Kemal and Ahmed Waqar Qasim, "Precise Estimates of the Informal Economy", http://www.pide.org.pk/psde/25/pdf/AGM28/M%20Ali%20Kemal%20and%20Ahmed%20Waqar%20Qasim.pdf; Ahmed Gulzar, Novaira Junaid and Adnan Haider, "What is Hidden in the Hidden Economy of Pakistan: Size, Causes, Issues and Implications, http://www.pide.org.pk/psde/25/pdf/agm26/day2/Ahmed%20Gulzar.pdf; and Muhammed Farooq Arby, Muhammed Jahanzeb Malik and Muhammed Nadim Hanif, "The Size of Iinformal Economy in Pakistan, SBP Working Paper Series, No. 33, May 2010.
21. Muhammad Sabir, "Financial Implications of the 7th NFC Award and the Impact on Social Services", *The Pakistan Development Review*, 49:4, Part II (Winter 2010) pp. 393.
22. http://tribune.com.pk/story/466441/nfc-award-reasonable-finance-ministry-official-counters-shaikh/
23. Report of National Finance Commission 2009, Government of Pakistan, pp 21-22, http://www.finance.gov.pk/nfc/reportofthenfc_2009.pdf.
24. http://www.thenews.com.pk/Todays-News-13-15027-Economic-Survey-2011-12-Govt-scores-perfect-0
25. http://www.thenews.com.pk/Todays-News-13-18520-Prices-have-gone-sky-high-admits-PM
26. Hafiz A Pasha, "IMF Intrusions", *The News International*, 27 October 2013.
27. A Study on the Impact of the Eighteenth Amendment on the National Finance Commission Award, SPDP (UNDP), pp 14, http://sdpd.org.pk/documents/09july/Report-A%20Study%20on%20Impact.pdf
28. http://tribune.com.pk/story/655398/shouldering-responsibility-government-assures-imf-over-new-nfc-award/
29. http://www.dawn.com/news/709637/pakistans-energy-crisis-major-hurdle-in-economic-growth-adb

30. http://tribune.com.pk/story/568794/the-considerate-patron-pml-n-to-absorb-rs200b-in-additional-tariff-increases/
31. Mushtaq Ghumman, "What Constitutes Circular Debt", *Business Recorder*, 29 March 2014.
32. "NEPRA Endorses Massive Increase in Electricity Rates", *The News International*, 11 October 2013.
33. http://tribune.com.pk/story/653889/karachi-2013-the-deadliest-year-of-all/
34. "Cost of War: Chapter on War on Terror Losses Jettisoned", *Express Tribune*, 1 June 2012.
35. "Cost of War on Terror Dropped from Economic Survey", *The News International*, 12 June 2013.
36. Economic Survey 2010-11, p. 220.
37. Asif Saeed Memon, "The Disappearing Poor", *Dawn*, 29 July 2012.
38. http://www.pap.org.pk/statistics/population.htm#tab1.3
39. Muhammad Adnan "Crossing the Poverty Line", *The News on Sunday*, 10 June 2012.
40. Akmal Hussain, "Institutional Imperatives of Poverty Reduction", Institute of Public Policy, BNU, p. 27, http://www.akmalhussain.net/Papers%20Presented/data/Institutional%20Imperatives%20of%20Poverty%20Reduction_Final_5-10-08.pdf
41. Economic Survey 2012-13, p. 105.
42. CIA World Factbook
43. "Observatory of Economic Complexity", http://atlas.media.mit.edu/.

4

Identity Conflict in Pakistan: The Challenge of Ethno-Nationalism(s)

Savita Pande

Anthony P. Cohen defined "identity" as "the ways in which a person is, or wishes to be, known by certain others."[1] The term "identity politics" refers "primarily to activist social movements, which have struggled to resist oppressive accounts of their identities constructed by others, who hold power over them, and claim the right to self-determination. The most obvious aspects of this relate to 'race', ethnicity, gender, sexuality, and disability; ... it entails a call for the recognition of aspects of identity that have previously been denied, marginalised, or stigmatised..... It is about who has the right to represent, or to speak, and for whom."[2] National identities are understood in two contexts: one, ethnic, rooted in cultural-historical legacies and two, civic-territorial, deriving from modernity, both essential, notwithstanding differences between them. The two have been classified in common parlance as ethno-nationalism and civic nationalism.

This paper deals with the identity issue in the context of ethnicity based nationalism or ethno-nationalism where ethnicity or "ethnie" stands defined in terms of "a named human population with a myth of common origins and ancestry, shared historical memories, one or more elements of common culture, and a measure of solidarity, at least among the elites."[3]

Smith defines nation as "a large, vertically integrated and territorially mobile group featuring common citizenship rights and collective sentiment together with one (or more common characteristics), which differentiate its members from those of similar groups with whom they stand in relations of alliance or conflict."[4] Nationalism is, thus, the feeling of being "linked by either ethnicity or territorial bond, and the belief that the corporate interests of that group can best be protected by control of their own state."[5] Grounded in the matrix of ethnicity as an ideology, ethno-nationalism stands defined as "the sentiment of an ethnic minority living in a state (or across boundaries) that propels the groups to unify and identify itself as having capacity of self-government."[6]

Conceptually, the debate has also varied from whether ethnic conflict is inherent in the nature or the primordialist view (Smith, Connor) or is it created by the state, the instrumentalists (Steinberg, Brass).[7] The former explains ethnicity as given and explains their actions and politics on the basis of cultural attributes including kinship and descent, language, religion and customs, as well as historical territory. The latter treats ethnic politics as created or manipulated. Then, there are others, Constructivists (Brubaker and Anderson), who think that it is constructed from social interactions.[8]

The State of Pakistan

Nothing can be more ironical than the fact that a state, which came into existence on the basis of identity – Muslim nationalism – is still struggling to find its identity. This cannot be explained in terms better than the answer which Khan Abdul Wali Khan, then chief of the Pashtun nationalist National Awami Party, gave when a journalist asked him if he thought he was a Pashtun first, a Pakistani first or a Muslim first. He said, "He had been a Pashtun for 3000 years, a Muslim for 1300 years and a Pakistani for 25 years."[9] This also shows that acknowledging his multiple identities, he clearly traced his longest ancestry to his ethnic self – the Pashtun.[10]

To begin with, the idea was clear that Muslims needed a land of their own, protected from the potential Hindu majoritarian post-Independence. During the Pakistan movement, the dominant discourse was religious nationalism, subsuming regional identities; post independence the debate shifted to "son of the soil" versus "migrants". Post-Independence, as several identities emerged, the religious identity question had to grapple with the issue of ethnic identity. This is best explained in terms of "contending identities". Ijaz Khan says this is because of two levels of explanation in this realm, the parallel and horizontal: the former resting its case on religious basis of its creation, the latter on regional/provincial and ethnic identities, which included Pashtun, Baloch, Sindhi, Punjabi and since 1980s the Muhajir; as also Saraiki in Punjab, Makranis and Barohis in Balochistan and Chitralis, Gilgitis and Hazarawals in Khyber Pakhtunkhwa.[11] The religious identity has streams of thought: "those who consider Pakistani identity to be basically religious, to be more precise, Islamic, and those who, though agreeing to Muslim identity of Pakistan, argue that being Muslim does not mean being Islamic" – that notwithstanding the two are united against the ethnic/national identity contentions.[12] While both the Centrist as well as ethno-nationalists are united on issues of democracy, Islamisation, and militarisation of the State, ethno-nationalist agenda goes further: seeking recognition of their separate identity.[13]

Pakistan is a classic case where the Constitution does not recognise ethnic minorities, yet the political history of the state is essentially exploitation by the ethnic majority – Punjab. The state is interventionist in nature and while ethnic reality may be primordial, the conflict is instrumental. Thus, functionally speaking, Punjabi is ethnic majority, Sindhi, Balochi, Pashtuns are ethnic minorities. The Mohajirs, again functionally speaking, began as a majority, but became a minority subsequently. The "language based" identity legitimacy in Pakistan has led to provincial territory becoming a symbol of nationalism for the majority community (Sindhis), leaving minority communities (Mohajirs) "deterritorialised", the parties representing them practicing the strategy of "ethnic overbidding" (MQM) and of ethnic underbidding (PPP) for fear of losing constituency outside the province.[14] The issue became more complicated as Pashtun inflow began, the process of nativisation of the Mohajirs and Pashtuns brought them into collision, the conflict becoming bloodier during 2000 to 2005.[15]

Contradictions were exacerbated post-71, as founding ideology of two-nation theory "lay in ruins" with the result that "tensions between regional and Islamic expressions of Pakistani identity have remained resolved". Waseem stated that, "Territorial nationalism based on Indus Civilisation emerged in full swing only after the indigenous revival during the 1970 elections. After the emergence of Bangladesh in 1971, the rise of new ethno-regional identities posed a challenge to the state's notion of a national identity and led to new patterns of identity formation at the sub-national level."[16] For some time, there were attempts by scholars like A. H. Dani to trace Pakistani nationality "that acquired its distinctive features from Indus Valley civilisation rather than from Islam", an idea developed further by Aitzaz Ahsan.[17] The idea, of course, is debatable, as Ahsan's Pakistani "must embrace 'Indian-ness' to claim his identity" as by denying that "Pakistani denies the Indus".[18] Shaikh has argued that post 1971, the conflicted Pakistani was called upon to "declare allegiance to an ethnic territorial nationality while under pressure also to affirm his identity as a denationalised Muslim."[19] Part of the explanation lay in the fact that the 1973 Constitution exacerbated ethnic conflict by creating federating units identified with their core linguistic communities. Thus, Sindhis, Punjabis, Pathans and the Baluch got their homelands legalised in provinces creating fears in the minorities like Mohajirs and Pashtuns in Sindh as identity struggles arose related to sons of soil versus outsiders; resentment against other "settlers" post-90s in Balochistan, and post-2001 in Khyber Pakhtunkhwa and FATA to tackle extremism.

An additional factor appeared in the state's identity politics (read religious) with Zia's Islamisation, the extent of which drastically increased with the concomitant Soviet Union's occupation of Afghanistan (1979–1989). The Islamisation policy, says Ilhan Niaz, "helped move Pakistani identity further away from geography, culture and historical experience, and closer towards religion and sentimentality. Zia's legacy has proved enduring and no government, democratic or military, has been able to reverse its effects", notwithstanding General Pervez Musharraf's call for religious moderation.[20]

The state saw an effective tool in neutralising the rising ethnic aspirations by superimposing an Islamic identity, the juxtaposition becoming more pronounced with the rise of Taliban and again their resurgence. Thus, the line between Pashtunwali and Sharia law blurred, "notably since the 1980s as the two identity traits were combined and the tribal culture encompassed a stronger religious aspect. This was evident especially under the Taliban rule that drew punishments largely from Pashtunwali and, in fact, forced combined Pashtunwali-Sharia law within and outside the Pashtun society."[21]

The additional element of sectarian identity introduced in the 1980s further complicated issues giving it an even more violent dimension, reaching astronomical levels now.

The overdeveloped state's intervention is, again, also responsible for the rise and pattern of sub-ethnic identities, say Saraiki. What does all this mean for the region? What are the implications for India, considering every now and then, Pakistan raises the bogey of this "external hand"?

The Beginning

To begin with, Pakistan was ethnically divided mainly into the Bengalis (more than 50 per cent), Punjabis, Pakhtuns, Sindhis and Balochs, later joined by migrants from India's Muslim minority areas, known as Mohajirs. The ethnic landscape was peculiar… Punjabis were dominant in all sectors, besides them (considered as second fiddle) were the Pashtuns, being better placed in the Army, Sindhis as landlords and Mohajirs in business, bureaucracy and politics. In other words, the minorities were more functional than structural. As for the protection of minority rights constitutionally, even where they exist in the constitution, they remain mainly in writing. But, in case of Pakistan, where there is no legal acceptance of ethnic minorities (unlike religious minorities), these laws do not exist or as we can say functional minorities exist, that is, they are minorities vis-à-vis a majority, the situation is still worse. The ethnic majority is thus that of Punjabis and the rest – the Sindhis, the Baluchis and the Pashtuns, thus, are the minorities.[22]

Apart from the cultural differences, the two wings situated geographically apart, communication became a problem, only elites interacted and it also resulted in low investments in social and economic activities. Besides, the Eastern wing was geographically dense constituting 55 per cent of population at Independence, but had low urbanisation level. Thus, the provinces and territories of West Pakistan were merged into One Unit in 1955 to balance with East Pakistan, the parity formula serving the basis of the federation, which was reflected in the 1956 and 1962 Constitutions.[23] Representation from East Pakistan remained low in public life.[24] The state's ideology of using Islam and Urdu as symbols of integration saw strong reaction from the provinces where the ethnic nationalists reacted by consolidating their ethnic identities using language as an important constituent. The strongest language activism was the Bhasha Andolan, the Bengali language movement of 1948 and 1951.[25] Province-wide strikes on February 21, 1952, the brutal suppression of the Language Movement by the state kick-started Bengali nationalism.[26] In mid-50s, secular and democratic forces were organised to give vent to their dissatisfaction.[27] The Central government sought and got the consent of United Front in East Pakistan on parity with West Pakistan (One unit) by exploiting three issues: inter-party conflict in East Pakistan, lifting of Ban on Bhashani's entry into Pakistan; and the restoration of Democratic government in East Pakistan. The Awami League resented, demanding a bigger share in the ministry, and was eventually expelled from the United Front.[28]

Although the language movement itself was diffused by 1955, it continued to have implications in the undivided Pakistan leading eventually to the creation of Bangladesh. The Awami league opened its membership to all citizens of Pakistan changing the name of the party from Awami Muslim League to the National Awami League and emerged as a mass party. In 1966, the Awami League proposed a Six Points Programme seeking: "adult franchise in a parliamentary framework; two subjects i.e. defence and foreign policy, along with communications to be with the Centre; two controvertible separate currencies or one currency to be handled by two separate reserve banks for the two wings; power of taxation for the provinces; right of provinces to handle foreign exchange and foreign trade; and paramilitary forces for East Pakistan."[29] The refusal of Yahya Khan and Zulfiqar Ali Bhutto to allow the Awami League to form a government after the elections of 1971, eventually led to secession and the formation of Bangladesh.

The most prominent issue for the people of East Pakistan was economic deprivation, which could be seen by vast gaps in the economies between the two wings of Pakistan, especially between 1949-50 and 1969-70. While East Pakistan earned foreign exchange by exporting raw jute and jute goods, which constituted over 90 per cent of the total export earnings of Pakistan, it was West Pakistan, which benefitted in terms of investment and industrialisation, East Pakistan remained agricultural because the government failed to "implement industrialisation there... The government even failed to adopt a system of agrarian expansion."[30] "The people of East Pakistan became poorer between 1947 and 1971, the years they stayed in union with West Pakistan."[31] Says Salahuddin Ahmed, "In modern times Pakistan set an example of a neocolonialist country, where one part of the previous colonial country, after achieving independence, turned the other part into a new colony for utilising its export earnings and using it as a market for selling the finished products.... *this phenomenon aroused nationalism against neo colonialism.*"[32]

Sindhi Ethno-Nationalism

Sindhi ethno-nationalism became directed against both, Punjabis as well as Muhajirs. The latter (Muhajirs) enjoyed the power and privilege for the first eleven years, as junior partners of the Punjabi ruling elite. Despite constituting only 3.3 percent of the country's population, they held disproportionate rate of jobs in the government and advanced their businesses.[33] The divide became pronounced as Karachi was named the capital and separated from the province, adoption of Urdu as the national language and finally the One Unit plan, seen by Sindhis as "an effort by the centre to swallow up Sindhi identity."[34] Functionally, the dismissals of Chief Minister(s) and their replacements, musical chair like politics in the Assembly controlled by the Centre in the initial years after independence further fuelled Sindhi ethno-nationalism.[35] One Unit plan divided the Sindhi elites within themselves. After the One Unit Plan was undone, Sindhi nationalism was seen in two different directions: Awami Tahreek of Rasool Bux Palijo formed on March 5, 1970 claiming to combine proletarian internationalism with the nationalist question and Jiye Sindh of G.M. Syed projected the idea of an independent nation-state for the Sindhis by the name of Sindhu Desh in 1972.[36]

As refugees from India, the Muhajir had a separate and distinct identity not shared by any of the other ethnic groups, who were hostile to them, clinging to the basis of an "Islamic Nation", they supported the fundamentalist Jamaat-e-Islami or the traditionalist Jamiat-e-Ulema-e-Pakistan.[37] The emergence of Hyderabad and Karachi as economic centres led to their economic preponderance.[38]

With the rise of Ayub Khan in power, a Pathan, in the early 60s, the Muhajir power sharing saw a decline after being replaced by Pakhtuns as junior partners in the setting of the ruling power, Ayub's constituency being the Army with 20 per cent Pakhtuns. The decline in Mohajir power came with the twin steps of 1972 Sindhi Language Bill and the Quota system. On the former, rioting erupted as the Sindhi language got a status equal to Urdu in the province.[39] One of the most violent reactions to the bill came from the Mohajirs, who "attacked not just Sindhi people, but the representation of Sindhi language as well by burning the Department of Sindhi at the University of Karachi."[40] It was only when Z.A. Bhutto announced a formula for reconciliation and went on a tour to Sindh that the violence came to an end.[41]

Secondly, changes were introduced in the existing quota system (the system introduced by Liaqat Ali Khan in 1948 ostensibly for parity between Eastern and Western wings), the recruitment percentage of Muhajirs came down.[42] However, in terms of numbers, the Mohajirs continued to be over-represented in the bureaucracy in terms of their population. Also an Ordinance was passed, which provided for non-discrimination in the appointments or promotions in Civil Service on the basis of the knowledge of Sindhi or Urdu language for a grace period of twelve years, which expired in July 1984, when the Zia regime decided not to enforce the language requirement.[43] Besides, the lateral entry system from 1972-1977, economic separation of East Pakistan was a loss to Muhajir economic power, further exacerbated by Bhutto's nationalisation of banks and insurance companies.[44]

The Zia period also saw the rise of Mohajirs, who by now saw themselves as victims of double discrimination against military authoritarianism (Ayub Khan) and civilian landlords (of Bhuttos). On his return to higher education in 1978 from a stint in the Army (where he faced discrimination as well), Altaf Hussain founded the All Pakistan Muhajir Students Organisation (APMSO), a precursor to the political party Muhajir Quami Movement (MQM). The Mohajirs' support to the religious parties, thus, "was not a manifestation of their "fundamentalism"; for these refugees and their siblings, it was an attempt to join the Pakistani mainstream, as Muslims and not as "refugees". Since they could not rely on an ethnic identity of their own, as the Sindhis, the Punjabis, the Baluch and the Pathans, the Muhajirin could only rely on the larger Muslim political identity derived from Jinnah's 'two nation theory'. Their support of political Islam was, thus, inspired by their specific identity politics rather than by their endorsement of the islamist *weltanschauung*".[45]

Although Karachi had seen many a riot before, however, the ethnic clashes which occurred in the second half of the 1980s in the city were unprecedented in their scale and brutality.[46]

The MQM's operational techniques showed great sophistication in terms of propaganda and coordination among members, it was established as a party as many known names were wiped out.[47] The party, based in Pakistan's most cosmopolitan region, apart from being built around personality cult of its leader to the extent unknown even in Pakistan, adopted different forms of urban violence such as extortion, target killings, and kidnapping, even incorporating criminal gangs dealing in petty crimes as well as institutionalising the torture of political opponents and extortion of people in Mohajir neighbourhoods.[48]

A short-lived 1980s alliance between Syed and Mohajir collapsed with the formation of the Sindh National Alliance between Palejo and Syed. Post Zia MQM has formed alliances as per its convenience: These include those with the PPP and Nawaz Sharif's PML; Musharraf; and enjoyed power in both the national and Sindh governments. In 1988, it formed an alliance with the PPP on the basis of a 25 point charter of demands, the alliance was short lived. MQM's demands were never implemented and the MQM broke its alliance with the People's Party in 1989 and after the 1990 elections, entered a new alliance with the Islami Jamhoori Ittehad (IJI). In 1991, it proposed to change its name from Mohajir to Muttahida, though it has not yet implemented the change.[49] The establishment played its own card, first by orchestrating a split in the MQM, creating splinter group – MQM Haqiqi; and then launching a massive repressive Operation Clean UP in 1992, while the violence and killings continued along with extrajudicial killings.[50] In the meantime, there was a shift in the demand also. For instance, instead of demanding recognition of separate nationality, it sought withdrawal of criminal charges against MQM activists as priority demand; unofficially, it sought a fifth province (rather than fifth nationality) for the Mohajirs.[51] The War on terror created fresh round of refugees, which added to the number of the Pashtuns, many of whom found their way to Karachi. The ANP, exploiting grievances of the Pashtuns, incited hatred against the Muhajirs and other ethnic groups.[52] However in early 2008, when the Musharraf regime unravelled, the MQM supported PPP, which formed a national government. As a result, the MQM became a junior alliance partner of the PPP in both Pakistan's national and Sindh governments, a mutual bid to marginalise ANP. Majority of political violence in Karachi in recent years can be accounted for by the rivalry between Muhajir gangs backed by the MQM and Pashtun gangs associated with the ANP.[53]

The Pathan-Mohajir conflict "solidified because of considerable flow of Pathan Refugees from Afghanistan, who lived in the milieu of criminal gangs in Karachi". The influx had "complicated the efforts of Mohajirs, the majority in Karachi and the largest minority in Sind to establish themselves as a recognised fifth main ethnic group in Pakistan and to counter the policies recognising Sindhis as indigenous (and preferred people of the Province)."[54] As the conflict transformed into Muhajir-Sindhi riots in 1988, again dipped in revenge and counter revenge... the pattern continued in the 1990s relieved only by a shift to Shia-Sunni violence.[55]

There have been demands of a separate Mohajir province by different organisations.[56] While Altaf Husain's demand for support of new provinces has been interpreted as support for a separate Muhajir province, other parties have slammed it also. Thus, he said in September 2013, "Mohajirs have not yet demanded separation and we don't want to demand this. Our ancestors created the country and we want to save and protect it."[57] He also stated some months before in January 2013, "I want to tell the nationalist groups and PPP leaders that if they don't accept the mandate of urban Sindhis then [they should] create a separate province for them."[58]

Apart from Jamaat-i-Islami, ANP and Tehrik-i-Insaf, MQM's challenges have been listed as: "a number of militant groups (are) consolidating their own hold on parts of the city. Baloch groups, said to be cultivated by the agencies against Baloch separatists, work with the PPP against the MQM. The Taliban are also a rising force, first wiping out the ANP from its Pakhtun strongholds. There are a number of anti-Shia militant groups operating in the city. All of them are against the MQM".[59] Kidnappings for ransom, sectarian attacks and gang warfare have spiralled since 2008 till 2013.[60] In the long run, Sindhis fear of being deprived of the benefits of Thar coal development and privatisation of the Qadirpur gas fields.[61]

Pashtun Nationalism

Dating back as far as 2500 years, the distinct Pashtun identity is traced in code of Pashtunwali defined by characteristics of honour or *nang*; revenge or *badla*; hospitality or *melmastia*; followers of relatively moderate Ganafi Islam; though never had a land of their own.[62] Pashtun history was a saga of conquest and subjugation, undermining Pashtun unity cause, separating Pashtuns across Pakistan and Afghanistan.[63]

Pashtuns became a part of Pakistan despite the controversial referendum (won by 50.5 per cent, boycotted by many) at the time of independence, the choice of joining either India or Pakistan, with no option of independence (the demand for Pashtunistan sought by them in the "Bannu Declaration" on June 22, 1947), the parties raising the issue were banned, their leaders imprisoned, and their newspapers proscribed.[64] This despite the assertion by the leaders that their demand for Pukhtunistan did not mean an independent state, but an autonomous province within Pakistan, where Pukhtuns could live sans Punjabi domination and Ghaffar Khan's assurance to the governor, Cunningham, that no anti-Pakistan activity will be encouraged and that there was no question of declaring the independence of the province.[65] However, from the very beginning, a highly centralised and authoritarian rule in Pakistan was established, which had no room for any demands of provincial autonomy and regional self-assertion. Since 1950s, the dream of an autonomous state lived on, interspersed by Afghan-backed fighters continuing to attack Pakistani forces across the border. In 1955, relations between Pakistan and Afghanistan were severed as government-inspired demonstrations in Kabul and other Afghan cities led to the pulling down of Pakistani flags and hoisting Pashtunistan flag over the Pakistan embassy.[66] There is no doubt that Pashtuns, who came as refugees, were absorbed in Pakistan. The Pashtuns have claimed to have had a proportionally smaller share in Pakistan's power constructs, smaller share in economy than have the Punjabis and the Sindhis. Sayeed stated: "...there was no ethnic group in Pakistan in 1947 that was more conscious of its separate linguistic and cultural identity than the Pukhtuns."[67]

Straddled across Pakistan and Afghanistan, the Pushtuns demand for Pushtunistan never saw the light of the day, partly because, initially, the Afghan Pashtuns saw it from the Afghan perspectives only, although they supported Pakistani Pashtun demand for self-determination, which could be seen in providing them, weapon, training and sanctuaries in the 60s and 70s.[68] After Punjabis, Pukhtuns formed the largest constituent of Indian Muslims in the Army, in the newly formed Pakistan.[69] Despite their better placement in the system, which was ruled by the Army for many years. Also, compared to Sindhis and Baloch, Pakhtuns are stated to be better placed in terms of owning local land and resources, administrative control and placements in bureaucracy.[70] This is contested by others, who point to the exploitation of the Pakhtuns in matters of Kalabagh dam, banking, earning excise duty from tobacco produced in the province, depriving the latter; exclusive use by the federal government, natural gas and oil in the Kohat (Gurguri) and Karak districts of Pukhtunkhwa, etc.[71]

The Afghan and Pakistan versions varied on the issue of Pashtunistan. The former thought it would resolve, once and for all, the border dispute with Pakistan and secure direct access for the landlocked state to the Arabian Gulf and Indian Ocean.[72] However, problem lay in lack of willingness in any Afghan leader to cede Afghan territories for Independent Pashtunistan.[73] Nevertheless, Even Zulfiqar Ali Bhutto decided to build ties with Afghan groups hostile to Daoud (including Hekmatyar) as he renewed his Pashtunistan rhetoric following the July 1973 coup in Kabul.[74] The policy of backing rebels continued after Bhutto, and through the 1980s, however, while Hekmatyar and his *Hezb-eIslami* were well-provisioned by ISI despite their non-effectiveness, the policy of depending on one group was given up in favour of backing eight; even refugees were required to affiliate with one party or the other.[75]

Without getting into Pashtun "homeland" debate, not many would dispute the shift in Pushtun activity to Pakistan from Afghanistan. Among the factors responsible for the shift has been massive migration of Afghan refugees (numbering two million) post overthrow of Daud as a result of Soviet intervention in 1978, the earlier migrations due to calamities etc. were not colossal. Thus Pushtuns may represent only about 15 per cent of the population of Pakistan, but their numerical strength is twice those in Afghanistan, the latter in number equal to those in Khyber Pakhtunkhwa alone; also constitute 20 per cent of the population of Karachi (the largest urban community of Pashtuns).[76] Ethnicity was still a primary identity, as majority of Communist leaders were Pushtuns; most of the Mujahideen groups were Pushtun and the victims of Jihad were also Pushtuns; not surprisingly the migrant refugees were also Pushtun. Pakistan's motives were clear: furtherance of Afghanistan and Kashmir policies and neutralising Pushtunistan by patronising Pushtun groups. The rise of non-pushtun groups as leaders like Burhanuddin Rabbani of *Jamiati Islami Afghanistan* and Ahmad Shah Masood of the Northern Alliance in post-Soviet withdrawal led Pakistan to, as a counter, propagate Hekmatyar and upon his failure, Taliban.[77] Before 1979, Islam played "a supplementary and secondary role" in the articulation of Pashtun nationalism. It was after the Soviet invasion of Afghanistan in 1979 that radical forms of Islam began to supplant the consciousness of Pashtun nationalism.[78] Pashtun nationalists believe that the superimposed Islamic fundamentalism undermines 50 million Pashtuns on either side of the Durand Line. Mishali Ram says, unlike Afghanistan where Talibanisation did not spread to non-Pushtun areas, "Pakistani Taliban actively promotes its ambition to change the entire makeup of the state. Rather than Pashtun nationalism and separatism, their stronghold in the Pashtun tribal areas serves to advance a wider ideological aspiration of bringing Pakistan in the bosom of Islam and Sharia law. Thus, the Pakistani Taliban has, in fact, developed into a cluster of insurgents that draws from other militant groups outside the Pashtun areas, mainly in the Punjab. *Nevertheless, while linked to regional and global developments of extremist political Islam, the insurgencies in both Afghanistan and in Pakistan's tribal areas are mainly ethnically oriented. Pashtun affiliation and tribal culture, specifically expressed by Pashtunwali, drive the rebellion.*"[79]

The alliance in Global War on Terror as Pakistan changed its Afghanistan Policy drastically, pitched the country's Punjabi-dominated army against the predominantly Pashtun people of the region. In its anti-Taliban operation in Swat in May 2009, killing and dislocating many and destroying Mingora, the Pakistani Army was pitched against Pushtun residents, giving advantage to Taliban which whipped up ethnic issue. Saikal says "even if admittedly, the Pashtuns also make up a good proportion of the Pakistani army, but this will not stop the Taliban from exploiting the ethnic factor to the maximum".[80] The offshoot of this policy was the debate between those, who characterised Taliban phenomenon as Pushtun nationalism and those who thought otherwise that by attacking innocent civilian Pushtuns, the movement had in fact done a great damage to Pushtun nationalism, which got exacerbated with Pakistan's alliance with the US in fighting the Taliban.[81]

Saikial says, caught between "adversarial forces" and a shared sense of common desperation and victimisation may lead them to forget their "historical divisions, and *rally behind the Taliban leadership in pursuit of their historical goal of an independent "Pashtunistan"*.[82] Echoing Selig Harrison, the clash between the "Punjabi army" and "Pushtun Taliban" will ignite a civil war leading the Pashtuns on both sides of the Durand Line to unite for the formation of an independent Pashtunistan... in fact, he uses Haqqani's term of "Islamic Pushtunistan".[83] Saigol says, "In contemporary times, Pashtun nationalists find themselves besieged from all sides.... The state of Pakistan is spilling Pashtun blood in the tribal regions. The al-Qaeda and Taliban militants are shedding Pashtun blood in both Pakistan and Afghanistan. The Americans and NATO forces are spilling Pashtun blood in Afghanistan. In Pakistan, they are pitted against the centralised and authoritarian state as well as the Punjabi majority. In Afghanistan, they are pitted against the Tajiks and Uzbeks and the erstwhile Northern Alliance. All this is going to reinforce feelings of oppression and injustice. It is likely to strengthen nationalist sentiment even further.... *It is an open question whether history unites the Pashtuns on both sides of a porous and permeable borderland by erasing the imaginary line drawn on a map coloured with tragedy.*"[84]

The Baloch Nationalism

The Baloch nationalism, rooted as it is in their claim to have a separate status from the colonial time, have seen repression of the worst order. The conflict has seen phases of ethnic insurgencies in 1948, 1958, 1973 and the latest since 2006, continuing today. The issue is complicated partly because of fractured leadership and divided loyalties to Sardars, thus intertwined around the three largest tribal groups: the Marri, Bugti, and Mengal tribes. The issues range from, besides historical grievances of political and economic subjugation, the construction of the Gwadar mega-port, expanded natural gas exploration, the war in Afghanistan, and the military's harsh response to nationalist demands seen in missing persons, killing and dumping. Apart from actual and perceived marginalisation, economic exploitation (by Punjabis at the Centre), the conflict also has a Pushtun-Baloch angle. Pashtuns in the north of Balochistan have achieved greater economic progress than the Balochs within the province because of colonial policies. Sectarian dimension entered as militancy rose and Hazaras became target of killers.

The ethnies are constructed on the basis of language.[85] Interestingly, unlike the 1981 Census, the 1998 Census does not distinguish Brahui speakers from Baloch speakers, even though the two languages are linguistically as distinct and unrelated, leading to a debate over majority status of Balochis in the Province.[86] As for Pushtuns-Baloch relationship, the two speak different languages, organisationally Pushtuns are better off economically, more egalitarian, while the Baloch more hierarchical.[87] Although, the former has sided with the latter on issues of provincial autonomy, it has been an active ally under NAP though "not all Pashtuns supported the Baloch (nor did all of the Brahuis)."[88] After the formation of Pakhtunkhwa NAP in 1970, led by Abdus Samad Achakzai, particularly Pushtun nationalism sharpened, with Balochis reportedly having no problems if Pushtun areas became part of Khyber Pakhtunkhwa.[89]

At the heart of the matter is the issue of missing persons – persons picked by security agencies from the state under the garb of anti-terror, anti-insurgency acts. There is a huge discrepancy in the number of the missing persons themselves.[90]

The missing is now seen killed and dumped.[91] Last few years saw 570 dead bodies strewn throughout the province; besides over 402 non-Balochs have been killed in 498 incidents, and over 486 injured in multiple attacks in the same period.[92] The Human Rights Commission of Pakistan (HRCP) reported 140 such bodies found in the province between July 2010 to May 2011.[93] The insurgency is now entwined with sectarian killings, specially Hazara, as banned outfits like Lashkar-e-Jhangvi allegedly keep targeting Shias throughout Balochistan. From 2008 to 2012, 758 members of the Shia community were killed in 478 incidents, of these, 338 victims were Hazaras.[94]

Resource exploitation is personified by gas exploration. Thus, although gas obtained from "Balochistan accounts for 30 per cent of Pakistan's total gas production, Balochistan consumes only 17 per cent of its own output, while the remaining 83 per cent goes to the rest of the country, primarily to the Punjab"; the central government charges a much lower price for Balochistan gas than for gas produced in other provinces and pays lower royalties.[95] It is, therefore, not surprising that Sui gas, which is extracted under the direct control of the Pakistan armed forces, is constantly attacked by the insurgents.[96] The undeveloped resources, 19 trillion cubic feet of gas reserves, six trillion barrels of oil reserves and extensive copper and gold deposits cannot be developed pending amicable resolution with the Baloch; foreign investment ventures in Baluchistan licensed by the central government are paralysed because Baloch leaders, demanding equitable share, challenge the right of the central government to conclude these licensing agreements without their participation.[97]

Seraiki

The most recent issue of ethno-linguistic identity is that of Seraiki identity, the movement for which started in 1960, when for the first time a move was launched to divide Punjab.[98] Bahawalpur retained a province like status till 'One Unit' plan came, but when it was disbanded; it became part of Punjab leading people of Bahawalpur to form Bahawalpur Suba Mahaz (BSM). As part of anti-One Unit movement, the Bahawalpur movement had sought Saraiki area as compensation for having lost its identity as a separate princely state after accession to Pakistan. Following a repressive attack on a protest rally in April 1970, the BSM galvanised into action and contested and won the provincial seat in the 1970 elections (despite Bhutto wave elsewhere). After the creation of 'One Unit', movement for Bahawalpur was launched by Riaz Hashmi, who in the 1980s merged his political agenda with the movement for Seraiki province.[99] The BSM contested the 1970 elections and secured a majority on the provincial and national assembly seats, the only region against the Zulfiqar Ali Bhutto wave. The PPP had gradually extended its sway over Bahawalpur by making political deals and aligning the powerful figures in the area with the PPP. The Bhutto era gave boost to nationalism in southern Punjab as the movement for the restoration of Bahawalpur province turned into the demand for Seraiki province.[100]

The PPP may have indulged in wheeling dealing in the province and the BSM disbanded, but the sentiment remained—languages like Multani, Riasti, Jatki, Dervi and Jangli – faded as Seraiki got overshadowed. Interestingly, the "Mahaz members elected apparently did not continue vigorous agitations for a Bahawalpur province, and the party fragmented by 1972."[101]

The convening of a National Seraiki Conference in Multan in 1974 introduced a new discourse on Seraiki identity, which, over time, became firmly and widely accepted and owned by the speakers of Seraiki language in different regions of Punjab, as well as the other three provinces and caused gradual fading of other names of the same language — Multani, Riasti, Jatki, Dervi and Jangli. But the imposition of martial law frustrated people's hopes for a separate province. The struggle, however, continued due to the efforts of Ustad Fida Hussain Gadi, who had formed Seraiki Lok Sanjh in mid-1980s to promote literary and cultural activities. The demand continued to be raised at different period of time by different Seraiki organisations or their leaders.[102] In 1975, the movement was joined by lawyers of Lahore High Court from Seraiki speaking areas and a Seraiki forum was established by Taj Langah, a Lawyer of Multan; in national Census of 1981, Seraiki was listed as a separate language; on April 6, 1984, Seraiki Suba Mahaz came up, which became the Pakistan Seraiki Party later, forming a constituent of PONM (Pakistan Oppressed Nations Movement) demanding a separate Seraiki province.[103] Zia's regime without consulting linguistic experts, recognised Seraiki as an independent language in the 1980s, which according to Husain Ahmad Khan was a triumph for Seraiki political advocates and the intelligentsia.... This was the period when the Seraiki Qaumi Movement (SQM) gained momentum. The SQM centres were in Karachi, Khanpur, Katora and Ahmadpur Sharqia.[104] The main political parties carrying on the movement included Pakistan Seraiki Party, Seraiki Qaumi Movement, Seraikistan Qaumi Movement, Seraiki National Party, Seraiki Qaumi Ittehad and Seraki Sooba Mahaz and their main grievances include growing number of settlers in the province and all projects like Sutlej Valley Project, where Seraiki generates more income than is spent on it, they demanded rise in job quotas for themselves.[105]

Interestingly, on May 9, 2012, a resolution was passed in the Punjab Assembly, demanding the creation of two new provinces: Bahawalpur and Janoobi Punjab (southern Punjab). The parliamentary commission on carving up new provinces, however, ignoring the demand, instead proposed one province including both aforementioned areas. The provincial assembly named the new provinces, and the commission preferred to make them into one with the new name of Bahawalpur–Janoobi Punjab. The PPP's idea behind the proposal for a South Punjab province was to woo the Seraiki people. It forced the PML-N to agree on the division of Punjab, notwithstanding the difference in the number of provinces as the PML-N, wanted the creation of two provinces, Bahawalpur and Seraiki or South

Punjab. The issue, anyway is not free of implications; it blocked the demand for Hindko province in Khyber Pakhtunkhwa or a separate province demand by Mohajirs, to name two. Prior to the 2013 elections, PPP's main focus was to seek the parliamentary approval for the creation of a fifth province. It passed a resolution to the effect, differences in the party notwithstanding.[106] The federal Government set up a fourteen member Commission headed by Farhatullah Babar from PPP to finalise the details – a move flayed by the PML (N), the ruling Party in Punjab demanding the creation of two new provinces, Southern Punjab and Bahawalpur provinces.[107]

Post 2008, politics over the province saw the PPP led Federal government passing a resolution of new province of South Punjab in the National Assembly on May 3, 2012; Provincial Assembly of Punjab unanimously passing two separate resolutions in favour of the creation of the province of South Punjab and restoration of the Bahawalpur province.[108]

The MQM, understandably, supports more provinces in the country.[109] The ANP that wanted a Seraiki province in Punjab and a Pukhtoon province in Balochistan changed their stance as MQM has filed a bill for the Hazara province to be stamped in Khyber Pakhtunkhwa, and calls have also come up for Malakand to be established as a province. The ANP is, thus, worried that it will have less land to govern if two more provinces are carved out of Khyber Pakhtunkhwa.[110] Ever since the issue of the re-naming of the former NWFP province became hot, there were rumblings of dissent in the Hindko speaking areas of Pakhtunkhwa.

Conclusion

One can safely conclude on the role of state in the ethnic conflict of the state, the debate is whether state action has caused the polarisation or the other way round. While Ayesha Jalal and Iftikhar H. Malik belong to the former category, arguing that the conflict was exacerbated by the long and repressive military rule, which impacted marginalised ethnic groups. Theodore P. Wright claims that ethnicity forced the bureaucratisation or militarisation of the state. In the early 1950s, the muhajirs, wary of losing, delayed the elections and amended the constitution to centralise the state power, which generated conflict and instability, a point also stressed by Rehman.[111] Whatever be the merits of the argument, the fact remains that instrumental aspect of the conflict cannot be denied, even if it is assumed that instrumentalism is possible because of primordialism. This was seen in the case of Mohajirs where changes in the state structure introduced by Bhutto and Zia-ul-Haq, alienated the Mohajirs, who reinvented their ethnic identity on the lines of a repressed community. Although Mohajir ethnic identity consciousness existed since independence; post 1971' Mohajir identity evolved not only against Punjabis and Sindhis, but also upper class Mohajirs. Again, state action defined Mohajir identity beyond MQM, as the establishment supported the rival faction Haqiqi. Thus, mere existence of identity including ethnic may not be sufficient, it needs to be mobilised (or manipulated). This applies to nationalism also, including ethnicity based or ethno-nationalism. Ethno national movements, sub-national movements for organised along ethnic, religious or cultural lines.[112] These groups engage in violent conflict against the state, they either calculate cost and benefit of such a conflict or are motivated by a sense of deprivation. Thus, the formation of Seraiki or Haqiqi based MQM mobilisation can also fall under the manipulation.

The context of identity has been brilliantly summed up as: "The elite of West Pakistan felt that they had a culture 'superior' to East Pakistan. Bear the fact in mind that it was One Unit at that time and, hence, all of what is Pakistan was one province. The Bengalis, it may seem, had somehow betrayed the cause by insisting on also being Bengalis, in addition to Pakistani. That sentiment lives and thrives in today's Pakistan. The celebration of individual culture and heritage is seen to be suspect and drawing 'divisions' and we should all just say that we are Pakistanis only, etc. That is perfect nonsense, of course. We are Punjabis, Baloch, Sindhis, Seraiki, Pashtun, Hazara, etc. and that is integral to us being Pakistanis.... If there is going to be a 'Pakistani' identity, it will have to be a sum of proud and clear ethnic identities. The JI and the bleeding green model failed in December 1971 and it is the right time to reflect on this."[113] In November 2009, the release of a British Council-commissioned report produced by Nielsen Research said "72 per cent felt that they were Muslims first and Pakistanis second."[114]

The Bangladesh independence movement earlier and the Baluch movement subsequently, in Pakistan are classic cases of the Punjabi-Muhajir establishment's failure to counterbalance their ethno-nationalism with

Islamic appeals. Since independence, generally and in 2004 particularly, Baluch leaders have successfully mobilised ethno-nationalist sentiments against the establishment, irrespective of change in governments. Yet it must be added that the Baloch movement is not a secessionist movement irrespective of the rhetorical claims of some of the leaders or fears expressed soon after the formation of Bangladesh. The state has failed in the strategy of containing Pashtun nationalism by cultivating the Taliban supporting their Sunni extremist irredentism. The Taliban did not assuage Pakistan establishment's fears of either Pashtunistan or recognise the Durand line. The use of force strategy has not worked, it fuelled insurgencies further, be it Baluchistan or Sindh, temporary peace notwithstanding temporary respites or dismissals of the government.

Nothing beats the case of Seraiki province, where while all party agree with the logic of a separate province, want the division on administrative ground![115] The unstated reason is supporting the division culture, ethnicity and language lines would be detrimental to national unity and identity (or more accurately, in this case, to Punjabi identity)....There are numerous nationalities in Pakistan...the state has to realise that the only sustainable option is cherishing these distinct nationalities and not suppressing them, if the aim is to evolve even a semblance of a Pakistani identity...the easy and absurd solution devised by the state is to deny any and all ethnic differences and sweep it under the blanket cover of a singular religious identity. The problem with this monolith, grossly inaccurate generalisation is not only that it is dishonest, it also does not work".[116]

Discussing the Islamic versus Muslim identity scenario, Sameena Yasmin says, taking a cue from the Iranian revolution, "If orthodox ideas of Pakistani identity at the societal level continuously gain strength, they may lead to a variant of an 'Islamic state' that may not wish to participate in the project of countering Jihadi ideas....The possible (state) responses range from the government silencing or ignoring the orthodox projection of their version of Pakistan's identity to inaction. In either case, the secondary struggle would impact on Islamabad's ability to effectively continue the primary struggle vis-à-vis Jihadis."[117] Notwithstanding the Islamic state versus state for the Muslims debate, the fact remains that the state imposed Islamisation as a means to counter the ethnic aspirations, although one must admit, there were other reasons for Islamisation – legitimacy being one of the top ones. There are two serious implications, if the ethnic and Islamic entities, instead of contradicting, reinforce each other, one may reach "Islamic Pashtunistan" of Hussain Haqqani, cited by Selig Harrison. Externally, a Jihadi-tolerant state (actually promoting state) may continue to pose problems in Kashmir where proxy war is going on since 1989 in the name of Jihad. The possibility of Taliban as well as state (read Army troops) being re-diverted to the border with India remains high after US withdrawal (even if partial).

An oft debated issue in the conflict is if inter-ethnic conflict in Pakistan bodes well for India since not only does it weaken Pakistan economically, it also takes the attention of the security establishment away. The counter argument is that a stable Pakistan is in Indian interest, going by the spill-over effect theory, i.e., instability and insurgency anyway spill over. In any case, going by the precedence of the formation of Bangladesh, secession did not mean stability or peace at India's borders. In any case, there is no secessionist movement underway and even if there is a remote possibility, there is no guarantee that it would bode stability or peace at Indian borders. In any case, Pakistan's accusations of Indian hand would continue, it being customary to blame neighbouring states, particularly hostile, for ethnic insurgencies.

NOTES

1. Anthony P. Cohen, "Culture as Identity: An Anthropologist's View," *New Literary History*, vol. 24, no. 1, Winter (1993), p. 195, http://canadatree.tripod.com/canadatreehome/id10.html.
2. David Buckingham, "Introducing Identity." in David Buckingham (ed.), *Youth, Identity, and Digital Media* (Cambridge MA: The John D. and Catherine T. MacArthur Foundation Series on Digital Media and Learning and The MIT Press, 2008), p. 1.
3. Anthony Smith, "Ethnic Cores and Dominant Ethnies", in Eric P. Kaufmann (ed.) *Rethinking Ethnicity, Majority Groups and Dominant Minorities* (London and New York: Routledge, 2004), p. 16.
4. A.D. Smith, *Theories of Nationalism*, p. 175.
5. Taj Mohammad Breseeg, *Baloch Nationalism: Its Origin and Development* (Karachi: Royal Book Company, 2004), p. 17.
6. Stephanie Lawson, "The Politics of Authenticity: Ethno-national Conflict and State", in Kumar Rupensinghe (ed.) *Conflict Transformation* (New York: St. Martin's Press, 1995), p. 116.
7. Anthony D. Smith, *Nationalism and Modernism: A Critical Survey of Recent Theories of Nations and Nationalism*, (New York & London: Routledge, 1998); Walker Connor, *Ethno-nationalism: The Quest for Understanding*, (Princeton: Princeton University Press,

1994); Stephen Steinberg, *The Ethnic Myth: Race, Ethnicity, and Class in America*, (New York: Atheneum, 1981); Paul R Brass, Ethnicity and Nationalism: Theory and Comparison, (New Delhi: Sage, 1991).

8. R Brubaker, Ethnicity without Groups, (Cambridge, MA: Harvard University Press, 2004); B. Anderson, Imagined Communities: Reûections on the Origin and Spread of Nationalism, (London: Verso, 1991) 2nd ed.
9. B.R. Singh, "The AFPAK Conundrum", http://www.greaterkashmir.com/news/2014/Feb/2/the-afpak-conundrum-7.asp, 01 February 2014.
10. Rubina Saigol, "The Multiple Self: Interfaces between Pashtun Nationalism and Religious Conflict on the Frontier", *South Asian History and Culture*, vol 3. no. 2, (2012), p. 197.
11. Ijaz Khan, "Contending Identities of Pakistan and Democratic Governance", *Peace and Democracy in South Asia,* vol. 2, nos. 1 & 2, (2006), p. 50.
12. Ibid, p. 51.
13. Ibid.
14. Mohammad Waseem, "Urban Sindh: Region, State and Locality", in Mona Kanwal Shaikh, Farzana Shaikh, Gareth Price (eds.) *Pakistan: Regional Rivalries: Local Impact* (Copenhagen: Danish Institute for International Affairs, 2012), p. 62.
15. Ibid.
16. Mohammad Waseem, "Politics of Ethnic Identities in Pakistan: Patterns of Ethnic and National Discourse", http://www.brookings.edu/~/media/research/files/papers/2011/3/01%20pakistan%20waseem/01_pakistan_waseem.pdf, p. 2.
17. Farzana Shaikh, *Making Sense of Pakistan* (New York: Columbia University Press, 2009), pp. 56-57.
18. Aitzaz Ahsan, *The Indus Saga and the Making of Pakistan* (Karachi: Oxford University Press, 1997).
19. Farzana Shaikh, Making Sense of Pakistan (New York: Columbia University Press, 2009), p. 56.
20. Ilhan Niaz, "Identities and the State in Pakistan: A Study of Mentality", *Asian Affairs,* vol. 43, no. 3, (2012), p. 463.
21. Meirav Mishali-Ram, "When Ethnicity and Religion Meet: Kinship Ties and Cross-Border Dynamics in the Afghan-Pakistani Conflict Zone", *Nationalism and Ethnic Politics,* vol. 17, no. 3, (2011), p. 270.
22. Selig S Harrison, *Pakistan: The State of the Union*, (Washington DC: Special Report, Centre for International Policy, 2009), p. 15, 19.
23. Under the one-unit scheme, the provinces and states of western wing were merged into the province of West Pakistan; East Bengal was recognised as the province of East Pakistan, both provinces given equal representation in the unicameral legislature of Pakistan under the first constitution of 1956—the centralised federation, however, marginalised Bengalis, Sindhis, Pashtuns, and the Baloch. Ayaz Khan," Non Consociational or Federal Federalism and Ethnic Strife of Pakistan", *Asian Social Science,* vol. 7, no. 7, (July 2011), p. 226
24. Rounaq Jahan, *Pakistan Failure in National Integration* (New York: Columbia University Press, 1972), p. 13.
25. Tariq Rahman, "Language, Power and Ideology in Pakistan", Teluq, University of Quebec, (2002), http://www.teluq.uquebec.ca/diverscite/SecArtic/Arts/2002/rahman/txt.htm.

26. Members of the left oriented Youth League defied the Section 144 orders that were imposed, nine people were killed in the police firing. M Rafique Afzal, *Pakistan: History and Politics 1947-1971* (Karachi: OUP,2001), p. 100; Since the 1950s, when the Bengali Language Movement challenged the West Pakistani domination of the former East Pakistan, the people and the press in West Pakistan agreed that this was the work of Hindus, communists and anti-state elements, who wanted to destabilise the state. Tariq Rahman, "Language, Power and Ideology in Pakistan", Teluq, University of Quebec, (2002), http://www.teluq.uquebec.ca/diverscite/SecArtic/Arts/2002/rahman/txt.htmhttp://www.teluq.uquebec.ca/diverscite/SecArtic/Arts/2002/rahman/txt.htm.
27. Since the 1950s, when the Bengali Language Movement challenged the West Pakistani domination of the former East Pakistan, the people and the press in West Pakistan agreed that this was the work of Hindus, communists and anti-state elements, who wanted to destabilise the state. Tariq Rahman, "Language, Power and Ideology in Pakistan", Teluq, University of Quebec, (2002), http://www.teluq.uquebec.ca/diverscite/SecArtic/Arts/2002/rahman/txt.htmhttp://www.teluq.uquebec.ca/diverscite/SecArtic/Arts/2002/rahman/txt.htm
28. M. Rafique Afzal, *Pakistan: History and Politics 1947-1971* (Karachi: OUP, 2001), p. 150.
29. Mohammad Waseem, *Federalism in Pakistan*, http://www.forumfed.org/pubs/Waseem-Fed-Overview.pdf, August 2010, p. 08.
30. Mahfuz R Chowdhury, *Economic Exploitation of Bangladesh* (Lincoln NE: iUniverse. Inc, 2004), p. 43.
31. Ibid, emphasis added.
32. Salahuddin Ahmed, *Bangladesh: Past and Present* (New Delhi: APH Publishing, 2004), p. 305, emphasis added.
33. In 1951, out of 95 senior civil services jobs, 33 were held by the Muhajirs and 40 by the Punjabis. In 1959, out of 48 top military elite positions, 11 were held by Muhajirs, i.e. 23 percent of the total. In the same year, of the total top (Class 1) bureaucracy, 3,532 positions, the Muhajirs' share was 1,070, i.e. 30 percent of the total. Tariq Rahman, *Language and Politics in Pakistan* (Karachi: OUP, 1996), p. 121.
34. Alyssa Ayres, *Speaking Like a State: Language and Nationalism in Pakistan*, (Cambridge: Cambridge University Press, 2009), p. 51.
35. Feroz Ahmed, *Ethnicity and Politics in Pakistan* (Karachi: OUP, 1998), p. 44.
36. Siddiqi, p. 88; Alyssa Ayres, *Speaking Like a State: Language and Nationalism in Pakistan*, (Cambridge: Cambridge University Press, 2009), p. 52.
37. Farhan Hanif Siddiqi, "Intra-ethnic Fissures in Ethnic Movements: the rise of Mohajir identity politics in post-1971 Pakistan", *Asian Ethnicity*, vol. 11, no 1, (2010), p. 31.
38. "The Karachi-based industrial houses controlled 96 per cent of Muslim-owned private industries, over 80 per cent of the assets of private commercial banks, and almost 80 per cent of the insurance companies", Adeel Khan, *Politics of Identity: Ethnic Nationalism and the State in Pakistan* (Sage, January 2005), p. 168.
39. This Act made Sindhi and Urdu compulsory subjects for class IV to XII. Article 5 of the Act stated that the Government may constitute and set up Academies and Boards for cultural advancement and promotion of the Sindhi language. Article 6 of the Act said that the Government may make arrangements for progressive use of Sindhi language in offices and department including Courts and Assembly. K.M. Arif, *Khaki Shadows, Pakistan: 1947-1997* (Karachi: Oxford University Press, 2001), pp. 214-215.

40. Alyssa Ayres, *Speaking Like a State: Language and Nationalism in Pakistan* (Cambridge: Cambridge University Press, 2009), p. 53.
41. T. Rahman, "Language and Politics in a Pakistan Province: The Sindhi Language Movement"', *Asian Survey*, vol. 35, no. 11, (November 1995), p. 1014.
42. "The revised quota of November 1949, which reduced the Bengali and non-Punjabi areas' share by two per cent and allocated 20 per cent to a merit category, gave even more benefits to the Mohajirs, whose literacy rate at 70 per cent was the highest in Pakistan. By 1950, when Mohajirs comprised two per cent of Sindh's population, their share of the successful candidates in the civil service examination was 46.6 per cent... Although the Mohajirs' share at levels below officer ranks in the military has been small, in the senior positions (above the rank of Brigadier) it was disproportionately high in 1968 at 23 per cent as they held 11 of 48 positions.
    Adeel Khan (2004) "Mohajir Ethnic Nationalism in Pakistan: El Dorado Gone Sour", *Asian Studies Review*, 28: 1, p. 43".
43. F. Ahmed, "Pakistan's Problems of National Integration: The Case of Sind", in S. Akbar Zaidi (ed.), *Regional Imbalances and the National Question in Pakistan* (Lahore: Vanguard Books, 1992), p. 168.
44. Asaf Hussain, *Elite Politics in an Ideological State: The Case of Pakistan* (Dawson: Folkestone, 1979), p. 149; Rashid Amjad , "Industrial Concentration and Economic Power", in Hassan Gardezi and Jamil Rashid (eds.), *Pakistan, The Roots of Dictatorship: The Political Economy of a Praetorian State* (London: Zed Press, 1983), p. 255.
45. Laurent Gayer (2003), "A Divided City: "Ethnic" and "Religious" Conflicts in Karachi, Pakistan", paper presented at the 1st Pakistan Seminar organised by the International Institute for Asian Studies and the International Institute for the Study of Islam in the Modern World, Amsterdam, 24 March, p. 10, http://www.sciencespo.fr/ceri/sites/sciencespo.fr.ceri/files/artlg.pdf
46. Laurent Gayer (2003), "A Divided City: "Ethnic" and "Religious" Conflicts in Karachi, Pakistan", paper presented at the 1st Pakistan Seminar organised by the International Institute for Asian Studies and the International Institute for the Study of Islam in the Modern World, Amsterdam, 24 March, p. 10, http://www.sciencespo.fr/ceri/sites/sciencespo.fr.ceri/files/artlg.pdf; Alyssa Ayres, *Speaking Like a State: Language and Nationalism in Pakistan*, (Cambridge: Cambridge University Press, 2009), p. 55; From 1982-1988, eighty students were killed on various campuses across Pakistan. Zahid Hussain, Ali Hasan, and Farrah Khan, "The Campus Mafias", *The Herald*, (October 1988), p. 52; Under Zia, there was a downturn in the share of Mohajirs in government jobs, the case was otherwise with Sindhis. "The Mohajir share of 46.8 per cent of senior positions in 1974 declined to 31.5 per cent in 1983. At the same time, Sindhis' share almost doubled by jumping from 3.6 per cent in 1974 to 6.8 per cent in 1983. Moreover, between 1974 and 1989 Mohajirs lost over 50 per cent of their share in the officer level posts when their share of 30.2 per cent dropped to 14.8 per cent", Charles H. Kennedy, "The Politics of Ethnicity in Sindh", *Asian Survey* , vol. 31, no.10, (2010), cited in Adeel Khan, p. 48.
47. Zaffar Abbas, "Karachi's New Guard", *The Herald*, (December 1988), p. 24.
48. This was known as bhatta (protection money) and the practice was notorious throughout Pakistan. The bhatta system more than anything, exemplifies the manner in which perfectly ordinary people are sucked into whole sale corruption. Talat Aslam, "Police: The Lawless Brigade", *The Herald*, (March 1987), p. 59. Also see Oskar Verkaaik,

Migrants and Militants: Fun and Urban Violence in Pakistan (New Jersey: Princeton University Press, 2004), p. 167.

49. Hassan Mehdi, "Day of the Dissidents" *The Herald*, (January 1991), p. 119
50. Ahmad Rais Khan, "Pakistan in 1992: Waiting for Change", *Asian Survey* , vol. 33, no. 2 (February 1993), p. 131; Ayaz Amir, "The Acid Test," *The Herald*, (June 1992), p. 32; Adeel Khan, *Politics of Identity: Ethnic Nationalism and the State in Pakistan* (Armidale: Sage, 2005), p. 180; As many as 200 were killed in extra judicial killings; Azhar Abbas, "Future Shock" *The Herald*, (March 1996), 46a; Idrees Bakhtiar, "Apocalypse Now", *The Herald*, (January 1996), p. 52.
51. Adeel Khan, *Politics of Identity: Ethnic Nationalism and the State in Pakistan* (Armidale: Sage, 2005), p. 180.
52. "When Sindhi flood survivors from outside Karachi tried to find refuge in the city during after devastating floods, the MQM strongly objected and at its instigation, the city's police force opened fire on some of the helpless refugees". Ali Ismail," Hundreds killed in National-ethnic Violence in Pakistan's Largest City" *World Socialist Website*, December 03, 2010, http://www.wsws.org/en/articles/2010/12/kara-d03.html.
53. Ali Ismail, "Hundreds killed in National-ethnic Violence in Pakistan's Largest City" *World Socialist Website*, December 03, 2010, http://www.wsws.org/en/articles/2010/12/kara-d03.html; Naeem Sahoutara, "Karachi Violence: New outfit Muhajir Republican Army Blamed for Unrest", *The Express Tribune*, August 30, 2013, http://tribune.com.pk/story/597289/suo-motu-case-new-outfit-blamed-for-karachi-unrest/
54. Donald L Horowitz, *The Deadly Ethnic Riot* (Berkeley CA: University of California Press, 2001), p. 415
55. Ibid., p. 416; "Sectarian violence did not affect Karachi until 1993 but claimed 57 lives in 1994, 98 in 1995, 13 in 1996, 28 in 1997, 8 in 1998, 58 in 2001 and 4 in the first four months of 2002. In 2001 and 2002, sectarian terrorists stopped targeting mosques and imambargahs, which had become heavily guarded, to focus on Shia "professionals" (doctors, lawyers, etc.). Laurent Gayer (2003), "A Divided City: "Ethnic" and "Religious" Conflicts in Karachi, Pakistan", paper presented at the 1st Pakistan Seminar organised by the International Institute for Asian Studies and the International Institute for the Study of Islam in the Modern World, Amsterdam, 24 March, p. 17.
56. "Jamaat e Islami has Ties with Al Qaeda", *The Express Tribune*, December 04, 2013, http://tribune.com.pk/story/640878/jamaat-e-islami-has-ties-with-al-qaeda-altaf/.
57. For instance in Members of the Muhajir Province Movement protested and staged demonstrations in the Liaquatabad area of Karachi, demanding their own separate province, "Mohajirs Demand Separate Province", *The Express Tribune*, April 03, 2012, http://tribune.com.pk/story/359152/muhajirs-demand-separate-province/; "MQM is Going to Make MAHAJIRISTAN or MUHAJIRISTAN", *CNN Pakistan*, Blogspot, July 10, 2011, http://cnnpakistan.blogspot.in/2011/07/mqm-is-going-to-make-mahajiristan-or.html.
58. "Administrative Units: MQM Chief Demands New Provinces" *The Express Tribune*, September 11, 2013, http://tribune.com.pk/story/602710/administrative-units-mqm-chief-demands-new-provinces/; "Jamaat e Islami has Ties with Al Qaeda", *The Express Tribune*, December 04, 2013, http://tribune.com.pk/story/640878/jamaat-e-islami-has-ties-with-al-qaeda-altaf/
59. "MQM targeted with malicious propaganda for raising voice on Sindh's rights: Altaf",

The Express Tribune, January 05, 2014, http://tribune.com.pk/story/655066/mqm-targeted-with-malicious-propaganda-for-raising-voice-on-sindhs-rights-altaf/.

60. Javed Qazi, "The City and Ethnicity", *The Friday Times*, September 06-12, 2013, vol. xxv, no. 30, http://www.thefridaytimes.com/beta3/tft/article.php?issue=20130906&page=5.2y.
61. "Crackdown Brings Apparent Lull in Karachi Violence", *The Daily Times*, October 06, 2013, http://www.dailytimes.com.pk/default.asp?page=2013\10\06\story_6-10-2013_pg1_3.
62. Selig Harrison, "Pakistan: State of the Union", Special report, (Washington DC: Center for International Policy, April, 2009), http://www.ciponline.org/images/uploads/publications/pakistan_the_state_of_the_union.pdf, p. 21.
63. L. Dupree, *Afghanistan,* (Princeton: Princeton University Press, 1980), pp. 126–27.
64. A. Saikal, *Modern Afghanistan: A History of Struggle and Survival* (London and New York: I.B. Tauris, 2006), pp. 26-27.
65. Many Pashtuns boycotted the referendum—of the 572,799 eligible voters, only 292,118 participated. S.S. Harrison, *Pakistan: The State of the Union* (Special Report) (Washington DC: Centre for International Policy, 2009), p. 13.
66. Khalid B. Sayeed, *Pakistan: The Formative Phase 1857–1948* (London: Oxford University Press, 1968), pp. 271–2; Adeel Khan, "Pukhtun Ethnic Nationalism: From Separatism to Integrationism", *Asian Ethnicity*, vol. 4, no. 11, (2003), p. 78.
67. S.M.M. Qureshi, 'Pakhtunistan: Frontier Dispute between Afghanistan and Pakistan', *Pacific Affairs*, vol. 39, nos.1–2, (1966), pp. 105–106.
68. Khalid B. Sayeed, *Pakistan: The Nature and Direction of Change* (New York: Praeger, 1980), p. 17
69. Iqbal Khattak, "Kabul Trained Baloch, Pushtoon Youth in 1970s: Ex-ANP Leader", *Daily Times*, February 15, 2010, http://www.dailytimes.com.pk/default.asp?page=2010%5C02%5C15%5Cstory_15-2-2010_pg7_4
70. Stephen P. Cohen, *The Pakistan Army* (Karachi: Oxford University Press, 1984), pp. 42, 44.
71. David Page, *Prelude to Pakistan: The Indian Muslims and the Imperial System of Control 1920–1932* (Karachi: Oxford University Press, 1987), p. 12 cited in Adeel Khan, "Pukhtun Ethnic Nationalism: From Separatism to Integrationism", *Asian Ethnicity*, vol 4, no. 11, (2003), pp. 78, 87.
72. Mohammad Raza and Humayun K Marufkhail, "The Pashtuns and the Future of the Pakistan Federation", in Selig Harrison ed., *Pakistan: The State of the Union* (Washington DC: Center for International Policy, April, 2009), pp. 56-57.
73. Amin Saikal, "Afghanistan and Pakistan: The Question of Pashtun Nationalism?" *Journal of Muslim Minority Affairs*, vol. 30, no. 1, (2010), p. 8.
74. Ibid.
75. W. Maley, *The Afghanistan Wars* (New York: Palgrave MacMillan, 2002), p. 74, Bhutto and his adviser Nasirullah Babur even toyed with the idea of restoring Zahir Shah.
76. Ibid., p. 75.
77. Robert Boggs, "Pakistan's Pashtun Challenge: Moving from Confrontation to Integration", *Strategic Analysis*, vol. 36, no. 2, (2012), p. 209.
78. W. Maley, *The Afghanistan Wars* (New York: Palgrave MacMillan, 2002), pp. 66-76.
79. Rubina Saigol, "The Multiple Self: interfaces Between Pashtun Nationalism and

Religious Conflict on the Frontier", *South Asian History and Culture*, vol. 3, no 2, (2012), p. 210.

80. Meirav Mishali-Ram, "When Ethnicity and Religion Meet: Kinship Ties and Cross-Border Dynamics in the Afghan-Pakistani Conflict Zone", *Nationalism and Ethnic Politics*, vol. 17, no. 3, (2011), p. 270.
81. Amin Saikal, "Afghanistan and Pakistan: The Question of Pashtun Nationalism?" *Journal of Muslim Minority Affairs*, vol. 30, no. 1, (2010), pp. 8 – 11.
82. For a detailed perspective of the two views, see Rubina Saigol, "The Multiple Self: interfaces Between Pashtun Nationalism and Religious Conflict on the Frontier", *South Asian History and Culture*, vol. 3, no2, (2012), pp. 197-214; Reforms in FATA have also triggered severe apprehensions in the Pushtun Communities. Robert Boggs, "Pakistan's Pashtun Challenge: Moving from Confrontation to Integration", *Strategic Analysis*, vol. 36, no. 2, (2012), p. 211; Selig S Harrison, "The Pashtun Time Bomb", *The New York Times*, Opinion, August 1, 2007, http://www.nytimes.com/2007/08/01/opinion/01iht-edharrison.1.6936601.html?_r=0.
83. Amin Saikal , "Afghanistan and Pakistan: The Question of Pashtun Nationalism?", *Journal of Muslim Minority Affairs*, vol. 30, no. 1, (2010), pp. 8-12, emphasis added.
84. Selig S Harrison, "The Pashtun Time Bomb", *The New York Times*, Opinion, August 1, 2007, http://www.nytimes.com/2007/08/01/opinion/01iht-edharrison.1.6936601.html?_r=0.
85. Rubina Saigol, "The Multiple Self: interfaces Between Pashtun Nationalism and Religious Conflict on the Frontier", *South Asian History and Culture*, vol. 3, no2, (2012), pp. 210-211, emphasis added.
86. Census Report of Pakistan 1998, Pakistan Census Organisation, Government of Pakistan, www.statpak.gov.pk/depts/pco/statistics/other_tables/pop_by_mother_tongue.pdf), cited in Farhan Hanif Siddiqi, *The Politics of Ethnicity in Pakistan: The Baloch, Mohajirand Sindhi Movements* (London: Routledge Contemporary South Asia Series, 2011) p. 53.
87. Feroz Ahmed, *Ethnicity and Politics in Pakistan* (London: Oxford University Press, 1999), pp. 176–77; According to the 1981 Census, the Brahui speakers comprised 20.7 per cent of the total population of Balochistan, Population Census Organisation, Government of Pakistan, 1981 Census Report of Pakistan. (Islamabad: Population Census Organisation, 1984) p. 10, cited in Siddiqi, *The Politics of Ethnicity in Pakistan,* p. 126.
88. Paul Titus, "Honor the Baloch, Buy the Pushtun: Stereotypes, Social Organization and History in Western Pakistan", *Modern Asian Studies*, vol. 32, no 3, (July 1998), pp. 657- 676.
89. Farhan Hanif Siddiqi, *The Politics of Ethnicity in Pakistan: The Baloch, Mohajir, and Sindhi Movements* (London: Routledge Contemporary South Asia Series, 2011) p. 53.
90. Farhan Hanif Siddiqi, "Security Dynamics in Pakistani Balochistan: Religious Activism and Ethnic Conflict in the War on Terror", *Asian Affairs: An American Review*, vol. 39, no 3, (2012), p. 167.
91. In 2008, the Federal Interior Minister said that 1,110 were missing, in 2011, while the Baloch Home Minister said that only 55 were missing; Baloch Chief Minister said that he "had a list of 800 missing persons"; Pakistan Human Rights Commission gave the figure of 600; Defence of Human Rights puts it at 1,700; some nationalists at 9000, others even higher, Pakistan Institute for Peace Studies, *Conflict and Insecurity in*

Balochistan (Islamabad: Narratives, 2011), p. 114-15. In a press statement, the Commission on the Inquiry of Enforced Disappearances said that the total number of cases currently stands at 621, a figure contested by Nasrullah Baloch, the chairperson of the NGO, the Voice for Baloch Missing Persons, "23,000 is the number of registered cases. From this, a whole 14,000 came during the current government's tenure." On January 1, 2011, the Commission on Enforced Disappearances reported a total of 138 cases of missing persons. From January 1, 2011 to February 28, 2013, 861 new cases were received by the commission, increasing the total number of cases to 999, out of which 378 cases have been disposed off. Thus, the current balance of the cases under investigation is 621. However, nationalist groups and non-governmental organisations in Balochistan report a much higher figure. "Baloch Missing Persons: 621 or 23,000? A Matter of Contested Figures", *The Express Tribune,* March 9, 2013, http://tribune.com.pk/story/518080/baloch-missing-persons-621-or-23000-a-matter-of-contested-figures/.

92. While exact circumstances of Balach Marri's death were not disclosed, a BLA spokesman said, "Marri might have been killed in an operation inside the Pakistani border" and AFP meanwhile, quoted a local TV channel as saying that "Marri had been killed in Afghanistan", "Balach Mari killed: BLA", *Daily Times,* November 22,2007, http://www.dailytimes.com.pk/default.asp?page=2007%5C11%5C22%5Cstory_22-11-2007_pg1_7; In the 2009 Turbat killings, "The victims were members of the committee that was recently formed by the Government of Pakistan to investigate the case of missing persons in the province, notably abducted UN worker John Solecki," "Balochistan Death Sparks Strikes", *BBC South Asia,* April 10, 2009, http://news.bbc.co.uk/2/hi/south_asia/7993352.stm.

93. Zahid Ghishkori, "Violence is on the rise in Balochistan: Report", *The Express Tribune,* January 2013, http://tribune.com.pk/story/488311/violence-is-on-the-rise-in-balochistan-report/.

94. Human Rights Commission of Pakistan, Balochistan, Blinkered Slide into Chaos: Report of an HRCP fact-finding mission (Lahore: June 2011), 35–42, http://www.hrcp-web.org/pdf/balochistanreport 2011.pdf

95. Zahid Ghishkori," Violence is on the Rise in Balochistan: Report", *The Express Tribune,* January 2013, http://tribune.com.pk/story/488311/violence-is-on-the-rise-in-balochistan-report/

96. Selig Harrison, "Pakistan: State of the Union", Special report, (Washington DC: Center for International Policy, April, 2009), p. 21, http://www.ciponline.org/images/uploads/publications/pakistan_the_state_of_the_union.pdf.

97. It said, "After rationalization of gas revenue receipts for Balochistan, the District or Agency from which gas or oil is being produced should be given at least 15 per cent of the revenue received by the provincial government 'and that ensuring maximum provincial representation' should be ensured immediately on the boards of PPL, OGDC, and Sui Southern: Privatisation of PPL should be brought to the CCI; and require that oil and gas companies should invest five per cent of total expenditures on social sector projects; and that areas where gas is produced should get gas on a priority basis". Senate of Pakistan, *Report of the Senate Committee on Balochistan,* Report no. 7, November2007, http://www.senate.gov.pk/uploads/documents/1308267066_685.pdf.

98. Selig Harrison, "Pakistan: State of the Union", Special report, (Washington DC: Center

for International Policy, April, 2009), http://www.ciponline.org/images/uploads/publications/pakistan_the_state_of_the_union.pdf, p 21.

99. Shafqat Tanveer Mirza writes that for the first time, the slogan of local and non-local was raised in Multan in 1962 elections by Sajjad Qureshi, who took on Frooq Sheikh, a Punjabi speaking from Chiniot. Sajjad Qureshi raised the point that Multani is a separate language. Shafqat Tanvir Mirza, "The origin and politics of the Seraiki movement", *Dawn*, May 24, 2009, http://www.dawn.com/news/881086/the-origin-and-politics-of-the-seraiki-movement.
100. Nukhbah Taj Langah, "The Discontents of Seraiki Nationalism", *The Friday Times.* June 07-13, 2013, vol. XXV, no. 17, http://www.thefridaytimes.com/beta3/tft/article.php?issue=20130607&page=13.
101. Riaz Missen, "Seraiki Nationalism in Focus", *Dawn*, May 02, 2009, http://www.dawn.com/news/881140/seraiki-nationalism-in-focus
102. Alyssa Ayres, *Speaking Like a State: Language and Nationalism in Pakistan*, (Cambridge: Cambridge University Press, 2009), p. 58.
103. In 2009 Abdul Qayyum Jatoi, a PPP MNA from Muzaffargarh and also Federal Minister for Defence Production, asked the government to create a Saraiki province by August 14 that year and threatened to launch a movement if the demand was not met. "Seraiki National Alliance Demands Separate Province" *The News*, June 19, 2011, http://www.thenews.com.pk/TodaysPrintDetail.aspx?ID=53353&Cat=7
104. Umbreen Javaid, "Saraiki Political Movement; Its impact in South Punjab", *Journal of Research Humanities*, vol. 40, no. 2, (July 2004), pp. 50-51.
105. "The Origin and Politics of Seraiki Movement", *Dawn*, May 24, 2009, http://www.dawn.com/news/881086/the-origin-and-politics-of-the-seraiki-movement/2emerged. According to Tariq Rahman, this was based on the successful model of MQM.
106. Muhammad Feyyaz, "Demand for a Seraiki Province in Pakistan", *Background Paper*, (Islamabad: Institute for Legislative Development and Transparency, 2011), p. 10.
107. Raja Asghar, "Fury in PPP over Ally's Provinces Bill", *Dawn*, February 08, 2012, http://www.dawn.com/news/693795/fury-in-ppp-over-allys-provinces-bill.
108. Yasmin Roofiand Khawaja Alqama, "Ethnic Dilemma in Pakistan and Division of Punjab: End or Beginning of the New Era of Conflict", Journal of Politics and Law, vol. 6, no. 1, (2013), p. 159.
109. Yasmin Roofi and Khawaja Alqama, "Ethnic Dilemma in Pakistan and Division of Punjab: End or Beginning of the New Era of Conflict", *Journal of Politics and Law*, vol. 6, no. 1, (2013), pp. 158-159.
110. "More provinces to strengthen country", *The News*, Online International Edition, January 30, 2011, http://www.thenews.com.pk/article-10333-More-provinces-to-strengthen-country.
111. Ali Tahir, "Why Divide Punjab?" *The Express Tribune*, January 10, 2012, http://blogs.tribune.com.pk/story/9711/why-divide-punjab/.
112. Ayesha Jalal, *Democracy and Authoritarianism in South Asia: A Contemporary Perspective* (Cambridge: Cambridge University Press, 1995); Iftikhar H. Malik, *State and Civil Society in Pakistan: Politics of Authority, Ideology, and Ethnicity* (New York: St. Martin's Press, 1997). Theodore P. Wright, Jr., "Indian Muslim Refugees in the Politics of Pakistan," *Journal of Commonwealth and Comparative Politics*, vol. 13, (July 1974), pp. 189-205, 200; J. Rehman, "Self-Determination, State-Building and the Muhajirs: An

International Legal Perspective of the Role of Indian Muslim Refugees in the Constitutional Development of Pakistan," *Contemporary South Asia*, vol. 3, no. 2 (1994), pp. 111-129.

113. Walker Connor, "When is a Nation", *Ethnic and Racial Studies*, vol. 13, no. 1, (1990), p. 92.
114. SaropIjaz, "Knowing Thyself", *The Express Tribune*, December 26, 2013, http://tribune.com.pk/story/648765/knowing-thyself/.
115. Ilhan Niaz, "Identities and the State of Pakistan: A Study in Mentality", *Asian Affairs*, vol. 43, no. 3, (2012), p. 462.
116. Kashif Zafar, "New Federating Units: Bahawalpur Politicians Oppose Seraiki Province", *The Express Tribune*, July 02, 2011, http://tribune.com.pk/story/200696/new-federating-units-bahawalpur-politicians-oppose-seraiki-province/
117. Saroop Ijaz, "So What is Our 'Pakistani' Identity?" *The Express Tribune*, July 11, 2014, http://tribune.com.pk/story/202975/so-what-is-our-pakistani-identity/.
118. Samina Yasmeen, "Pakistan, Militancy and Identity: Parallel Struggles", *Australian Journal of International Affairs*, vol. 67, no. 2, (2013), p. 157.

5

Radicalisation in Pakistan

Alok Bansal

The attack on Army Public School in Peshawar on 16 December 2014, where terrorists from Tehrik-e Taliban Pakistan (TTP) killed 141 people including 132 school children, shows that the terrorists are willing to stoop to any level to achieve their perceived objectives.[1] The manner in which the terrorists tried to justify their dastardly actions quoting incidents from Islamic lexicon showed the level of radicalisation in Pakistan.[2] The repeated cycle of suicide blasts across Pakistan, continuing sectarian violence in Sindh and Quetta, and incidents of crowd meting out instant justice are indicative of the growing trend of intolerance and religious fundamentalism in the Pakistani Society. The fact that an ideology can motivate a person to wilfully end one's life, in quest of his or her objectives shows the extent of one's motivation and is often termed as Radicalism in popular parlance. The 2013 elections have further accentuated the radicalisation, as the right wing political parties, which have advocated softer approach towards Taliban, triumphed in the elections. The fact that Tehrik-e-Taliban Pakistan (TTP) could prevent three 'secular' parties, who had been part of the government, from campaigning in 2013 elections, shows the power that it wields in Pakistan. Both Pakistan Muslim League-Nawaz (PML-N), which emphatically won the elections, as well as Pakistan Tehrik-i-Insaaf (PTI), which polled the second largest number of votes have supported negotiations with Taliban, which implies some sort of accommodation with the dreaded terror outfit.

Radicalism, like terrorism or fundamentalism, does not have a globally accepted definition and the usage of the term has often varied with time and according to the perceptions of individuals. It is generally defined as holding or following of radical or extreme views or principles or practices. Thus, the term is an offshoot of the word "Radical", which according to Encyclopaedia Britannica was first used by the English Whig parliamentarian James Fox in 1797, when he asked for "radical reform" of the electoral system. Consequently, its initial usage pertained to calling all those supporting the movement for parliamentary reforms as Radicals. The word was first used in a political sense in the 18th century Great Britain and was initially confined to the upper and middle classes. Subsequently, in early 19th century, when the labourers and artisans joined the protests for parliamentary reforms, they were called as "popular radicals". Contrary to current usage, in many European and Latin American countries, Radicalism evolved as a variant of Liberalism. Sometimes, it has been less doctrinaire and more moderate, whilst at other times, it has been more extreme. Many radical parties were formed by left wing liberals in Europe and other parts of the world.

According to Collins English Thesaurus, the word "Radical" is generally used as an adjective for extreme, complete, entire, sweeping, violent, severe, excessive, thorough or drastic. It is also used to denote an extremist, fanatic, militant or revolutionary. Webster Learner's Dictionary, defines Radicalism as radical political ideas and behaviour or the opinions and behaviour of people, who favour extreme changes, especially in government. According to the *Journal for the Study of Radicalism* published by the Michigan University Press, defining 'radicalism' has been a troublesome proposition and in the absence of a universally accepted definition, the journal considers it to be an idea that "applies to those, who seek sudden social transformation, often, though not always, through violent means. But of course, there are also those, who question the very basis of a society, as well as those, who can be described as reactionary." For the purpose of this paper, Radicalism is broadly defined as an extreme world view, backed by aggression, force and possibly violence, which also encompasses complete rejection of alternate view points and has extremely low tolerance for ambiguity.

Consequently, in the case of Pakistan, terms like fundamentalism and extremism are often substitutable with radicalism and Talibanisation is one of the major manifestations of radicalism.

Radicalisation in Pakistan is not only challenging the writ of the state and its institutions, it is also accentuating the sectarian divide and aggravating the persecution of minorities. Taliban has been controlling large tracts of land in Federally Administered Tribal Area (FATA) and some parts of Khyber Pakhtoonkhwa (KP), where the writ of the government and its institutions has been virtually absent. Of late, it has started asserting similar control over parts of Karachi, where political parties, not supportive of Taliban ideology, have been forced to close down offices and population not amenable to their ideas has been pushed out. This has been the clearest manifestation of the level to which the state has ceded its authority in Pakistan. Similarly, the sectarian violence in the first six months of 2013 claimed over 500 lives. The minorities have been targeted frequently under the garb of blasphemy laws. Attack on All Saints Church in Peshawar on 22 September 2013 was also a manifestation of growing intolerance of minorities. A mentally deranged man was burnt inside the police lockup in Bahawalpur district by an irate crowd for allegedly indulging in blasphemy. There have been numerous cases, where mere accusation of blasphemy has led to murder of the accused. These are clear pointers towards a rapidly radicalising polity.

Radicalisation in Pakistan is nothing, but a natural manifestation of the 'Two Nation Theory', which automatically made religion the central issue in the new state. It is popularly believed that radicalism is a consequence of General Zia-ul-Haq's policies of Islamisation to legitimise his regime and American instigated, Saudi funded and ISI operated 'jihad' in Afghanistan. However, the truth is that the process of radicalisation had started right from the time Pakistan came into existence and Zia only accelerated it. The idea of Pakistan was not very popular in the region that eventually came to constitute Pakistan; consequently, successive Pakistani governments have used religion to justify the call for Pakistan. Moreover, having been established on the basis of religion, it has always been difficult for the state to deemphasize Islam from governance. The Objectives Resolution adopted by the Constituent Assembly of Pakistan in March 1949 vested the sovereignty with Allah alone. This gave the *Ulema* a permanent right to veto any parliamentary resolution, if they perceived it to be against their understanding of Islam. This ensured that religion acquired a permanent place in the body politic of the state. Zulfiqar Ali Bhutto, generally perceived to be a secular politician, furthered the process of radicalisation by banning alcohol and giving state the "Right of Taqfir".[3]

Afghan Jihad and General Zia's religious proclivities furthered the process of radicalisation. He institutionalised the religious interface into the functioning of state and its various organs. It was during his rule that the sectarian divide also came into its own and various armed sectarian outfits emerged on the Pakistani horizon. His actions radicalised society, and coupled with Pakistan's perceived geopolitical interests in Afghanistan, led to the creation of Taliban. Similar process was replicated against India and radical Islamic outfits were used to further Pakistan's perceived interests in Jammu and Kashmir. Consequently, these outfits were allowed to carry out their radical Islamic propaganda and recruitment with the tacit connivance of the state. Emergence of TTP and its subsequent accommodation by the state has provided further fillip to the process of radicalisation and, today, no institution of the state is immune to the virus of radicalisation. It even threatens the cohesion of the Pakistan Army, which is believed to be the only functioning institution in the country. The paper aims to look at the growing radicalisation and cult of violence in Pakistan, which has acquired dangerous levels.

Pakistan Movement and the Initial Years

The 'Two Nation Theory' has been the main contributor to radicalism in Pakistan, right from the time of its inception, and even earlier, it was instrumental in leading the demand for Pakistan. The theory that led to the partition of India and creation of Pakistan, propounded that the Muslims of the Sub-continent were a separate nation and could not stay with others in a unified nation. As the Indian National Congress, the party leading the movement for Indian independence was opposed to the partition and asserted that different communities in India have been living in harmony for centuries; the Muslim League highlighted the separateness. Their whole argument was premised on the belief that Muslims of the sub-continent always had a distinct culture and had prevented its assimilation in the predominant Hindu culture of India.[4] After independence, to avoid being overwhelmed by the predominant Hindu culture, they needed a separate homeland to lead their life according to their belief. This required them to highlight the uniqueness of Islam and lay emphasis on religion, even though many of their leaders were not overtly religious in their personal life. This resulted in various theological arguments being put in support of the demand for Pakistan.

The whole theory was communally biased and, accordingly, made Islam the central tenet in the new state. Consequently, the state-building process in Pakistan has not been easy. Constitutionally, Pakistan is an Islamic state. Many have argued that Jinnah used the Muslim identity to secure a separate state, but by no means had he aspired for an Islamic state, least of all a theocratic state. Some analysts even state that Mohammad Ali Jinnah, the leader of the Muslim League, wanted a secular state. To support this argument, people often cite his speech of 11 August 1947, when he was elected the President of the Constituent Assembly, where he stated that any individual "no matter to what community he belongs, no matter what relations he had with you in the past, no matter what is his colour, caste or creed, is first, second and last a citizen of this State with equal rights, privileges and obligations".[5] He went on to add that the religion of an individual was not the business of the state and asserted that the minorities were free to visit their places of worship.[6] However, in March 1948, in an address to the Bar Association in Karachi, he unambiguously asserted that Pakistan will be an Islamic state adhering to the principles of *Shariah*. It needs to be appreciated that Jinnah was not an ideologue or a visionary; he was just a brilliant lawyer, who used different arguments at different times to advance his case.[7] Many believe that religion hardly mattered for Jinnah, but nothing could be further from truth. There is no doubt that Jinnah, who drank, ate pork and hardly prayed, was fairly secular in his personal life. However, it must be appreciated that he was born in the Ismaili faith, but converted to the IthnaIshari (Twelver Shia) faith in his later life.[8] This clearly shows that religion was by no means irrelevant for him. His speech of 11 August 1947 must be seen in a context, as it was made at a time when Pakistan did not want the entire Muslim population from India to migrate to the newly created state. At that point of time, the Government of Pakistan also did not want the wholesale migration of non-Muslims from Pakistan, as they controlled the economy and bureaucracy.[9] More significantly, on

14 August 1947, during the formal transfer of power, when Lord Mountbatten, during his speech to the Constituent Assembly, suggested Akbar as the role model for the state of Pakistan, Jinnah rejected it out of hand and stated that Pakistan had a better role model, the Prophet.[10] Since then, the state, which was established on the basis of religion, has been looking at various Islamic role models and it has become virtually impossible for the state to deemphasize Islam from governance.

After Jinnah's death, the state gave up even its pretence of secularism. The Objectives Resolution adopted by the Constituent Assembly of Pakistan in March 1949 vested the sovereignty with Allah alone. It was incorporated into the Constitution as an annexure and stated:

> "Whereas sovereignty over the entire universe belongs to Allah Almighty alone and the authority which He has delegated to the State of Pakistan, through its people for being exercised within the limits prescribed by Him is a sacred trust; This Constituent Assembly representing the people of Pakistan resolves to frame a Constitution for the sovereign independent State of Pakistan; Wherein the State shall exercise its powers and authority through the chosen representatives of the people; Wherein the principles of democracy, freedom, equality, tolerance and social justice as enunciated by Islam shall be fully observed; Wherein the Muslims shall be enabled to order their lives in the individual and collective spheres in accordance with the teachings and requirements of Islam as set out in the Holy Quran and the Sunnah."[11]

This only gave the *Ulema* a right to veto any parliamentary resolution, if they perceived that it was against their understanding of Islam. This ensured that religion acquired a permanent place in the body politic of the state. In the initial years, it did serve a crucial purpose, as the idea of Pakistan was not very popular in the region that came to constitute it. Successive governments propagated the idea of an all-inclusive Islamic identity with the aim of subsuming the ethnic identities of various groups residing within its boundaries. The official history that was taught in the schools depicted Pakistan as an Islamic entity totally disconnected with Hindu India and consequentially disregarded ethnic, cultural or linguistic identities.[12]

At the time of its creation, the biggest threat to nascent Pakistani nationalism emanated from the ethnic aspirations of its residents, more so from Pakhtoon nationalism, which had successfully countered the appeal of Pakistan movement during the 1946 elections under the British. Consequentially, in order to nip this grave threat in the bud, an all-inclusive Islamic identity was promoted to subsume the ethnic identities of the citizens. Of various parts of Pakistan, radical elements grew roots in Pakhtoon territories of Federally Administered Tribal Areas (FATA), which had been virtually autonomous under the British rule. The biggest challenge to Pakistani nationalism in 1947 emanated from the quest for a separate home land by the Pakhtoon nationalists. Consequently, the first political step of the Pakistan government was to sack the secular Congress Government of North West Frontier Province (NWFP),[13] headed by Dr Khan Saheb, the elder brother of Khan Abdul Ghaffar Khan.

After the dismissal of the provincial government, in order to counter Pakhtoon nationalism, the security establishment helped the religious political parties and *Mullahs* to spread their influence in the Pakhtoon belt. Thus, the seeds of radicalisation in the Pakhtoon belt of Pakistan were sown in 1947 itself. To further weaken the Pakhtoon nationalism and to fragment the Pakhtoons, FATA was not merged with NWFP or brought into the political mainstream and was kept frozen in a medieval milieu. In FATA, in the absence of any social, political and economic development and with state sponsored religious indoctrination, the environment was extremely conducive for radicalisation of the society, which eventually manifested itself in the form of Taliban. The process was fairly successful in countering Pakhtoon nationalism, but in due course, it gave rise to a bigger Frankenstein, that of radical Islam.

After the Objectives Resolution, which gave Islam a pre-eminent position in the state, the next step was to define the Muslim identity. At an Ahrar Conference in Rawalpindi on May 01, 1949, a public demand was made to declare Ahmediyas as non-Muslims. After the Rawalpindi conference, the voices for declaring them non-Muslims began growing and became shriller. On January 15, 1950, a meeting of Ahmediyas was pelted with stones. Subsequently, at various public meetings, Ahmediyas were declared as apostates and it was hinted that the just punishment for apostasy was death. Sporadic cases of violence against Ahmediyas started and by January 1953, there were strong demands for declaring Ahmediyas as non-Muslims.[14] On January 21, 1953, Khwaja Nazimuddin, the then Prime Minister of Pakistan, was delivered an ultimatum in Karachi by a deputation of *Ulema* to declare Ahmediyas as non-Muslims and to remove Chaudhry Zafarullah Khan, who was the Foreign Minister, and other high ranking Ahmediyas from office within one month. The ultimatum was rejected and leaders of the parties, who were making these demands, were arrested. However, this resulted in wide-spread rioting in Punjab and the situation became so grim that the army had to be called in and the city of Lahore had to be placed under Martial Law for over two months. Subsequently, the Government of Punjab, in June 1953, constituted a judicial commission comprising of Justice Munir and Justice Kayani to inquire into the circumstances that led to the disturbances. The Commission sat from July 1953 till February 1954 and submitted its report on April 10, 1954.[15]

One of the significant observations of the judicial commission was that it was not feasible to infer whether Ahmediyas were Muslims, as no two *Ulemas* could agree on the basic definition of a Muslim.[16] The court inferred that "no two learned divines are agreed on this fundamental. If we attempt our own definition as each learned divine has done and that definition differs from that given by all others, we unanimously go out of the fold of Islam."[17] The report warned about the emerging ideological dangers and cautioned against the idea of projecting Pakistan as an Islamic state and the state attempting to define as to who is a Muslim. Alas! The warning was not heeded. In 1965, during the first indirectly organised presidential elections when Fatima Jinnah was contesting against Ayub Khan, his cronies got a fatwa issued that Islam did not allow a female head of state. In due course, such attempts to use Islam to delegitimise individuals assumed monstrous proportions.[18]

Although, the government in the fifties and sixties withstood the pressure from radical elements to declare Ahmediyas as non-Muslims, the demands for the excommunication of Ahmediyas and other minority sects from Islam started gathering steam. This period also saw the persecution of minorities and their migration from Pakistan. The centrality of Islam within the state and its structures kept rising, although the process of radicalisation was relatively slow outside the tribal belt.

Liberation of Bangladesh and the Bhutto Era

General Yahya Khan, who succeeded Ayub Khan as the President, focussed on using the Islamic identity to maintain unity and to defend Pakistan. Accordingly, religious parties were encouraged to attack Yahya's opponents both in the Western as well as Eastern wing of Pakistan as enemies of Islam. The liberation war of Bangladesh was projected by Yahya as a struggle for Pakistan's Islamic identity, which was under threat from the corrupted Bengali Muslims of East Pakistan and Hindu India. General Niazi, who led the Pakistani forces in the Eastern Wing, urged dedication to Islam and invoked the spirit of *jihad* to defeat the enemy, whose only aim was the disintegration of the Islamic Republic. To pursue these ideals, the Jamaat-e-Islami was encouraged to set up two counter-insurgency outfits in the Eastern Wing. Yahya stated that Pakistan's enemies wanted to undo their country, whose people's life was "pulsating with love of the Holy Prophet" and proclaimed that every person in Pakistan was a *Mujahid*. Despite Yahya Khan's liberal use of Islamic ideology and symbolism to defend Pakistan's integrity and ideology, 1971 war was catastrophic for Pakistan and led to the breaking away of more populous Eastern Wing and almost 80,000 Pakistani soldiers becoming prisoners of war.[19]

The loss of the Eastern Wing had a tremendous impact on Pakistani psyche; not only did it negate the 'Two Nation Theory', it also dented the national pride, as the masses had always been indoctrinated about the myths of an imaginary glorious past. However, rather than learning from history, the Pakistani masses were made to believe that Pakistan's defeat and disintegration had been brought about by non-adherence to Islamic tenets by the ruling elite.[20] Consequently, religion gained further significance and the Two Nation Theory, rather than being discarded, was used with renewed vigour in a new direction.

This theory that propagated exclusion required an object of hate; during the Pakistan movement, it was the Hindu majority and subsequently, even after the creation of Pakistan, most of the ills plaguing the country were blamed on them. So much so that even the Bangladesh crisis was blamed on the corrupting influence of Hindu Bengali. After the separation of Eastern Wing, when the numbers of non-Muslims became insignificant in Pakistan, the fanatic adherents of the exclusivist 'Two Nation Theory' turned their ire towards their co-religionists, who differed from their own version of Islam. Consequently, violence was used to settle scores not only between Shias and Sunnis, but also between different strands of the same sect.

Meanwhile in 1974, the Pakistani State acquired the Right of Taqfir and declared Ahmediyas as non-Muslims by a constitutional amendment.[21] Since then, there have been repeated demands for declaring adherents of various other sects and sub-sects as apostates.

Despite his secular convictions, Zulfiqar Ali Bhutto used religion to revive the flagging national morale. He did so by acquiring the nuclear technology and talking of the Islamic Bomb. He made deliberate efforts to improve relations with Muslim oil producing states, who had hit the oil jackpot only recently. In February 1974, Pakistan hosted the second summit of the Organisation of the Islamic Conference (OIC) with grandeur. It was used to seek credit from friendly Arab states to soften the blow of the global oil shock for the cash starved economy of Pakistan. This period also saw a large migration of Pakistani nationals to these oil rich states to work. They sent to Pakistan valuable remittances that shored up Pakistan's foreign exchange reserves, but also brought back an admiration for a more puritanical version of Islam. The manner in which the Islamic Organisation of Petroleum Exporting Countries (OPEC) countries, who are predominantly Muslim, withstood the pressure from the West led by the United States, won them the admiration of Pakistani middle classes. They saw this as a global reassertion of Islam and consequently, "sought to emulate the Saudi variant of Wahabi Islam."[22] Bhutto also started supporting two Islamic anti-government militias, Jamiat-e-Islami and Hizb-e-Islami to pressurise the Afghan government.[23] This led to greater radicalisation in territories along the Afghan border. At the same time, along with the remittances, the Islamic charities from the Middle East also started sending in funds and this resulted in mushrooming of *Madaris* across Pakistan, which started propagating Islam that was prevalent there.

Under relentless onslaught from the religious political parties for his socialist policies, which were considered as anti-Islam, Bhutto graduated on to the concept of 'Islamic socialism' and churned out a narrative that used "core Islamic principles of justice, equity, and poverty" to alleviate poverty and to tackle socio-economic challenges of Pakistan. With the passage of time, as the challenge from Islamic political parties increased, he kept turning more and more conservative and pandered to the religious political parties. He took several steps that enforced the primacy of Islam, weakened the secular structure of state and irrevocably enhanced the pace of radicalisation in Pakistan. He banned liquor, shifted weekly holiday to Friday, appointed a Minister for religious affairs in the central cabinet and invited the *Imams* of Mosques in Mecca and Madina to visit Pakistan.[24] He also officially renamed, Pakistan as an Islamic Republic, established a Council of Islamic Ideology and provided state funding for the poor *Imams* in various mosques. To further aggravate the sectarian tensions, he decried that the school syllabi for Shias and Sunnis should be different.[25] However, his most damaging step was the introduction of Taqfir in the body politic of Pakistan. When parties like Jamaat-e-Islami used the call of Saudi ideologues to demand excommunication of Ahmediyas from the fold of Islam, Bhutto conceded the demand and declared them a minority, thereby undermining their claim as equal citizens of Pakistan.[26] This opened the flood gates and since then, there have been numerous demands to declare adherents of various sects and sub-sects of Islam as heretics. The sectarian violence gathered steam and has become a grave threat to the unity of Pakistan.

More significantly, this period saw drastic changes in the orientation of the Pakistani Armed Forces. They turned more conservative and with the banning of liquor, the atmosphere in the hitherto 'secular' officers' messes transformed irrevocably, with Islamic practices making slow and steady ingress and separation of sexes. The entire nature of the social interaction amongst officers changed irrevocably and Islamic lexicon governed the military discourse. Islamic ideology made rapid ingress into what was till then largely 'secular' Armed Forces of Pakistan. Bhutto also appointed an avowed Islamist, General Zia-ul-Haq as the Chief of Army Staff, who changed the Army's motto to 'Faith, Piety and *Jihad*' from 'Unity, Faith and Discipline' as given by Jinnah.[27]

Zia's Islamisation Drive

General Zia-ul-Haq deposed Bhutto after the street demonstrations against him organised by the religious political parties started turning violent with amazing regularity. After seizing power, Zia sought legitimacy through the liberal use of terms from the Islamic lexicon. He called himself a 'soldier of Islam' and asserted that Pakistan was created on the basis of Islam and could survive only as long as it stuck to Islam and, therefore, felt that the Islamic system was an essential prerequisite for Pakistan. He believed that

Islam was a revolutionary process that could transform Pakistan and there "ushered in an era of religious obscurantism that affected every facet of domestic life and foreign policy".[28]

Zia was deeply influenced by the violence that he witnessed during the partition in 1947, which shaped his thinking vis-a-vis India. After capturing power, he began the process of Islamisation by changing the laws to make them in conformity with the holy Koran. Many believed that his Islamisation drive was more for effect, but he nevertheless put the laws on books, which keep haunting Pakistan to this day. His rule created permanent fissures in Pakistan, by imposing harsher Islamic law and active support to Afghan *Mujahedeen*, which introduced the Kalashnikov culture in Pakistan. Zia sincerely believed that Pakistan, like Israel, was created on religious basis, needed Islam and its ideology for cohesion and felt that the country would disintegrate without its binding force.[29]

Zia went about systematically Islamising all the major institutions of the government. In army, apart from changing the slogan to incorporate *Jihad*, he also introduced a column for assessing religious sincerity in officers' annual confidential reports. More significantly, Deobandi proselytising groups like Tablighi Jamat were accorded greater access to the military officers. He also used the Islamic political parties to counter political opposition and went to the extent of appointing many of their members as ministers. He introduced separate electorate for minorities, thereby ensuring their complete political marginalisation. In judiciary, he introduced *Shariat* benches at the High Court and an appellate *Shariat* Bench at the level of Supreme Court to determine if a particular legislation was in conformity with Islam. His most regressive step was to introduce the *Hudood* Ordinance, which sanctioned medieval punishments like flogging, stoning and amputation.[30]

Islamic zeal also governed Zia's foreign policy of bringing Afghanistan under Pakistan's influence. Confluence of Pakistan's perceived strategic interests with the US attempts to weaken its Cold War adversary made Pakistan the staging ground for launching Islamic warriors into Afghanistan.[31] The Saur Revolution in Afghanistan and the subsequent movement of Soviet Army into Afghanistan led to large scale migration of Afghan nationals East of Durand Line. They had familial ties and shared common traditions and culture with those residing in FATA and KP. They were housed in camps, which harboured the Islamic warriors fighting the Soviets, who were staying in the camps in Waziristan Agency near Miramshah, from where they would cross the Durand Line to take up arms against the Afghan government forces.[32] General Zia's regime in Pakistan, which had made no secret of its Islamist leanings, welcomed the refugees with open arms to emphasise its solidarity with the Islamic *Ummah*.[33]

The refugees were settled by the Pakistani authorities on the basis of ethnic and tribal affiliations to prevent as much antagonism as possible. Moreover, numerous Islamic fighters from the Arab world and other Muslim countries joined the Afghans to participate in a war, which the West had propagated as the 'holy war' against the infidel Soviets. These *Mujahedeens* were trained by the ISI, funded by Saudi Arabia and armed by the US. Zia felt that this *Jihad* could usher in "a new era of greatness for the Muslim nations of Asia and Africa". To pursue these objectives, Zia started propagating in Pakistan an extreme variant of Islamic ideology. Islamic political parties like Jamaat-e-Islami and Jamiat Ulema-e-Islam became key allies of the government in recruiting Afghan refugees to become *Mujahedeens*. In the process, these parties not only expanded their presence across Pakistan, but also wielded enormous power on account of their proximity with power. Poor students from all over Pakistan were enrolled into *Madaris*, where they were taught only an obscurantist version of Islam, without any modern subjects. This process of indoctrination included preparation of textbooks with violent images and militant teachings and was funded by the US and Saudi Arabia. Zia encouraged Islamic warriors from across the globe to come into Pakistan and set up shop. Zia's fascination with bringing Afghanistan under Pakistan's sphere of influence turned the latter into a global hub of *Jihadi* terrorism.[34]

Zia's 'Islamisation' rendered Islam into a divisive force, pitting secular against religious forces, Sunni against Shia and Muslim against non-Muslims. He not only encouraged the religious organisations, he also helped create many *Jihadi* militias to further Pakistan's perceived interests in Afghanistan and Kashmir. Many of these, in due course, transformed themselves into sectarian monsters. In his zeal to Islamise the society, he introduced laws and measures in accordance with conservative Sunni interpretations of Islam.[35] He made any disrespect to the companions of the prophet (Sahabahs), a cognisable offence (Some Shias indulge in Tabarra, criticism of first three caliphs, who were Sahabahs). Meanwhile, the Iranian Revolution of 1979 established an Islamic Republic dominated by Shia theocracy and it gave a renewed confidence to the Shia masses across the Islamic world. Persecuted for centuries under the Sunni dominated regimes, the revolution invigorated the Shia masses far beyond the Iranian borders. It also led to the resurgence of Shia thought across Pakistan. Till then, most Shias in Pakistan did not know their rituals that differentiated them from Sunnis, even though their mosques, graveyards, namaz and many festivals had been different from Sunnis. Consequent to the revolution, many Shias in Pakistan started going through the collection of Shia Hadiths that had not been translated from Persian and Arabic. As a result, when Zia ordered that *Zakat* be collected centrally and deducted from individual bank accounts; it was vehemently opposed by the Shias. They asserted that their faith did not allow them to pay *Zakat* to the state; instead they were required to pay *Khums* to their clergy, which was twice the amount Sunnis paid. The Shias protested en-masse in Islamabad and in one of the rare occasions, Zia backtracked and exempted Shias from paying *Zakat*.[36] The Shias were now required to tell the bankers their faith so as to prevent *Zakat* from being deducted. This led to an identity formation and many Shias, who were ambivalent regarding their faith, also started identifying themselves as Shias. More significantly, as Census are not conducted on the basis of sect; the bank records became a means of identifying Shias.

During this period, threatened by Iranian revolution, Saudi rulers intensified their efforts to export Sunni-Wahabi Islamism to other parts of the Muslim world. Pakistan, thus, became the main battleground in Iran-Saudi battle. The *Jihadis*, supported and trained in Pakistan to resist the Soviets, received Saudi financial backing and, thus, assumed anti-Shia undertones. This aggravated the sectarian conflict in Pakistan, with Saudi Arabia spending millions of dollars to fund radical Sunni outfits in Pakistan and the rise of Ayatollah Khomeini galvanising the Pakistani Shia.[37] A number of Sunni political parties, including Jamiat-ul-Ulema-i-Islam (JUI), now began employing aggressive anti-Shia rhetoric, declaring many Shia practices to be in violation of the Islamic belief system.[38] The Shia community's increasing reliance on Teheran to organise and assert its demands created uneasiness within the Pakistani military and led to demands by extremist Sunni groups to declare Pakistan as a Sunni state and the Shias as heretics.[39] To curb Shia assertiveness, Zia and his intelligence agencies authorised and sponsored Haq Nawaz Jhangvi, Vice President of JUI in Punjab, to establish a new anti-Shia outfit called Sipah-e-Sahaba (SSP).[40] Jhangvi launched a virulent anti-Shia campaign in Jhang, where Shia landlords dominated the political and economic landscape. The small traders and poor farmers of the area, who were Sunnis, joined his campaign. Conservative Deobandi and Ahle-Hadith *Madaris* in the region provided many activists and leaders for this cause and created an environment conducive to violence.[41] In the wake of these developments, an Iran-educated, charismatic cleric named Allama Arif Hussain al-Hussaini decided to set up a Shia religious political party in 1987. This alarmed Zia as well as the Saudis and led to Shia-Sunni clashes in Hussaini's hometown of Parachinar in 1987. Hussaini was assassinated on August 5, 1988 in Peshawar, allegedly at the behest of President Zia. Many in the Shia community also openly accused the governor of the NWFP, Lt. Gen. Fazle Haq of being involved in the murder. Haq was killed by unknown gunmen in 1991. Twelve days after Hussaini's death, President Zia's plane crashed as a result of sabotage, killing him and many senior army officers, along with the U.S. ambassador to Pakistan and the U.S. Defence Attaché, who were also on board. While Zia's death is shrouded in mystery, many believe it to be the handiwork of Shia groups.

Birth of Taliban to 9/11

Many of the foreign fighters invited by Zia stayed on in the tribal areas once the conflict in Afghanistan ended. These foreigners married local women and became son-in-laws of the soil. Although the last Soviet troops left Afghanistan on February 15, 1989, Pakistan continued to supply weapon and shelter to *Mujahedeen* in the Pakhtoon belt. Even after General Zia's death, ISI continued to be in the forefront of guiding *Mujahedeen* operations.[42] However, the power in Kabul was annexed by groups that were not under the direct control of ISI and as ISI's attempts to push in its nominee Gulbudin Hekmatyar failed, it created a new force to capture power in Afghanistan – the Taliban.

In October 1994, the city of Kandhar fell to an obscure militia of religious students. The romanticised version of their first combative encounter describes how Mohammed Omar, the local *Mullah* and a former *Mujahedeen,* who had lost his right eye in 1989, was asked to take action against a tyrant military commander. He, therefore, recruited the religious students – the 'taliban' – who executed the tyrant and thereafter began to confront various *Mujahedeen* groups. Talibans were mainly Pakhtoons, who had either, like Mullah Omar, fought the Soviets or had grown up as refugees in various *Madaris* that had been set up in Pakistan with financial assistance from the United States and Saudi Arabia.[43] The Taliban movement derived its recruits from the Pakhtoons of Afghanistan and Pakistan, who had been indoctrinated in Pakistani *Madaris* and were trained and armed by the ISI.[44] It received enormous support from the Pakistani security establishment and this resulted in their astounding successes against the *Mujahedeen.* The Talibans were deliberately fashioned as a military and political force by the ISI for the purpose of installing a client government in Afghanistan that could provide Pakistan strategic depth during times of conflict with India.[45] The reasoning that led to Pakistan's propping up of the Taliban, were similar to their support for Hekmatyar earlier. When it was apparent that Hekmatyar could neither seize Kabul nor sanctify the Durand Line, Pakistan shifted its support to the Taliban. The aim was to exploit a Pakhtoon movement thriving on the popular rejection of the existing political order for the growing chaos and anarchy within the country. Pakistan's establishment perceived that with its puritanical Islamic ideology, the Taliban would bridge Afghan ethnic divisions.[46]

It was perceived that the Taliban would provide Pakistan the strength and confidence to deal with India. Though the concept of 'strategic depth' has not been explained, it appeared that Pakistan wanted to use the Afghan territory to train militants for operations in Kashmir and to set up a government that would not rake up the 'Pakhtoonistan' issue.[47] This need became particularly acute in the 1990s, as war over Kashmir appeared to be a distinct possibility. Pakistan supported insurgency, was escalating in the Kashmir valley. Pakistani support to the Taliban was also due to the dramatic increase in the influence and visibility of Islamist forces in the Pakistani polity. This was the result of Zia-ul-Haq's policy of using Islam to legitimise his regime. An integral part of this strategy was the bestowing of state patronage on fundamentalist religious groups and institutions in order to build support. It also manifested itself in the increasing Islamisation of the officer corps of the armed forces as loyalty to the regime came to be tested on the basis of religiosity and the public observance of Islamic rituals.[48]

By the end of 1996, the Taliban had captured Kabul and were in most of Afghanistan. The Taliban had come to power largely by paying off the leaders of various tribes with Pakistan and to a lesser extent, Saudi money. In a tribal society, tribesmen follow their leader rather than an abstract ideology.[49] A large number of those fighting with the Taliban were Pakistani nationals – students of *Madaris* in tribal Pakistan. This interaction led to the spread of radical ideology in the tribal region, which had not been overtly religious in the past. This marked a significant change and the society in the tribal areas started moving from a tribal society to an Islamic society, where Mulla, an object of derision till then, started gaining in stature and became all powerful.

A huge *Jihad* industry was set up by funding various *Madaris* in NWFP and FATA. These seminaries combined Sunni Wahabism with Deobandi ideology to produce a cocktail of religious bigotry and sectarian hatred.[50] In the sectarian labyrinth of Pakistan, Taliban's alignment with Deobandi-Wahabi combine altered the sectarian power balance irrevocably. This Taliban backed sectarian violence not only targeted Shias whom many Deobandi *Ulemas* had already termed as heretics, but also targeted the majority sub-sect of the sub-continent, the Barelvis, who were not considered as being adequately Islamic. There were retaliations by Barelvis and Shias, but Deobandis being better armed and more significantly better organised, invariably triumphed. The theological complexities of this conflict become quite clear from the attacks on numerous shrines of Sufi saints revered by the Barelvi masses in Khyber Pakhtoonkhwa, Sindh and Punjab.

The emergence of the Taliban government provided a huge psychological boost to their ideological compatriots in Pakistan. It also provided them a safe haven from where they could launch attacks and retreat for rest and recreation. This surge in sectarian violence took place at a time when there was administrative paralysis in Pakistan, as post Zia regimes were generally weak, instable and corrupt. Despite some attempts to rein in the radical genie, Zia's prodigies stuck to their mission of turning Pakistan into an outpost of puritanical Islam being practiced in Saudi Arabia. Soviet defeat in Afghanistan as well as collapse of communism led to the delusion of Islamic grandeur that was harnessed by the ISI to shape Pakistan's security discourse.[51] It also provided inspiration to the radicalised Pakistani youth, who considered it a part of their sacred duty to fight wherever they perceived that there was oppression of Muslims. This led to the privatisation of *Jihad* and armed groups emerged from traditional religious movements to fight for Islam. Consequently starting from 1980s, the country saw mushrooming of 24 armed militant groups operating across Pakistan in pursuance of their internal and external agenda.[52]

The major militant groups were Lashkar-e-Taiba (LeT), Jaish-e-Mohammed (JeM), Harkat-ul-Mujahideen (HuM) and Harkat-al-Jihad-al Islami (HJI). All of them had similar orientation and drew bulk of their recruits from the unemployed youth of Punjab and KP, while HuM and HJI were closely associated with Taliban, the LeT drew support from Wahabi groups in Saudi Arabia. Their growth was not surreptitious, but in full media glare with the connivance of the state. They exhorted the populace to join *Jihad* by catchy slogans like "A martyr ensures salvation for the entire family". They not only collected funds publicly, but also supported the families of these 'martyrs'. They were publishing newsletters, pamphlets as well as producing audio and video tapes. Pakistan's powerful security establishment perceived them as "instruments of Pakistan's regional policy".[53] Consequently, by the time the Al Qaeda attacked the World Trade Centre in New York, there was no dearth of militant groups sympathetic to the Taliban and willing to do its bidding.

War on Terror and Talibanisation of Pakistan

Pakistan drastically changed its policy options in Afghanistan after 9/11. Until then, the ISI had used the Pakhtoon belt to train militants against successive governments in Kabul for over two decades. It had also sponsored an Islamist ideology amongst Pakhtoons residing on both sides of the Durand Line.[54] After the Taliban regime was overthrown, many Taliban and Al-Qaeda cadres, which had hitherto been active in Afghanistan, withdrew into FATA.[55] In due course, they regrouped and moved to the tribal areas to pose a challenge to the new regime in Afghanistan. Slowly, the autonomous tribal belt on Pakistan's border, where the tribal population had already been radicalised, became the refuge for thousands of Taliban and Al Qaeda fighters.[56] Their presence in the region was so visible that in the aftermath of the October 2005 earthquake, Ayman Al Zawahiri appealed for funds to help quake victims even though the "enemy Musharraf's government was agent of the US". This not only helped them garner funds from Islamic charities, but also to improve their standing amongst the local population.[57]

Once the Taliban started attacking Afghan government positions from their safe havens in Waziristan, there was immense pressure on Pakistan not only to disengage from the Taliban, but also to eliminate them and their Al Qaeda allies, which had been considered as the country's "strategic" asset in Afghanistan. Initially, Pakistani forces avoided interfering with them, intending to use them in Afghanistan after the US withdrawal. However, this policy had to change under sustained US pressure when the Pakistani troops were forced to enter South Waziristan Agency in FATA and directed the local Taliban to surrender the foreign militants. The aim was to create a distinction between the local Taliban and Al Qaeda led foreign militants.[58] By 2003, around 80,000 army and paramilitary troops had been deployed in Waziristan.[59] However, instead of going for the militant leadership known to the ISI, the troops moved only in the areas, where militant activity became too visible to hide. Consequently, only the Arabs and the Central Asian militants of no significance to Pakistan were captured or killed.[60] Military operations in South Waziristan started in February 2004 when the U.S. military complained that the territory was not just a hideout for Al Qaeda and Taliban fighters, but also a launching pad for operations in Afghanistan.[61] However, the Pakistan Army suffered heavy casualties, when the Taliban ambushed troops and took officials hostage and as the establishment did not want to completely demolish the potential assets, it sued for peace.[62]

As the Army could not establish the writ of the state, the Pakistan government tried different strategies to control the militants. It struck deals with them in South Waziristan, initially with Nek Mohammed and subsequently with Baitullah Mehsud. In April 2004, the army came to an informal understanding with the local Taliban led by Nek Mohammad at Shakai. The 'Shakai Agreement' allowed Taliban a free run in South Waziristan and numerous other incentives in return for an assurance that foreign militants would not use the territory to launch cross-border attacks.[63] The agreement provided legitimacy to the pro-Taliban militants and destroyed the existing civilian administration led by the political agent in the Agency. The agreement left only two forces in the region; a bruised and demoralised military and a buoyant Taliban. The local Taliban never fulfilled their part of the agreement with respect to the foreign militants.[64]

Nek Mohammad vowed to continue supporting Al Qaeda and other foreign militants and was subsequently killed in a drone attack on June 18, 2004. He was succeeded by Abdullah Mehsud and by this time, South Waziristan had turned into a Taliban citadel and the continuing military operation was resulting in heavy military and civilian casualties. Subsequently, some militant commanders of the South Waziristan *Shura* were paid hefty amounts for relinquishing hostilities.[65] However, each of these deals only helped Taliban to consolidate its position and spread its influence. After Abdullah Mehsud was dead, Baitullah Mehsud took over the reins of Pakistani Taliban and in December 2007 created the Tehrik-e Taliban Pakistan (TTP),[66] a loose conglomerate of 40 radical organisations aligned with Taliban.[67]

The peace deals signed by authorities not only enhanced the stature of the militants in a tribal society, but also provided them a fortress to consolidate and propagate their ideology. The radical ideology espoused by Taliban spread from South Waziristan to North Waziristan and the state once again failed to deal with the menace militarily and acquiesced to sign another peace deal with the radicalised militants termed as Miramshah Agreement on September 5, 2006.[68] However, like previous attempts in South Waziristan, it failed to usher in peace.

The Miramshah agreement virtually ceded state authority to the Taliban in North Waziristan. The government, in accordance with its policy of accommodation with the militants, also wanted to strike another deal with the Taliban in Bajaur Agency, but a drone attack on the militants by the US on the eve of the peace deal scuttled it. By 2006, Bajaur and Mohmand agencies in FATA and the adjoining regions in NWFP and Balochistan had come under the influence of the radical groups aligned with Taliban. Various peace deals showed the state's unwillingness to counter the radical thought. It also accepted by its with-drawal the creep-ing Talibanisation of the tribal areas. Subsequent murder of tribal leaders, who had cooperated with the government, ensured complete supremacy of the Taliban in the region. It allowed the Taliban to enforce their ideology in FATA, the adjacent districts of KP and to use violence against those, who dared to oppose them.[69]

The year 2007 saw a sharp geographical expansion of the areas affected by Islamic radicalism and militancy in NWFP. In the aftermath of Lal Masjid operations in Islamabad, Tehrik-e-Nifaz-e-Shariat-e-Mohammadi (TNSM), led by Maulana Fazalullah, which had allied with the Taliban and had set up a FM radio station to propagate their views, virtually took over the entire Swat Valley. Despite the presence of over 3000 troops, the Taliban not only captured the region but also appointed its own administrators. A large number of troops and policemen surrendered and a large number of them were captured by the militants. All these personnel were released after being disarmed. Subsequently, Taliban expanded their operations to hitherto peaceful regions, like the Orakzai Agency in FATA and Lower Dir district in NWFP.

The Taliban also adopted an aggressive posture and started attacking security forces in their strongly held citadels in FATA. Sararogha Fort in South Waziristan, Ladha Fort and Seplatoi Fort in North Waziristan, Darra Adamkhel, the town well-known for manufacturing arms and the 1.6 Km long Kohat Tunnel, which connects Peshawar valley to the southern parts of NWFP, were all captured. This belligerent behaviour of the Taliban was meant to show to the populace their level of confidence in dealing with the security forces head on. It also led to a large-scale displacement of Pakhtoons from the region.[70] Militants also realised that liberal education posed the biggest threat to their radical ideology and systematically destroyed schools and educational institutions in the region, especially those educating the girls. All the girls' schools in Bajaur Agency were destroyed or closed down and over 64 schools were destroyed in Swat Valley alone.[71] In its desperation to bring peace to the region, the caretaker provincial government of NWFP again yielded to radical militants and proposed the implementation of *Shariah* regulation in the entire Malakand Division of NWFP. It even agreed to take away the right to file a writ in the High Court and the Supreme Court. A *Shariah* court at the division level was proposed as the final authority of justice.[72] It was only a protest by the lawyers and sections of judiciary that prevented the law from coming into force.

After the 2008 elections, the ANP government in NWFP negotiated a peace deal with Maulana Sufi Mohammad, who had founded TNSM, now a component of TTP. After negotiating a peace deal with him, it negotiated a ceasefire and eventually a peace deal with Maulana Fazalullah, his more radical son-in-law, who had been leading the Taliban in Swat valley.[73] These deals virtually gave the militants a free run within the region and agreed to enforce *Shariah* (Nizam-e-Adl) not only in Swat Valley, but in over half the territory of NWFP. In return, the militants agreed not to attack government personnel and properties and to hand over the foreign militants to the government.[74] The agreements in Swat were followed by agreements in Mohmand and Bajaur agencies granting autonomy for the militants in their area of influence. Meanwhile, negotiations with Baitullah Mehsud were completed and a ceasefire was agreed upon. The Army was withdrawn from the tactical positions it was holding in Waziristan under the garb of redeployment.

The Taliban used the deals as tactical pauses to consolidate their positions, while diverting their fighters to other areas. This resulted in insurgency spreading to newer regions in NWFP. The pitched battles fought in Kohat and Bannu showed their growing strength. The signing of peace deals with militants without any credible mechanism for violators only emboldened the militants.

The Taliban, wedded to hardcore Sunni thought, not only fought the security forces, but also supported the Sunni tribes to exterminate the Shia tribes in the Kurram Agency. The security forces moved into the region only after 300 lives had been lost in an internecine warfare. The Taliban exploited the sectarian fault lines to spread their influence and ideology into newer areas. In Dera Ismail Khan district in NWFP, a Taliban suicide bomber killed 32 and injured over 50, when he blew himself inside a government hospital after the body of a local Shia had been brought in.[75] Even the Shia soldiers captured by Taliban were eliminated, while Sunnis were released.[76] Government inaction in the face of these sectarian provocations further exacerbated the sectarian tensions.

After consolidating their presence in the Pakhtoon belt, the Taliban moved into the Pakistani heartland of Punjab. It followed a two pronged strategy. It supported the landless and marginal farmers against the landed gentry in South Punjab, a strategy it had followed successfully in Swat. More significantly, it exploited the existing sectarian differences in Punjab.

The fact that most feudal lords in South Punjab were Shias further helped its cause. It aligned itself with Sunni sectarian outfits like Sipah-e-Sahiba and Lashkar-e-Janghavi to target Shias and other sectarian minorities.[77] They not only attacked Shia and Ahmediya places of worship, but also attacked Barelvi clerics and revered Sufi shrines like Data Ganj Baksh in Lahore.[78]

They also occupied a number of mosques and *Madaris,* which their sympathisers used as an ideal platform to propagate their radical ideology. The Lal Masjid in the heart of Islamabad openly advocated '*Jihad*' against the government and decadent society. The clerics of the mosque, Maulana Abdul Aziz and Abdul Rashid Ghazi had good contacts with many leaders of al-Qaeda and Taliban, including Osama bin Laden. Their Friday sermons were pro-Taliban and exhorted the followers to undertake *Jihad* against the Americans. The students from the seminaries attached to the mosque started enforcing their own puritanical code of conduct.[79] Women students occupied a children's library and vandalised CD shops in the markets nearby. People, including policemen, were picked up and incarcerated within the mosque complex. Only after the students picked up Chinese nationals in July 2007 did the army move in, but by then it was too late. Hundreds were killed in the operation, many of them women and children. Many Special Forces soldiers, who were deployed, refused to fight and had to be court martialed. Ayman al-Zawahri, appealed to all Pakistanis to overthrow Musharraf's regime, as he was destroying Islam at America's behest. The operation won many recruits to the Taliban cause, as many female students were killed in the operation.[80]

By 2008, the Taliban was attacking security forces and Army installations using suicide bombers and explosive laden vehicles. The Punjabi Taliban had emerged as a band of tough hardcore Islamists.[81] More significantly, they infiltrated Pakistan's security establishment, most attacks on security forces bore clear indications of insider collusion. Both Islamabad and Rawalpindi, the political and military nerve centres were targeted repeatedly by them.[82] Operation Rah-e-Rast in Malkand Division not only brought a large number of IDPs, but also carried Taliban influence into Punjab and Sindh. In the aftermath of the operations, there was a sudden spurt in terrorist violence in Punjab. The Taliban attacked security forces in Mianwali, the Sri Lankan cricket team in Lahore and police training academy in Manawan. There were attacks on Shia places of worship in Dera Ghazi Khan and Chakwal as well as suicide attacks in Rawalpindi and Islamabad indicating Taliban's growing influence in the most populous of Pakistan's provinces. Feudal elements in Punjab accentuated the process of Talibanisation by making contributions to *madaris* propagating radical Deobandi view of Islam.[83]

Along with Punjab, Taliban made deep incursions into Karachi, Pakistan's largest metropolis and its economic capital. Altaf Hussain, the MQM leader has on numerous occasions warned about the dangers of creeping Talibanisation of Karachi. Many coeducational institutions in parts of Karachi have been threatened with dire consequences if they refuse to change; some others have received letters from the Taliban with similar threats.[84] Farooq Sattar, the federal minister and leader of MQM in parliament, warned the country that, the Taliban were closing in on Islamabad with an aim of taking over the entire country.[85]

Radicalisation in Pakistan crossed the Rubicon, when Salman Taseer, the Governor of Punjab, was assassinated by his own bodyguard, Mumtaz Qadri. The fact that the assassin could empty two magazines, without any of the other guards taking any steps to incapacitate him or to defend the governor, indicated that all of them were in collusion with the assassin.[86] According to some reports, the assassin had even informed other guards that he was going to kill the Governor. The subsequent treatment of the assassin shows how far the radical virus has permeated the Pakistani society. The assassin was garlanded in the court premises by the lawyers in Lahore and his house became a venue of pilgrimage. Most clerics refused to even lead the funeral prayers for the slain governor and party colleagues of the slain governor have been shy of openly supporting him. Eventually, a party member performed his last rites, but even he had to leave the country to save his life.

Salman Taseer had advocated steps to avoid misuse of blasphemy laws to target the minorities. He had shown the courage to visit and seek clemency for a poor illiterate Christian lady, who was in prison on trumped up charges of blasphemy and had been sentenced to death.[87] After his assassination, no political party dared to support him and when *Fateha* was being read for the assassinated governor in the parliament, the members of the religious parties kept sitting, showing complete disrespect to the deceased soul.

The assassination shattered a lot of misconceptions. Firstly, the oft repeated assertion of the liberal elite that majority of Pakistanis are liberal, but are often overshadowed by a vocal minority of radical elements. A candle light vigil organised by the friends of slain governor could hardly gather 100 people in Lahore, a city where he was the governor, on the other hand, Jamaat-e-Islami mustered over 25,000 men in support of the assassin in Karachi, just on a day's notice. So much was the fear amongst the liberal elite that people were unwilling to come and speak on television chat shows. Secondly, it shattered the myth that Barelvi Muslims following Sufi traditions are liberal. Not only was Mumtaz Qadri, a Barelvi Muslim, he has been strongly backed by the Barelvi clerics, who have been in the forefront demanding his release. It appears that there is a competition of sorts between various sects and sub-sects, as to who is more radical.

Even more galling was the stoic silence of two significant institutions of the state, the judiciary and the Army. Pakistan's judiciary, which had in the past justified coups and had given to the world the most ludicrous 'Doctrine of Necessity' had started showing some spine. Chief Justice Iftikhar Chaudhry was projecting himself as a crusader and took *suo motu* notice in numerous cases against the government and the Army. However, he consistently avoided taking any position against the Taliban and maintained complete silence on the issue of Salman Taseer's assassination. Even when an Anti Terrorism Court in Islamabad High Court, pronounced Mumtaz Qadri guilty and sentenced him to death, the court was ransacked by the irate lawyers supporting Qadri and the Chief Justice asked the judge to proceed on leave. The judge, who delivered the judgment against Qadri, has since left the country, but neither the Supreme Court nor its 'crusader' Chief Justice took any cognisance of this case. The Army, which has dominated the body politic of Pakistan for much of its existence and has a view on every issue concerning Pakistan from trade to entertainment, also kept mum.

Today virtually all parts of Pakistan, including its heartland of Punjab have been afflicted by the virus of radicalism. In 2013 elections, 55 candidates from Punjab belonged to 10 different sectarian groups, and, of these 40 belonged to the outlawed Sipah-e-Sahaba, which has now transformed into Ahle Sunnat Wal Jamaat.[88] Almost every day some hapless citizen or the other is killed by various radical outfits across the country. Despite numerous attacks on security forces, sectarian and religious minorities as well as lady health workers administering polio drops, the government and most political parties have in the past wanted negotiations with TTP. Despite daily killings of political, military and civic activists, the overwhelming public opinion was in favour of talks and this shows the level of radicalisation in Pakistan. Although after the killing of school children, the public opinion has turned against the Taliban and has become supportive of military operations against them. However, even after such a dastardly act, there are numerous elements within the society like the cleric of *Lal Masjid,* Maulana Abdul Aziz, who have refused to out rightly condemn the attack in Peshawar.

Impact of Radicalisation

The most serious implication of the process of Talibanisation is the radicalisation of the Armed Forces. As the armed forces draw their manpower from the same society, its composition is bound to reflect the biases of the society. General Zia had ensured that a whole generation of Army personnel listened to fundamentalist Mullahs and interacted with members of *Tableeghi Jamaat*, consequently, they believe that they are in the Army, not only to fight for Pakistan, but also for the glory of Islam. General Musharraf, after two assassination attempts, did try to cleanse the Army of radical elements and succeeded in purging overtly religious generals. However, the junior officers and other ranks by and large reflect the prevailing views of the society. Most of them still believe that the war against Taliban is America's war and have reservations about fighting them.

Every single attack on a military installation has borne clear marks of collusion by elements from within. Many Pakistani Air Force (PAF) and army personnel including six officers were convicted for attempts on General Pervez Musharraf in December 2003, when he was the President. An army soldier, Abdul Islam Siddiqui, was hanged on August 20, 2005 after Court Martial for the same offence. In April 2012, one of the six convicts, an air force technician Adnan Rashid, who had been sentenced to death, was freed by Taliban in a daring jail break in Bannu.[89] As early as 2006, six middle ranking officers were court-martialled for refusing to fight in FATA.[90]

On another occasion, an anti-aircraft gun was discovered on the flight path of General Musharraf's plane, when he was taking off from Rawalpindi Air base on a pitch dark night. In September 2006, most of the 40 men arrested for attacks on Musharraf were mid-ranking PAF officers. The conspiracy was uncovered when an Air Force officer used a cell phone to activate a rocket aimed at Musharraf's residence in Rawalpindi. The rocket was recovered, and its activating mechanism, also a cell phone, revealed the officer's telephone number.[91] The Pakistan Air Force confirmed in 2009 that it had acted against at least 57 personnel following the December 2003 assassination attempt against the then President, Pervez Musharraf. Six of these men were sentenced to death; others were arrested or dismissed from service. Over 100 PAF men faced disciplinary action in the aftermath of the murder attempt. However, the possibility of some of the accomplices having evaded arrest cannot be ruled out.[92] There have also been numerous instances of sabotage in the PAF to prevent aircraft from being deployed against the militants.

In one of the most bizarre cases, 200 armed security personnel led by a colonel were taken captive along with their officers and equipment by 20 Taliban in South Waziristan.[93] During subsequent attacks on Kohat Cantonment in 2008, there were reports that some tribal cadets of Army Cadet College had joined the militants. During five years of MMA rule, large portions of the NWFP including cantonments were infiltrated by pro Al-Qaeda elements. Former army personnel were also involved in the attack on GHQ, which was carried out with the possible collusion of insiders. In 2010, two former army officers along with two serving officers including a colonel were convicted by a court martial for planning an attack on the Shamsi airbase, which was being used by the Americans to fly their drones.

Pakistan has always tried to deny the existence of such elements within its security establishment. Investigative journalist, Syed Saleem Shehzad was believed to have been brutally silenced for publishing a story, which highlighted the presence of Al Qaeda cells within the Pakistani Navy. The attack on PNS Mehran was another case of collusion by serving personnel. Kamran Ahmed, a former naval commando and his brother Zaman Ahmed were arrested for aiding the attackers. Another marine commando from

Waziristan, who had been posted at PNS Mehran, was arrested in January 2011 for having links with Al Qaeda and the Taliban.

Saleem Shehzad, in his book *Inside Al Qaeda and the Taliban: Beyond Bin Laden and 9/11,* which was published just before his death, writes that many ex-officers of the Armed Forces have joined various radical organisations and numerous serving officers are collaborating with Al Qaeda and Taliban. A number of junior officers and other ranks still place faith above country and, accordingly, many former officers, who were earlier involved with Afghan and Kashmiri '*Jihad*', have joined Al Qaeda. The book talks about Captain Khurram Ashiq from the elite Zarrar Company of Pakistan SSG, who along with his brother Major Haroon Ashiq joined Al Qaeda after resigning from the Army. However, they continued to use their connections within the army to facilitate Al Qaeda aims. Haroon allegedly killed Major General Ameer Faisal Alavi in Islamabad and kidnapped Karachi film maker Satish Anand with assistance from another officer, Major Basit. He was subsequently arrested while attempting to kidnap an Ahmadi for ransom and is currently lodged in Adiala Jail in Rawalpindi.[94]

A few days before his murder, Saleem Shehzad had described the attack on PNS Mehran as "the violent beginning of an internal ideological struggle between Islamist elements in the Pakistani armed forces and their secular and liberal top brass."[95] He also warned about a nexus of serving and retired soldiers, which could instigate mutiny against the top military brass.[96] Most analysts believe that the Pakistani military is the glue that binds a fissiparous state like Pakistan and one can well imagine the implications of an ideological war within this institution. Of late, the disciplined façade of army has been showing cracks as many mid-level officers and soldiers have harboured latent sympathies for their opponents. This has resulted in large-scale surrenders by the personnel of the security forces. Many Pakhtoon soldiers were unwilling to take up arms against their kith and kin.[97]

The arrest and subsequent court martial of Brigadier Ali Khan of Pakistani Army, who was posted at the General Headquarters (GHQ) for links with pan-Islamic radical outfit Hizb-ut-Tehrir, has once again highlighted the existence of radical Islamist elements within Pakistan's Armed Forces. The prosecution had alleged that the Brigadier had planned to spread mutiny and hatched a conspiracy in collusion with an F-16 pilot to bomb the GHQ during corps commanders' meeting. The Brigadier allegedly had support of 400 armed men, including some generals and personnel of 111 Brigade.[98] The fact that Brigadier Khan is a third generation army officer, with a brother, son and son-in-law in the Army, shows the gravity of the situation. Even before Brigadier Khan, two serving army officers were court martialed for links with Hizb-ut-Tahrir.[99] However, the immediate concern for the international community is the prospect that there could be some officers like Brigadier Khan in Strategic Planning Directorate (SPD) that is responsible for the security of Pakistani nuclear stockpile.

Adnan Rashid, the former air force personnel, who had been sentenced to death and was released by Taliban after Bannu jail break, in a recent video, asked the Pakistani soldiers not to obey their generals and air marshals and offered them amnesty if they joined TTP.[100] This sort of statement coming after an attempt at taking over a fully loaded warship by serving and retired naval officers, allied with the militants, is extremely dangerous. For the first time since Pakistan's creation, there is a threat to the cohesion of the Pakistan Army. This, in Pakistan's case, could be catastrophic, as it is probably the only functioning institution in the country. According to Stephen Cohen, most States have an army, but in Pakistan's case, the army has a State. Consequently, with the erosion of army's cohesion, the state's monopoly on instruments of power is weakening and, in due course, would strengthen the fissiparous forces. Pakistan appears to be losing its internal sovereignty to radical elements.

The growing radicalisation is eroding the state structure within Pakistan and the manner, in which the state has been capitulating, makes the Lebanonisation[101] of Pakistan a distinct possibility and that might be catastrophic for all its neighbours including India. If Taliban transforms into Pakistan's Hezbollah, it could pose serious threats to Indian security. There have been firings by non-state actors on Indian Territory from across the international borders, India did not respond militarily then, but India would have to evolve its reaction, if it becomes the norm.

The Taliban already enjoys complete domination over most parts of FATA and great influence over large areas in KP and northern Balochistan. Its influence in Punjab and urban Sindh is growing. This makes Taliban a grave menace in the region and the international community is justifiably concerned about the increasing area under Taliban control in Pakistan. There have been serious concerns about the nuclear arsenal falling into the hands of militants. It must also be understood that the Taliban today is quite different from what it was prior to 9/11. It is no longer insular and is closely linked to the global Islamic movements. Its aims and objectives are no longer confined within a geographically defined area.

The onward march of the radical ideology as symbolised by the Taliban, if unchecked, would eventually lead to the emergence of Pakistan as a citadel of radical Islam, with liberal elements either pushed out or silenced. Such a state would start exporting its ideology across the world. It is important to note that many Islamic militants from across the world – from the Philippines to Chechenya, including Indonesians, Maldivians, Bangladeshi, Tajiks, Uzbeks, Arabs and Uighurs – come to Pakistan for indoctrination. This would cause a conflict that would transcend regional boundaries. It needs to be appreciated that TTP and all other radical organisations in Pakistan are closely aligned with global Islamic movement including Al Qaeda. Even in the most populous Pakistani state of Punjab, where many of these organisations were created and nurtured by the security establishment, they have switched their loyalty from the Pakistan Army to Al Qaeda.[102] Al Qaeda is in the region because it believes that it was the prophet's prophesy that '*Khurasan*'[103] (present day Afghanistan, Pakistan, Iran and Central Asia) will be the initial theatre for 'End of Times' battles for the establishment of global Islamic Emirate. It also talks of *Ghazwa-e-Hind* (battle for India), before Imam Mahadi reveals himself to command the Muslim forces to defeat the western forces led by *Dajjal* (Anti-christ). The Taliban, under Al Qaeda's influence, is set out to fulfil this prophecy.[104]

The growing influence of Taliban poses two pronged challenges for Pakistan's neighbours. Firstly, as the foot-soldiers of Taliban move out of their citadels, it would lead to a net accretion in the ranks of the armed militants, challenging the state in Pakistan's neighbourhood. Secondly, by giving them a free hand, Pakistan would end up creating a bastion of Islamic fundamentalism in this region, which will become the nerve centre for propagating Islamic radicalism in the entire neighbourhood. As it is, Afghan Taliban, Uzbek, Uighur, Tajik and Kashmiri militants have established fraternal ties with TTP and many of their militant camps are now located in the region under their control. As the militants entrench themselves and propagate their extremist ideology, there is never going to be any dearth of volunteers willing to cross the Line of Control (LoC) or the international borders to blow themselves up. So the increasing influence of militants in the region poses a direct threat to the security interests of Pakistan's neighbours.[105]

With this sort of an ideology, it is quite evident that the Talibanisation will not stop at Pakistan's frontiers and all its neighbours will have to face non-state actors based in Pakistan, promoting radical ideology. Every single deal with the Taliban in Pakistan has seen their foot soldiers move to newer areas. Peace deals in Swat had seen many of them move to Kashmir and Afghanistan, sometimes even with the connivance of state actors.[106] Besides India and Afghanistan, growing influence of the Taliban will give strength to Islamic militants fighting in Tajikistan, Uzbekistan and even China. Its intolerance of Shias will soon bring it into conflict with the Iranian regime as well.

Conclusion

The instruments that were created during the Afghan war against Soviet Union have begun to haunt Pakistan. It is ironical that the *Jihadi* outfits that were created by the Pakistani state are posing both material as well as ideological threat to the state. There is a tendency amongst the Pakistani elite to blame the fringe extremist elements and Mullahs for the menace of religious extremism, without acknowledging that it is enshrined in the constitution and in the doctored history that is taught in its schools. Sections of Pakistan Constitution, such as those relating to the Objective Resolution, the text of oaths of high offices, the notorious Eighth Amendment, the council of Islamic ideology and the *Shariah* court go a long way in promoting religious extremism. While the *Jihadi* outfits could serve certain perceived tactical and strategic objectives of the state, but in the long run, they are part of the pan-Islamic agenda that aims to capture the Pakistani state. Even today, the Pakistani security establishment is loath to disassociate itself completely from these outfits and to condemn them unequivocally.

For the first time since 1947, there is a credible threat to the cohesion of Pakistan army. There is a distinct possibility that with the withering of the Pakistani state, its nuclear stockpile could fall into the hands of these radical non-state actors, who could use it to make crude radiological bombs.

This could pose a serious threat to India and other states in the region. Moreover, if the state weakens and the fault-lines aggravate, the state structure might crumble leading to an internecine war and large-scale bloodshed. This may result in mass exodus of population, especially those unwilling to live in a Talibanised state. Most of them will head to the only country, which is culturally familiar to them, namely India. The Indian state is in no position to deal with millions of refugees on its soil. This influx of millions of refugees would pose a serious problem of governance and could impose serious economic and social strain on the Indian state.

NOTES

1. "Pakistan Taliban: Peshawar School Attack Leaves 141 Dead", from http://www.bbc.com/news/world-asia-30491435 (accessed 27 Dec 2014).
2. "Taliban Spokesman: "The Peshawar Attack is in Complete Accordance with the Prophet's Teachings"" from http://www.jihadwatch.org/2014/12/taliban-spokesman-the-peshawar-attack-is-in-complete-accordance-with-the-prophets-teachings (accessed 27 Dec 2014).
3. Taqfir refers to the practice of declaring somebody, who calls himself a Muslim, as apostate.
4. Ayesha Jalal, "The Past as Present" in Maleeha Lodi (ed.) *Pakistan: Beyond the Crisis State*. (New Delhi: Rupa & Co, 2011), p. 10.
5. Akbar Ahmad, "Why Jinnah Matters", in Maleeha Lodi (ed.) *Pakistan: Beyond the Crisis State*. (New Delhi: Rupa & Co, 2011), p. 23.
6. Ibid, pp. 23-24.
7. Waqqas Mir, "I am Sorry Mr Jinnah", *The News on Sunday*, December 29, 2013, Karachi Edition, Dialogue, p. 31.
8. Khaled Ahmed, *Sectarian War: Pakistan's Sunni-Shia Violence and its Links to the Middle East*. (Oxford: Oxford University Press, 2011), p. xx.
9. Vazira Fazila-Yacoobali Zamindar, *The Long Partition and the Making of Modern South Asia: Refugees, Boundaries, Histories*. (New York: Columbia University Press, 2007).
10. Akbar Ahmad, n.5, pp. 24-26.
11. From http://www.pakistani.org/pakistan/constitution/annex_objres.html (accessed August 1, 2013)
12. Ayesha Jalal, n. 4, p. 11.
13. Now called Khyber Pakhtoonkhwa (KP)
14. Report of the Court of Inquiry constituted under Punjab Act II of 1954 to enquire into the Punjab Disturbances of 1953, Lahore, 1954, pp. 13-25.
15. Ibid, pp. 1-2.
16. Ibid, pp. 215-218.
17. Ibid, p. 218.
18. Ziad Haider, "Ideologically Adrift" in Maleeha Lodhi (ed.) *Pakistan: Beyond the 'Crisis State'* (New Delhi: Rupa & Co, 2011), pp. 116-117.
19. Ibid, p. 118-119.

20. Ayesha Jalal, n. 4, p. 14.
21. Ziad Haider, n. 18, p. 117.
22. Ayesha Jalal, n. 4, pp. 14-15.
23. Ziad Haider, n. 18, 120.
24. Ibid, pp. 119-120.
25. James P Farwell, *The Pakistan Cauldron: Conspiracy, Assassination & Instability*. (Washington DC: Potomac Books, 2011), pp. 60-61.
26. Ayesha Jalal, n. 4, p. 15.
27. Ibid.
28. Ziad Haider, n. 18, p. 120.
29. Mary Anne Weaver, *Pakistan in the Shadow of Jihad and Afghanistan*. (New York: Farrar, Straus and Giroux, 2002), pp. 56-61.
30. Ziad Haider, n. 18, 121.
31. Ibid, p. 122.
32. Victoria Schofield. *Afghan Frontier: Feuding and Fighting in Central Asia*, (London: Tauris Parke Paperbacks, 2003), p 294.
33. Ibid., p 295.
34. Ziad Haider, n.18, pp. 122-123.
35. Yunas Samad, "Pakistan: From Minority Rights to Majoritarianism" in Gyanendra Pande and Yunas Samad, *Faultlines of Nationhood*, (New Delhi: Roli Books, 2007), p. 108.
36. Khaled Ahmed. n. 8, pp. 29-30.
37. Hassan Abbas, *Pakistan's Drift into Extremism: Allah, the Army and America's War on Terror*, (New York: M. E. Sharpe, 2005), 89-132.
38. Mumtaz Ahmad, "Revivalism, Islamization, Sectarianism, and Violence in Pakistan" in Craig Baxter and Charles H. Kennedy (ed.), *Pakistan, 1997*, (Boulder: Westview Press), 1998, 108-109.
39. Husain Haqqani, "Weeding out the Heretics: Sectarianism in Pakistan," in Hillel Fradkin, Husain Haqqani and Eric Brown (ed.) *Current Trends in Islamic Ideology* Volume 4, (Washington DC: Hudson Institute,2006), pp. 82-83.
40. Sipah-e-Sahaba Pakistan (The Army of the Friends of the Prophet), is a Pakistani Deobandi organisation, and a former political party, established in the early 1980s in Jhang by Haq Nawaz Jhangvi. Its stated goal is to primarily deter major Shiite influence in Pakistan in the wake of the Iranian Revolution.
41. SVR Nasr, "The Rise of Sunni Militancy in Pakistan: The Changing Role of Islamism and the Ulama in Society and Politics", in *Modern Asian Studies*, Vol. 34, No 1, February 2000, Cambridge University Press, pp 142-143.
42. Victoria Schofield, n. 32, p 326.
43. Ibid, p 335.
44. Vivek Kumar Mishra, "Role of Pakistani Madrassa in Sustaining Taliban after 9/11", *World Focus*, September 2006, Volume 27, Number 9, pp 28-29.
45. Mohammad Ayoob, "South West Asia after the Taliban" in Musa Khan Jalalzai (ed.) *Afghanistan, Central Asia Pakistan and the United States*, (Lahore: Book Biz, 2003), pp 252.
46. Frederic Grare, "Pakistan-Afghanistan Relations in the Post-9/11 Era", Carnegie Papers, No 72, October 2006, pp 9-10.
47. Smruti S Pattanaik, "In Pursuit of Strategic Depth: The Changing Dynamics of

Pakistan's Afghan Policy", in K Warikoo (ed.), *Afghanistan: The Challenge*, (New Delhi: Pentagon Press, 2007), p. 139.

48. Mohammad Ayoob, n. 43, pp 252-253.
49. Norman Friedman.*Terrorism, Afghanistan, and America's New Way of War*, Annapolis: Naval Institute Press, 2003, p. 197.
50. Ayesha Jalal, n. 4, p. 15.
51. Ibid, p. 16.
52. Zahid Hussain, "Battling Militancy" in Maleeha Lodhi (ed.) *Pakistan: Beyond the 'Crisis State'* (New Delhi: Rupa& Co, 2011), p. 136.
53. Ibid, pp. 136-137.
54. M Ilyas Khan, "Back to the Drawing Board", *The Herald*, Karachi, February 2006, p 59.
55. Christian Wagner, "Peace in Waziristan", German Institute for International and Security Affairs *SWP Comments* 25, October 2006, p. 2.
56. Mohammad Ayoob, n. 45, p 245.
57. Vinod Anand, "Prospects of Security and Stability in Afghanistan", *World Focus*, September 2006, Volume 27, Number 9, p 11.
58. Frederic Grare, n. 46, pp. 6-7.
59. "Pakistan's Tribal Areas: Appeasing the Militants", International Crisis Group, Asia Report No 125 dated December 11, 2006, p 14.
60. M Ilyas Khan, n. 54, p 60.
61. Rahimullah Yusufzai, "No End in Sight", *Newsline*, April 2006, p 27.
62. Rahimullah Yusafzai and Sailab Mahsud, "Waziristan Clashes Death Toll Rises: 16 Troops, 23 Military Vehicles Lost", *The News,* March 18, 2004.
63. Shabana Fayyaz, "Towards a Durable Peace in Waziristan", Pakistan Security Research Unit, University of Bradford, Brief No 10 dated April 23, 2007.
64. "Rebellion in Waziristan", Regional Institute of Policy Research and Training Peshawar Report dated February 22, 2007, p. 25.
65. Ibid.
66. TTP (the movement of the Taliban in Pakistan) a conglomerate of armed Islamic groups owing ideological allegiance to Afghan Taliban, came into being on December 14, 2007 when Shura (Council) of Taliban representatives from all the agencies in FATA and settled districts of Swat, Bannu, Tank, Lakki Marwat, Dera Ismail Khan, Kohistan, Buner and the Malkand Division met and elected Baitullah Mehsud as their head and set up a unified organization. Many of the groups that constitute TTP often clash with one another, but are united as far as the implementation of Shariat and opposition to US presence in Afghanistan is concerned. The organization was banned by the Pakistan government on August 25, 2008.
67. "Pakistan Security Report 2008" by Pakistan Institute for Peace Studies, p. 5.
68. Note 59, ibid, p 19.
69 Christian Wagner, no 55, p 5.
70. "Darra Fighting", Editorial, *The News*, January 27, 2008.
71. Massoud Ansari, "The Ticking Bomb", *The Herald*, August 2008, p. 68.
72. Delawar Jan Banori, "Shariah Regulation Draft for Malakand sent to President", *The News*, January 30, 2008.
73. Sufi Mohammad had founded TNSM after leaving Jamaat-e-Islami in 1992. He also led a 10,000 strong force to fight alongside Taliban, when US troops invaded

Afghanistan in the aftermath of 9/11. Many of his followers died in the misadventure and he was arrested on his return to Pakistan. The leadership of TNSM consequently passed on to his son-in-law Fazlullah, who used illegal FM radio station to give his sermons and to propagate his ideology. Over the years, he assumed an even more hardline stance and after the military operations in Lal Masjid at Islamabad, asked his followers to prepare for *Jihad* against the military government. In October 2007, after a few altercations with the security forces, his followers virtually took over the entire Swat Valley. The security personnel merely surrendered with weapons and towns after towns were taken over by the armed cadres of TNSM. It took the Pakistani Army more than a month to establish some semblance of control over the region. Sufi Mohammad meanwhile continued to languish in jail and years of incarceration mellowed him down. As Sufi Mohammad began showing his willingness to negotiate a settlement, Fazlullah distanced himself from his erstwhile mentor and when Sufi Mohammad negotiated the deal with the government, the hardline faction led by Fazlullah refused to abide by it.

74. In the peace deal signed with Fazlullah, the militants agreed that they would accept and honour the writ of the federal and provincial government and would not malign the religion of other citizens. They assured that government personnel and properties will not be attacked, vaccinations will not be opposed and all foreign militants will be handed over to the government. They also agreed to a ban on display of illegal weapons and FM broadcasts without due permission from the government and to cooperate with the government to investigate murder, robbery and other crimes. They consented to dismantling the training facilities for suicide bombers as well as explosive manufacturing facilities. The government, on its part, agreed to implement *Shariah* in entire erstwhile Malakand Division in letter and spirit, compensate all victims for the damages to life and property and to review all cases against militants in prison. It agreed that the Army would be sent back to the barracks gradually and an Islamic University would be set up at TNSM headquarters to be run jointly by the government and TNSM. It agreed to take actions against oppressors, bribe-takers, adulterers, thieves, dacoits and kidnappers in order to rid the society of such elements. Finally, an 11-member joint committee was set up to ensure the implementation of the deal.
75. "DI Khan Blast", Editorial, *The News*, August 21, 2008.
76. "A Sectarian War", Editorial, *The News*, August 23, 2008.
77. Anatol Lieven, *Pakistan: A Hard Country*. New York: Public Affair, 2011, p. 291.
78. Ibid, p. 133.
79. Arshi Saleem Hashmi, *The Arabist Shift from Indo-Persian Civilization & Genesis of Radicalization in Pakistan* Pak Institute for Peace Studies, p. 11.
80. Alok Bansal, "Pakistan: After Lal Masjid" from Sify.com, July 24, 2007.
81. Note 67, ibid, p. 11.
82. Ibid, p. 12.
83. Sabrina Tavernise, Richard A Oppel Jr and Eric Schmitt, "United Militants Threaten Pakistan's Populous Heart", *The New York Times*, New York Edition, April 14, 2009, p. A1.
84. Ardeshir Cowasjee, "The Price of Moral Cowardice", *Dawn*, April 19, 2009.
85. "Taliban Intend to Grab Capital, warns MQM", *Dawn*, April 17, 2009.
86. Mohammed Hanif, "How Pakistan responded to Salman Taseer's Assassination", *The Guardian*, January 6, 2011, p 4 of the G2 section.

87. "Punjab Governor Salman Taseer Assassinated in Islamabad" from http://www.bbc.co.uk/news/world-south-asia-12111831 (accessed January 5, 2011)
88. S Iftikhar Murshed, "A Thoughtless Action Plan" *The News on Sunday*, Karachi Edition, December 28, 2014, p. 6.
89. "Pak Jailbreak: Terrorist had Access to Mobile, Facebook" from http://www.rediff.com/news/report/pak-jailbreak-terrorist-had-access-to-mobile-facebook/20120416.htm (accessed on April 16, 2012)
90. Zahid Hussain, "Deadly Dilemma", *Newsline*, November 2006, p. 23.
91. Shaheen Sehbai, "Rumour Mills Go Rolling with Arrest of Eight Militants", *The News*, October 15, 2006.
92. "The Enemy Within?" Editorial, *The News*, June 26, 2009, p. 6.
93. "Tackling the Militants", Editorial, *Dawn*, September 2, 2007.
94. Syed Saleem Shehzad, *Inside Al-Qaeda and the Taliban: Beyond Bin Laden and 9/11.* (London: Pluto Press, 2011), pp. 82-103.
95. Syed Saleem Shahzad, "Pakistan's Military under al-Qaeda Attack", *Asia Times Online,* May 24, 2011.
96. Syed Saleem Shahzad, "Trouble Ahead in Pakistan's New US Phase", *Asia Times Online,* May 18, 2011.
97. Ayesha Siddiqa, "Dealing with Deals", *The Herald*, August 2008, p. 16d.
98. "Brig Ali Planned Air Strike at GHQ: BBC", *Daily Times*, March 2, 2012.
99. Alok Bansal, "Radicalisation of Pakistani Armed Forces", from CLAWS website http://www.claws.in/index.php?action=details&m_id=894&u_id=157 (accessed June 28, 2011).
100. "Taliban Says Pakistan Army Fooled Youth for Blood Game in Kashmir", *The Economic Times*, December 28, 2014 from http://articles.economictimes.indiatimes.com/2014-12-28/news/57462577_1_pakistani-army-proxy-war-indian-kashmir (accessed 29 Dec 2014).
101. 'Lebanonization' has come to refer to a process of national disintegration, where central authority erodes to a level that different power groups start acting independent of the central authority, not only as far as their interactions with one another is concerned, but also with entities outside the geographical frontiers of the state. It is distinct from 'Balkanisation', as the process of disintegration does not create clear cut smaller states as in the case of the latter. In recent times, the term has been used extensively for Somalia and Iraq before its recent stabilization.
102. Khaled Ahmed in Foreword to Mujahid Hussain. *Pakistani Taliban: Driving Extremism in Pakistan.* (New Delhi: Pentagon Security International, 2012), p. vii.
103. Khurasan refers to parts of Iran, the Central Asian Republics, Afghanistan and parts of Pakistan.
104. Syed Saleem Shahzad, n. 94, p. xvi.
105. Alok Bansal, "Implications of Peace Deals in Pakistan's Wild West", from IDSA website http://www.idsa.in/publications/stratcomments/AlokBansal130608.htm (accessed April 13, 2009).
106. Khalid Aziz, "The Swat Peace Agreement", *The News*, May 26, 2008.

ANNEXURES

Annesure 1: Party Position (Provincial Assemblies)

	Province	*KPK Assembly*					*Punjab Assembly*				
		99		22	3	124	297		66	8	371
S#	*Party Name*	*General*	*Ind*	*Women*	*Non-Muslims*	*Total*	*General*	*Ind*	*Women*	*Non-Muslims*	*Total*
1	PML-N	12	1	3	0	16	218	32	58	7	315
2	PPPP	3	0	1	0	4	7	0	1	0	8
3	PTI	35	1	10	0	46	23	0	5	1	29
4	MQM	0	0	0	0	0	0	0	0	0	0
5	JUI-F	13	0	3	0	16	0	0	0	0	0
6	PML	0	0	0	0	0	6	0	2	0	8
7	PMAP	0	0	0	0	0	0	0	0	0	0
8	JI	7	0	1	0	8	1	0	0	0	1
9	PML-F	0	0	0	0	0	0	0	0	0	0
10	NP	0	0	0	0	0	0	0	0	0	0
11	QWP	7	1	0	0	8	0	0	0	0	0
12	ANP	4	0	1	0	5	0	0	0	0	0
13	AJIP	3	0	1	0	4	0	0	0	0	0
14	BNP	0	0	0	0	0	0	0	0	0	0
15	NPP	0	0	0	0	0	0	0	0	0	0
16	PML-Z	0	0	0	0	0	2	0	0	0	2
17	JQM	0	0	0	0	0	0	0	0	0	0
18	PNML	0	0	0	0	0	1	0	0	0	1
19	APML	1	0	0	0	1	0	0	0	0	0
20	BNAP	0	0	0	0	0	1	0	0	0	1
21	MWMP	0	0	0	0	0	0	0	0	0	0
22	IND	11	0	0	0	11	5	0	0	0	5
	Total	96	3	20	0	119	264	32	66	8	370

(Contd.)

Annexure 1 (*Contd.*)

	Province	*Sindh Assembly*					*Balochistan Assembly*				
		130		29	9	168	51		11	3	65
S#	*Party Name*	*General*	*Ind*	*Women*	*Non-Muslims*	*Total*	*General*	*Ind*	*Women*	*Non-Muslims*	*Total*
1	PML-N	3	2	1	0	6	10	5	3	1	19
2	PPPP	69	2	16	5	92	0	0	0	0	0
3	PTI	3	0	1	0	4	0	0	0	0	0
4	MQM	39	0	9	3	51	0	0	0	0	0
5	JUI-F	0	0	0	0	0	6	0	2	0	8
6	PML	1	0	0	0	1	5	0	1	0	6
7	PMAP	0	0	0	0	0	10	0	3	1	14
8	JI	0	0	0	0	0	0	0	0	0	0
9	PML-F	8	0	2	1	11	0	0	0	0	0
10	NP	0	0	0	0	0	7	0	2	1	10
11	QWP	0	0	0	0	0	0	0	0	0	0
12	ANP	0	0	0	0	0	1	0	0	0	1
13	AJIP	0	0	0	0	0	0	0	0	0	0
14	BNP	0	0	0	0	0	2	0	0	0	2
15	NPP	2	0	0	0	2	0	0	0	0	0
16	PML-Z	0	0	0	0	0	0	0	0	0	0
17	JQM	0	0	0	0	0	1	0	0	0	1
18	PNML	0	0	0	0	0	0	0	0	0	0
19	APML	0	0	0	0	0	0	0	0	0	0
20	BNAP	0	0	0	0	0	0	0	0	0	0
21	MWMP	0	0	0	0	0	1	0	0	0	1
22	IND	1	0	0	0	1	3	0	0	0	3
	Total	126	4	29	9	168	46	5	11	3	65

Designed and Developed By IT-Wing Election Commission of Pakistan.

Annexure 2: Party Position (National Assembly)

S#	Province	FATA		Federal Capital		Khyber Pakhtunkhwa				Punjab			
	Party Name	*General Seats*	*Ind*	*General Seats*	*Ind*	*General Seats*	*Ind*	*Women*	*Total*	*General Seats*	*Ind*	*Women*	*Total*
		12		**2**		**35**		**8**	**43**	**148**		**35**	**183**
1	PML-N	2	1	1	0	4	1	1	6	120	12	32	164
2	PPPP	0	0	0	0	0	0	0	0	3	0	1	4
3	PTI	1	0	1	0	18	0	4	22	7	0	2	9
4	MQM	0	0	0	0	0	0	0	0	0	0	0	0
5	JUI-F	1	0	0	0	4	0	1	5	0	0	0	0
6	PML-F	0	0	0	0	0	0	0	0	0	0	0	0
7	PMAP	0	0	0	0	0	0	0	0	0	0	0	0
8	JI	0	0	0	0	3	0	1	4	0	0	0	0
9	ANP	0	0	0	0	2	0	0	2	0	0	0	0
10	NPP	0	0	0	0	0	0	0	0	0	0	0	0
11	PML	0	0	0	0	0	0	0	0	2	0	0	2
12	BNP	0	0	0	0	0	0	0	0	0	0	0	0
13	QWP-S	0	0	0	0	1	0	0	1	0	0	0	0
14	PML-Z	0	0	0	0	0	0	0	0	1	0	0	1
15	NP	0	0	0	0	0	0	0	0	0	0	0	0
16	AMLP	0	0	0	0	0	0	0	0	1	0	0	1
17	AJIP	0	0	0	0	1	0	0	1	0	0	0	0
18	APML	0	0	0	0	1	0	0	1	0	0	0	0
19	IND	6	0	0	0	0	0	0	0	2	0	0	2
	Total	10	1	2	0	34	1	7	42	136	12	35	183

(*Contd.*)

Annexure 2 (*Contd.*)

S#	Province / Party Name	Sindh				Balochistan				Total General Seats	Total Ind. Joined Party	Total Non-Muslims Reserved	Total Women Reserved	Grand Total
		General	Ind	Women	Total	General	Ind	Women	Total					
		61		**14**	**75**	**14**		**3**	**17**	**272**		**10**	**60**	**342**
1	PML-N	1	1	1	3	1	4	1	6	129	19	6	35	189
2	PPPP	33	0	6	39	0	0	0	0	36	0	1	7	44
3	PTI	1	0	0	1	0	0	0	0	28	0	1	6	35
4	MQM	19	0	4	23	0	0	0	0	19	0	1	4	24
5	JUI-F	0	0	0	0	4	0	1	5	9	0	1	2	12
6	PML-F	4	0	1	5	0	0	0	0	4	0	0	1	5
7	PMAP	0	0	0	0	3	0	1	4	3	0	0	1	4
8	JI	0	0	0	0	0	0	0	0	3	0	0	1	4
9	ANP	0	0	0	0	0	0	0	0	2	0	0	0	2
10	NPP	2	0	1	3	0	0	0	0	2	0	0	1	3
11	PML	0	0	0	0	0	0	0	0	2	0	0	0	2
12	BNP	0	0	0	0	1	0	0	1	1	0	0	0	1
13	QWP-S	0	0	0	0	0	0	0	0	1	0	0	0	1
14	PML-Z	0	0	0	0	0	0	0	0	1	0	0	0	1
15	NP	0	0	0	0	1	0	0	1	1	0	0	0	1
16	AMLP	0	0	0	0	0	0	0	0	1	0	0	0	1
17	AJIP	0	0	0	0	0	0	0	0	1	0	0	0	1
18	APML	0	0	0	0	0	0	0	0	1	0	0	0	1
19	IND	0	0	0	0	0	0	0	0	8	0	0	0	8
	Total	60	1	13	74	10	4	3	17	252	19	10	58	339

Designed and Developed By IT-Wing Election Commission of Pakistan

Index